Capitalism
and
Individualism

Capitalism and Individualism

Reframing the Argument for the Free Society

Tibor R. Machan

New York   London   Toronto   Sydney   Tokyo   Singapore

First published 1990 by
Harvester Wheatsheaf
66 Wood Lane End, Hemel Hempstead
Hertfordshire HP2 4RG
A division of
Simon & Schuster International Group

© Tibor R. Machan 1990

All rights reserved. No part of this publication may be reproduced, stored in a retrieval system, or transmitted, in any form or by any means, electronic, mechanical, photocopying, recording or otherwise, without prior permission, in writing, from the publisher.

Typeset in 10pt Plantin
by Witwell Ltd., Southport

Printed and bound in Great Britain by
BPCC Wheatons Ltd., Exeter

British Library Cataloguing in Publication Data

Machan, Tibor R., *1939–*
 Capitalism and individualism: reframing the argument for the free society.
 1. Political ideologies: Liberalism. Theories
 I. Title
 320.51

ISBN 0-7450-0561-6

1 2 3 4 5 94 93 92 91 90

Contents

Acknowledgments vii

Preface ix

1. Problems with Hobbesian individualism 1
2. Economic "Science": an amoral discipline 17
3. A metaphysical recasting of economic science 33
4. Classical (qualitative) individualism 56
5. Why capitalism? 76
6. The moral superiority of capitalism 98
7. Adding a moral component to anti-collectivism 118
8. Business and society: why anti-corporatism? 143
9. Living with capitalism 154

Bibliography 169

Index 175

Acknowledgments

In my efforts to develop the ideas in this book I have had a good deal of support. My former colleagues at the State University College, Fredonia – Morton Schagrin, Randy Dipert, Ken Lucey and Marvin Kohl – never tired of discussing the issues with me. And my colleagues at Auburn University continued to tolerate my endless exploration of the various ideas surrounding the work on this book. Then I was fortunate to have been asked by Liberty Fund, Inc., to direct quite a few of their conferences and four 10-week summer seminars, and I benefited greatly from the many exchanges during all of these. I have also had extensive conversations with such friendly adversaries as Professors Armen Alchian, Yale Brozen, James Buchanan, Milton Friedman, James Gwartney, Ernest van den Haag, F.A. Hayek, James L. Johnson, Henry Manne, Richard McKenzie, Douglas North, Steve Pejovich, Alvin Rabushka, Gordon Tullock, Walter Williams and Leland Yeager.

I have tried the patience of many of these individuals with my insistence that there is indeed a problem with classical liberalism, especially its economic imperialist versions. And their criticisms of my arguments probably have not registered as fully as they would have liked. They might also believe, perhaps rightly, that I sometimes overstate a point or two, as is always possible in any succinct statement of a complicated and important idea. Still, my argument benefited from the exchanges and I thank them all for their goodwill and generosity. Despite the fear often expressed to me that my line of approach may threaten liberty, my aim has been largely to show that the love of liberty must be the political result of a more important love, that of human life itself.

Most of all I have had the benefit of constant and intense exchanges with my friends Douglas J. Den Uyl, Douglas Rasmussen, J. Roger Lee, Sven Thommesen, Jeffrey Wallin, Eric Mack and David L. Norton. I am fortunate to have been stimulated to much thought by their suggestions and responses to my ideas. Jim Chesher has helped me immensely with the final preparation of the manuscript. Anonymous reviewers have also helped with this work. I have, in addition, received extensive assistance from Robert Bolick and the staff at Harvester Wheatsheaf.

I have also benefited from the generous financial support of the Lynde and Harry Bradley Foundation of Milwaukee, Wisconsin, and the John M. Olin Foundation of New York City. Some initial versions of portions of this book were published in the *Journal of Applied Philosophy*, *International Review of Economics and Ethics*, *Economic Affairs*, *The Freeman*, *Southern Economic Journal*, *Florida Policy Review* and *Liberty*. I thank the publishers for their permission to draw on those essays here.

I would like to thank my children, Erin, Thomas and Kate, for their patience with me as I took time away from them to work on this project. I also wish to thank Jamie Sinclair for what she endured during my work on this and other projects.

Preface: A Paradox of Capitalism?

I have for some time been thinking about how best to approach the task of answering the questions of political theory. What is a just society? What is the proper function of government? What is the best relationship between citizen, society and state? What kind of economic system is proper for human community life?

My interest was sparked in graduate school when I discovered that these kinds of question were deemed virtually unanswerable within the most prominent and respectable framework of thought in recent time, positivism. When I began my graduate work at the University of California, Santa Barbara, emotivism – the view that moral judgments have no truth value but express one's emotions relating to some topic, which is the substantive offshoot of positivist metaethics – was still prominent, although some philosophers had begun to waver. What was even more disconcerting is that those who were the best friends of freedom and upheld the legacy of classical liberalism, the economists, were the most adamant positivists and declared themselves most unbendingly against the view that one might, after all, learn moral and political truths.

In subsequent years I also discovered that one of the major difficulties faced by Western liberal societies has been that people seem unable to be morally inspired by its unique philosophy. The liberal political vision, understood in the tradition of John Locke, Adam Smith and John Stuart Mill, has had enormous success on the political front. It has on that score caught the imagination of many advanced civilizations. The economic achievements of societies that have more or less consistently followed that vision have also been impressive. They have encouraged the institution of market systems and, more recently, considerable privatization throughout the globe, including what used to be the socialist bloc. Most persons in such systems seem better off than they would be in the other types of system available to them.

Let me note straight away that by "the free market economy" or "capitalism" I do not mean societies in which trade is allowed by an authoritarian central government. Capitalism is here defined by reference to the legal principle of *the right to* private property, not by a public policy *permitting* exchange of various goods and services, a policy that might at any time be rescinded. That is the system for which a philosophical-ethical-theoretical grounding is wanted. (Although many critics of capitalism freely refer to various authoritarian systems by that term, Karl Marx knew well enough that what most clearly distinguishes capitalism from other political economies is the basic institution of private property rights, not just its occasional tolerance by some dictator or king.) This kind of political economy has failed thus far to command a dedicated following among the moral leadership of these societies. Numerous religious, literary and philosophical leaders keep denouncing the system as callous, greedy, alientating and otherwise dehumanizing.

The liberal vision is, of course, most loyally defended by economists: the last several Nobel prize winners in economics have all been ardent supporters of capitalism. These eminent scholars and figures do much to sustain the liberal vision, but they do not help to foster the awareness of its moral superiority. Mostly liberalism and its economic system, capitalism, are defended because they are a good engine of wealth creation; they produce abundant goods and services for most people and increase the standard of living for their citizens far more efficiently than all the alternatives that have been tried as organized social-political systems. It is thus mainly in terms of its instrumental worth, not its moral worth, that capitalism and thus Western liberal democracy gains its support.

Quentin Skinner of Cambridge University noted in his Tanner Lectures at Harvard University, "The Paradoxes of Political Liberty", that "We are very poor guardians of our own liberties." He referred to liberalism's "minimalist view of civic obligation" and lamented the "dangerous privatization" of certain values of Western civilization. In this he joined many others, including the late Leo Strauss, Daniel Bell, Irving Kristol, C. B. Macpherson and the noted columnist George Will, in suggesting that the most widely circulated kind of defense of capitalism is inadequate. It simply cannot give the support necessary to convince people to defend the system, to stand up for it proudly, to regard it as morally inspiring and even noble, even at a time when socialism is proving to be a practical failure.

In this work I will argue that the main trouble with defending capitalism is the definition of the concept of "human being" on which the defense usually relies. From this definition, put forward primarily by economists, it is not possible to generate a conception of the human good, except perhaps that most barren idea of subjective utility. In particular, most economists hold the view that human behaviour always amounts to pursuing self-interest, trying to maximize wealth, seeking to satisfy desires. Even those economists who dispute this have rarely developed a full alternative framework and thus, perhaps inadvertently, tacitly support the imperialist idea that the best tool for understanding the behavior of human beings in markets must also be the right view of human nature in general.

Critics argue, however, that this is quite inadequate, false to the fact and, moreover, self-defeating in the end. The assumption that we are all seeking just to satisfy ourselves does not even support the conclusion that we should actually stand up for our system. What if liberty, including capitalism itself, is under assault? If we are all just desire satisfiers, pleasure seekers, then we will not take on the often difficult task of defending our system, advocating it, supporting educational programs that show its merits, etc. People in the business community will just invest in immediate or longer-range profit making, and not in the uncertain, intangible task of spreading the word about capitalism, about how good it is for people. They charge that the economic human being, *homo economicus*, has no binding, rational reason for defending the features of his or her economic system that insure its survival in the long run. The economic human being is non-political and non-patriotic.

The critics do make a very good point. The defense of free political systems and markets cannot rely solely on economic arguments based on utility maximization, subjective value theory and the doctrine that what ultimately motivates human action in all realms susceptible to rational understanding is crass self- or vested interest. In the last analysis these arguments imply that people may even quite rationally act not to defend their freedom. This is the paradox of liberalism when taken as a general philosophy of life rather than as the political implication of a more fundamental moral understanding of human life.

But any theory that is incapable of self-defense is a self-defeating theory in the face of many competing ones that ask for courage and vigilance in their own support. Communism, socialism and the various theocratic or religiously inspired systems, such as Islamic fundamentalism, all call for valiant support from the people, promising honor, salvation and related moral rewards for such devotion. To reply to these systems something more potent is needed than merely saying, in the last analysis, "You will probably be wealthier in capitalism."

I will try to show that there is in general good reason to hold that human beings do indeed, and often should, act as prudent individuals. This is not, however, all there is to what they should do, to what they should regard as worthwhile, even in the framework of a sound capitalist outlook. They should also vigorously fight for and pursue certain (objective) values, of whose reality they can become convinced if only they examine the relevant evidence and arguments. Just because economic science does not offer a way to prove the value of individual liberty, including economic freedom, it does not mean there is no way rationally to support such values.

Once spelled out, a different approach to defending the free society will involve a different idea of human nature from that used by capitalist economists. That is just one of the differences between the economic and non-economic approach to defending values. Interestingly, Adam Smith, the "father of scientific economics", recognized the value of the moral defense of the free capitalist system in *The Wealth of Nations*, where he wrote the following:

> In [Greek] philosophy the duties of human life were treated of as subservient to the happiness and perfection of human life. . . . In [that] philosophy the perfection of virtue was represented as necessarily productive to the person who possessed it, of the most perfect happiness in this life. In the modern philosophy it was frequently represented as almost always inconsistent with any degree of happiness in this life, and heaven was to be earned by penance and mortification, not by the liberal, generous, and spirited conduct of a man. By far the most important of all the different branches of philosophy became in this manner by far the most corrupted.

I want to show that what is best about capitalism is that it enables its citizens to strive for a noble life on their own: it secures the freedom and independence of citizens, their personal sovereignty. Capitalism, in short, treats each mature individual as an adult moral agent, not as a ward or subject of the state.

At no point will I be talking about any actual, current political-economic system such as the United Kingdom or the United States of America. I would expect that, just as Marxists and other socialists discuss socialism and communism quite independently of the Soviet Union or the People's Republic of China, so those who would defend *laissez-faire* capitalism or the constitution of individual rights should be allowed to do so without being treated as apologists of the *realpolitik* of any actual political economic order. (Yet, no doubt, there is something in the widespread impression that the USSR embraces more socialist policies than do other nations, and that the USA has more kinship with *laissez-faire* capitalism than do other political communities.)

I want to demonstrate that the free system and its economic corollary, capitalism, accept that it is morally right for every person to act so as to become the happiest he or she can be. Here "happiness" is not left undefined but is tied to the nature of human beings and to the individual involved. Therefore this is not a subjectivist, undefined, arbitrary, "do whatever you desire" idea of human values, as critics have claimed and as many defenders have unfortunately agreed. Rather, the value of political liberty is an objectively demonstrable social priority for every individual; it is not optional whether it is such a primary value to a person. And it requires a great deal of moral effort for such liberty to be realized and maintained; that is, the full concentration and application of our essential human faculties. In this the alleged paradox of capitalism vanishes. The defense of liberty is no mere preference that many people might quite rationally omit from their list of priorities. It is not optional whether one should pursue liberty; rather it is a prominent civic responsibility.

If true, this outlook can defend both the free market and the imperative to strive to establish it. But more than that, such a defense of the system also preserves one of the most vital values of liberalism, as understood within the classical and neo-classical economic framework: its attention to human individuality and diversity. It seems to me that what has caught the imagination of economic champions of liberalism is its ability to satisfy such different conceptions of what is worth having and doing in life. But economists have drawn the wrong metaethical conclusions from this: that ethical relativism or subjectivism must be true. This is the fallacy of affirming the consequent. If subjectivism is right, then liberalism is right, and since liberalism is right, it is taken to have been proven that subjectivism is right. Both critics and proponents of liberalism accept this, and both are mistaken. Liberalism could well be right for reasons other than the alleged rightness of subjectivism. I want to argue that a proper understanding of individualism best explains the value of liberalism. And this understanding of individualism is not tied to ethical relativism or subjectivism.

I agree with the liberal that one ought to be free to pursue the values one chooses, which is impossible without economic liberty. Nevertheless, it is entirely consistent with this idea that one is also morally bound – which does not mean that one may be forced by others, that it be legally mandatory – to pursue some goals ahead of others. Defending human individual liberty, the core of liberalism, is just such a goal.

Let me finally say something about the limitations I face in this book. My aim is not to argue with everyone – welfare statist, socialist, fascist, etc. – although some of what I argue may have clear implications for whether the systems they believe in are sound. I do argue with many "middle-of-the-roaders" in my other books on political philosophy, including *Human Rights and Human Liberties* (1975), *Individuals and Their Rights* (1989a), *Marxism: A Bourgeois Critique* (1988), *Private Rights, Public Illusions* (1990) and *Liberty and Culture: Essays on the Idea of a Free Society* (1989b). Here I want to focus mainly on providing a better alternative to the *homo economicus* defense of the free market, capitalist political economy. Of course, that is not enough to show that such a political economy is superior to other systems. However, with the steps taken here, we can proceed to compare capitalism with those other systems and are likely to find its normative defense faring better than it has done thus far in the minds of many who have considered it and found it wanting. That is because, in the last analysis, politics is a normative endeavor, concerned with how human beings ought to live in each other's company.

Chapter 1

Problems with Hobbesian Individualism

HOBBESIAN INDIVIDUALISM AS A PREY FOR CRITICS

What makes a certain type of individualism such an appealing target for critics? What does this Hobbesian type of individualism amount to? What do its critics find wrong with it? How do the proponents of this view respond to their critics? Finally, are these responses adequate; do they fend off the complaints issued?

Neo-Hobbesian individualism considers persons as driven only by subjective motives. It sees all people as desire satisfiers who will act to fulfill what they desire in the best way they can. In the end people are passive, driven to act as they do and ultimately not deciding on their course of conduct of their own volition. Furthermore, none of the values persons embrace can be shown to have any objective validity: they are all a matter of personal preference. This is deemed to be a scientific outlook on human social life, understanding it in terms of laws of behavior and predictable events. Those who support this basic framework and use it to defend a free society, including and especially the free marketplace, would argue that for this kind of desire-satisfying person that kind of society, prizing mainly negative liberty, is best suited. It will best serve to make that person's life effective and prosperous as well as peaceful.

But neo-Hobbesian individualism – the position from which neo-classical economics emerges and which by some accounts supports a theory of natural rights and the libertarian political framework implied by it – suffers from serious flaws, the most serious being that it is evidently false to the facts. Human beings are not, and generally do not see themselves as, mere utility maximizers or desire satisfiers. Nor do they see their lives as being void of any objective values. Nor again are they or do they think of themselves as unable to choose what to do on their own initiative.

1

Defenders of neo-Hobbesian individualism accept much of the criticism but reply that what they believe is as much as we can affirm based on science. And anyway, the few things all people do seem to desire – prosperity, wealth, etc. – seem better achieved by the system implied by the neo-Hobbesian individualist picture, so what is wrong with it? People disagree over the means, not the ends, so why muddy the waters with a lot of talk about values and ideals, with what is good or right? We are dealing with a natural phenomenon, so why not make use of the methods of the natural sciences and leave such prescientific notions as ethics and morality out altogether? But this response is based on an obsolete view of science, and a discredited and largely false ontology and metaphysics; and it ignores some vital factors most ordinary persons rightly consider indispensable to a sound understanding of human affairs.

Let me now fill in some of the details. Later I will turn to a more successful individualist theory which will avoid the flaws of the neo-Hobbesian theory but retain some of its distinctive individualist and classical liberal implications.

QUANTITATIVE INDIVIDUALISM

The view of human nature that has been prominent among economists and some other social scientists may be dubbed, following David L. Norton's lead, quantitative individualism. It derives, ultimately, from Thomas Hobbes's atomistic materialism and nominalism. The view is atomistic in that it takes individuals to be ultimate, basic units in society, as distinct from regarding social groups (e.g. families, tribes, classes) as basic. It is materialist because all persons are treated as primarily composed of matter-in-motion and ultimately understandable by the laws of motion. And it is nominalist because the classification "human" is regarded as ultimately arbitrary, imposed by fiat, not as a matter of metaphysical or natural necessity. Our system of classification is deemed optional or nominal; that is, in name only.

This view affirms human individuality on the basis of the physical separateness of persons. Although quantitative, or numerical, individualism may not be so labeled by all those who embrace and discuss it, it is a widely known philosophical tradition. We find it not just in Thomas Hobbes but also in much of classical liberalism, and in classical and neo-classical economic theories.

The doctrine can be stated as follows. The respect in which something is an individual is that it is an entire or whole entity. It is entire and whole in that it exists separately from entire or whole entities other than itself. It has been grouped in the company of others, ultimately arbitrarily, and with no basic justification for it, by those who have chosen to classify reality as a matter of convenience, vested interest, personal desire or some other incidental motive; that is, by human beings.

An example of such an individual would be an auditorium chair. Although difficult to distinguish from others in the auditorium, it is nevertheless an individual, separate thing. Cows running in herds are also such individuals. And, of course, human beings are such individuals as well, although there may be more to their individuality. Each chair in an auditorium or each cow in a herd is quantitatively or numerically an individual but hardly an individual in any other respect. One may suppose that some unique attributes may obtain within each individual auditorium chair or herded cow but, from the point of view of being chairs or cows, those characteristics will not be relevant.

What would some of the universe's basic principles have to be for there to be individuals of the sort we have just considered? One plausible answer is that they would be those of Thomas Hobbes's reductive materialism. First, let us briefly note the historical connection between the conception of individuals along lines proposed by economists and Hobbes's viewpoint. Then let us look at the substance of that view.

There is a well-known historical connection between Hobbes's doctrine and individualism as most critics use the term. When, for example, David Norton speaks of *mechanistic* individualism as a doctrine "to which all modern individualism must acknowledge a debt",[1] he is referring to British individualism as first laid out by Hobbes. Was Hobbes's individualism motivated, as R. G. Tawney[2] and Karl Marx[3] maintain, by class interest? That really does not matter for now. Suffice it to keep in mind that it is to Thomas Hobbes that we must look to find the position's underpinnings.

The metaphysics of Hobbes's individualism is roughly this. Ultimately all of existence is composed of the same material stuff or matter-in-motion, however many shapes and forms this same stuff might take either accidentally or as a matter of our classification schemes. The Hobbesian mechanistic materialism, which in certain respects anticipates the views of Immanuel Kant and, of course, the contemporary pragmatist philosopher Willard Van Orman Quine,[4] accounts for differences in kinds by way of nominal classifications. As far as kinds or essentials or natures (as in the nature of cats or human beings) are concerned, any self-consistent classification would do, since in the last and only ontological analysis there is really, actually nothing beyond the uniform stuff of which existence is composed. Ultimately this renders the idea of human rights by nature (i.e. natural, basic rights), or any naturalist ethics, untenable.

As far as Hobbes's view applies to understanding human beings, it must be accepted that the beings we have come to identify as human are grouped together only because we have chosen to classify them so. Without our long accepted, shared but ultimately arbitrary interests, the very idea of "human being", not simply the English term, could well mean nothing at all. Or it might mean something very different from what it now happens to mean. Indeed, under nominalism it is difficult to figure out what it would be to "mean" anything. We simply decide to name various parts of nature in line with various arbitrary, albeit accustomed, objectives.

Let us put this Hobbesian view now in ways of particular interest to us: human beings are numerically individual combinations of the basic stuff of existence by virtue of our having come to classify them within a distinct group, but not for any other reason that we could rest on some independent reality.

This position had, and still has, a very strong intellectual appeal to those who wished to make clear, non-mystical, scientifically and naturalistically formed sense of the world around them. They probably also wished to cast an optimistic light on what could be done about many problems human beings faced. Indeed, contemporary positivism and behaviorism seem also to be inspired largely by the desire to help ourselves as we make our way in life and society. To look for the one overarching formula which will unlock the mysteries of existence need not be some naive ideological project, as many critics of Hobbes's materialist and individualist position maintain; it may simply be an effort to get things right.

Quantitative individualism, then, seems to be tied to a framework that is mechanistic in metaphysics and nominalistic in epistemology. Metaphysically all of reality, including real possibilities, is matter-in-motion. Epistemologically we have divided reality into classes which we think serve our convenience, needs and interests rather effectively. Nothing is objectively or inherently different from anything else, so far as we can tell. In turn, all beings are the same, and no fundamental, objective characteristic pertaining to beings outside what is fully accountable in terms of quantitative constituents (more or less of the same basic stuff) is identifiable in reality. Pebble, beast and person are all the same, however different they appear to us; and whatever their individuality consists of, ultimately it has to do with nothing more than their separability as beings subsumed within nominal classes.

If the framework within which quantitative individualism fits so well is correct, then quantitative individualism too would be correct and we would have to bite the bullet about all the "flagrant excesses" it "unleashes", leading to an economic, social, and political individualism that is "mechanical, egoistic, and smug". [5] I am inclined to believe that the roughly Hobbesian mechanistic materialism and nominalism, tied to

Galilean and Newtonian mechanics – with its promise of comprehending everything by reference to *the* laws of mechanical motion – is the most appealing and forceful framework from which quantitative individualism can emerge and has done so. There are other possibilities, but I will not discuss them here. In any case, they would seem less plausible since they would more readily admit a merger with a more robust individualism that I shall discuss later.

Certain crucial consequences flow from this reductive materialist, quantitative individualist viewpoint. There can be little doubt that, when the metaphysics of the situation line up as the Hobbesian reductivist would have it, there is no room for moral good and evil, and thus for justice, in human life and society in any but the most artificial sense.

Hobbes's own doctrine of natural law illustrates this clearly. It is but a scheme or technique necessitated by the presence of, firstly, the supposed drive for self-preservation and, secondly, numerous others who could be a threat but might also be instrumentally useful to the fulfillment of this drive. In Hobbes's philosophy we are fully determined, by motives produced by our circumstances, to forge a polity of a certain kind. There is no more room in this for the idea of natural morality and justice – which implies personal, individual responsibility for acting in a fashion that interpersonal morality requires, as well as the possibility of culpable failure to act that way – than for any other well-founded, non-conventional idea of merit, value or excellence.

In our time this is evident in the self-declared value-free status of much of contemporary social and, especially, economic science. For instance, F. A. Hayek, a leader of the Austrian school of economics and 1975 Nobel prize co-winner in economics, is quite adamant in denying that the market is just. As he puts it, "the question as to whether the resulting distribution of incomes [in a free economy] is just has no meaning". [6] Hayek approvingly quotes R. G. Collingwood saying that "A just price, a just wage, a just rate of interest, is a contradiction in terms. The question what a person ought to get in return for his goods and labor is a question absolutely devoid of meaning." [7] Milton Friedman, unofficial leader of the somewhat different Chicago school and another Nobel laureate, joins him on this score. The free market is quite indifferent as to matters of justice, and how could it be anything else? After all, justice implies the possibility of injustice, right the possibility of wrong, and in a deterministic socioeconomic universe there is no possibility of anything else but what in fact happens. And for Friedman, as well as for many others who speak from the viewpoint of neo-classical economics, " 'bad' and 'good' people may be the same people, depending on who is judging them". [8] In other words, as far as judgments of right and wrong are concerned, no objective truth is possible.

This viewpoint suggests also that human beings are ultimately not free to make moral choices. Even if there were some objective standard by which what they do and their various institutions could be evaluated as right or wrong, morally good or bad, they would be powerless to behave in ways other than those in which they actually do behave. Nobel laureate George Stigler's statement of the nature of human actions clearly suggests this. He tells us that "Man is an eternal utility maximizer – in his home, in his office (be it public or private), in his church, in his scientific work – in short everywhere."[9] Stigler's deterministic view is reaffirmed by his contention that we live in the best of all possible worlds: ours is just the world that our necessarily rational behavior produced.[10] That this is the general outlook to which we are led by neo-classical economics is well enough established.[11]

CRITICS OF ECONOMIC INDIVIDUALISM

The critics of the free market system that rests on Hobbesian individualism and its implications for social theory are full of complaints. They lament, most generally, that the market system lacks moral awareness and sensitivity: it makes room for greed, ambition and struggle, but lacks charity, generosity and compassion. As the protagonist in the film *The Revolutionary* put the point by way of a slogan painted on a brick wall, "Capitalism = the war of all against all".

The objections presented against the individualist, or egoist, constituents of capitalism may begin with those offered by Marx himself. His central thesis is that individualism is an ideology, a pseudo-philosophy that has as its historical mission to offer a temporary phase of humanity's history a degree of legitimacy and self-confidence. For Marx the capitalist system is a phase and individuality itself is an invention, as argued, for example, in John O. Lyons' *The Invention of the Self*, as well as in Alasdair MacIntyre's *After Virtue*.

More particularly, Marx complains that, among other things, the capitalist or bourgeois

> right of man to freedom is not based on the union of man with man, but on the separation of man from man. It is the right to this separation, the rights of the limited individual who is limited to himself.[12]

(For Marx the future will find all persons taking within themselves their "species-being", the collective nature of human beings; we will have come into our own, reached the state of true human freedom and collective emancipation.) This is the lament that unites Marxists and many non-

Marxists. Many other segments of our intellectual and academic community, non-Marxists yet still on the left of the political economic spectrum, are critical of individualism. For example, Robert Bellah, a sociologist at the University of California, Berkeley, has criticized individualism in various forums. Bellah, co-author of a prominent anti-individualist book,[13] argues that it is a mistake to link individualism to the ideal of a free society; quite the contrary, individualism is a threat to human liberty. (He cites Alexis de Tocqueville, among others, as an authority in support of his thesis.) It is, moreover, a serious enemy of community, fraternity and love of fellow human being.

The political–philosophical left is not alone in finding individualism fundamentally objectionable. Many from the right complain about it as well, including such luminaries as Walter Berns, George Will, Irving Kristol and Peter Berger.[14] Professor Harry V. Jaffa, one of the several widely published students of the late Leo Strauss, as well as one of the Aristotelians with Lockean leanings of the Strauss cadre (and both a political philosopher and a former champion of presidential candidate Barry Goldwater), expresses perhaps the most forceful philosophical objection to individualism when he says that "we must always look beyond that 'individual' [such as Shakespeare, Aristotle or Plato] to the species, and when we speak of species we are speaking of course of an order within a whole". Jaffa goes on to say that

> properly speaking, there is no such thing as individualism – for the very simple reason that there is no such thing as an individual . . . the word "individual" is an adjective. And an adjective ain't nothin' 'til there's a noun to which it is attached. It's an attribute without a substance.[15]

In all these cases the bottom line is that an individualist foundation of the natural rights system and its economic corollary, free market capitalism, impedes all efforts to forge a sound conception of justice. Individualism and justice are simply incompatible. And since individualism is the purported basis for natural rights politics and its economic system, capitalism, these too are incompatible with justice.

More particularly, there is no room for a moral perspective on human life in this outlook. It is ill-equipped to pay heed to the innumerable moral considerations that keep arising for us in our lives. This would not be so objectionable if neo-classical economics were not explicitly intellectually imperialistic, as is seen, for example, in the volume, edited by Gerard Radnitzky and Peter Bernholz, *Economic Imperialism*. In fact the economic viewpoint aims to comprehend all human affairs, and in this respect neo-classical economics aspires to be as much of a totalist viewpoint as does Marxism.

For decades we have heard about the lack of solid moral foundations for the free society. It has been expressed in a variety of ways, including with the charge that the free world is hedonistic, decadent, lacking in moral will and permissive in most of its social institutions. Not only Soviet Marxist propagandists and Islamic fundamentalists but also both conservatives and democratic socialists in the West make this charge. And, in a way, neo-classical defenders of capitalism fully concede the point.

Perhaps of greater interest to ordinary human beings, there is no natural place for human community life in the Hobbesian individualist system: human beings are treated as isolated, atomic beings, not linked with each other by a common nature. Critics, thus, lament the loss of community, the fragmentation of family life, the heavy influence of economic factors on where people live and how they establish their human associations; friendship, neighborliness and other normally desirable features of human existence are destroyed in a system that is hospitable to the free marketplace of economic exchange relations.

The commercialization of the professions is another concern widely expressed. There is no emphasis on professional ethics, especially in business, where anything seems to be permissible so long as the integrity of market relations is maintained. Doctors, dentists, artists, car manufacturers, masons, tailors, educators and scientists all become mainly commercial agents, with the focus on the craft waning and that on "the bottom line" becoming increasingly sharp and singular.

Paradoxically not even respect for the negative human rights of liberalism - the rights to life, liberty and property - can be said to find a solid base in this outlook. I have already noted how the idea of standing up for the principles of the free market seems to find no support in the neo-classical paradigm. But even the observance of principles such as human rights come to be no more than useful strategies to advance personal interests. If one could violate them with impunity, argues James Rachels for example, there would be every reason to do so and no reason not to.[16] The critics complain that life itself becomes unprincipled, that everything has its price, including love and friendship, which could well be betrayed for a good economic opportunity. As John Rawls notes, from within the Hobbesian egoist framework there is no possibility of genuine friendship: "Among persons who never acted in accordance with duty of justice except as reasons for self-interest and expediency there would be no bonds of friendship and mutual trust."[17] Such a person, Rawls argues, "lacks certain natural attitudes and moral feelings of a particularly elementary kind . . . [e.g.] resentment and indignation".[18]

There are many other arguments advanced against the individualism that follows the Hobbesian position. Nearly all criticisms directed at the free market system find their philosophical support in positions that reject the barrenness of the individualism associated with the Hobbesian tradition and most sharply exhibited in the works of neo-classical economists. They are the theorists who see each person as an isolated utility maximizer or desire satisfier. They are the theorists who treat all human decisions as forms of calculation in which the subjective costs and benefits that one is likely to incur from taking one or another action are weighed. Marx argued that "in modern bourgeois society, all relations are subordinated in practice to the one abstract monetary–commercial relation".[19] This clearly invites the most potent normative criticism of individualism since it denies individualist/capitalist societies the validity of all notions such as loyalty, betrayal, fidelity and honor.

Moreover, the *homo economicus* idea also generates the complaint that within a society so conceived the political institutions must become corrupted to serve only the wealthy or commercial members, not each member whose rights governments ought to protect. Here again Marx made the point in his unique fashion, maintaining that this is a necessary part of bourgeois society and that the idea that it could be avoided is nonsense. The intrusion of government in support of business is a natural consequence of the Hobbesian individualism that motivates capitalist systems. (Marx blamed Henry Carey, an American economist, for failing to realize "to what extent the state influences – public debt, taxes, etc. – themselves grow out of bourgeois conditions".[20])

If this Hobbesian, *homo economicus* individualism is the only version on which to rest the free market system, then that system is in serious trouble. Contrary to widespread opinion, mostly among neo-classical economists, it will not give adequate support to a theory of basic property rights in the Lockean tradition.[21] A Hobbesian theory of rights does not manage to secure the case for the institution of individual property rights. Only the Lockean natural rights theory, and even that only with serious revisions, manages to do this. It advances a viable, morally palatable conception of a just social order that supports the free market system. It will be important to see whether a kind of individualism that does support such rights is sound and can answer certain criticisms of capitalism.

THE HOBBESIAN ANSWER TO CRITICS

What do neo-classical economists maintain in the face of these laments? What is their answer?

As against Marx, the neo-classical, neo-Hobbesian theorists have mainly taken the tack of cross-examining their critics and showing that Marx has nothing coherent and feasible to offer. Or they have argued, in a related fashion, that Marx ignores the findings of the classical liberal, neo-classical, neo-Hobbesian school, for example the truth of the subjective utility theory of market or economic value. If the Marxist argues that capitalism exploits the workers, the strategy is to argue that Marx has ignored the fact that values are subjective and the exchange economy actually delivers to everyone what is best under the circumstances. For example, David Conway argues against Marx that

> Capitalism has the great virtue of allowing people to pursue their self-interest in ways that at the same time promote the interests of others. For the essence of exchange is that, where uncoerced, both parties are better off for having engaged in it.[22]

Thus he freely invokes the famous subjective theory of value which accounts for the economic value of commodities solely in terms of their "utility", or what I would call "preference fulfillment". In other words, Conway follows the neo-classical and Austrian economists in his account of what gives something its economic value. And he seems to accept, with others of this school, that once one's economic values have been secured, that alone accounts for being "better off". That is where he joins in the imperialism of the neo-classical school.

Some, such as Thomas Sowell, have gone to great lengths to defuse the Marxist line of attack.[23] They have argued against the entire Marxist edifice, all the way from calling into question the dialectical approach to studying history to dismissing the theory of human nature Marx advances.[24]

Essentially, however, the neo-Hobbesians argue that we must grasp the nettle. There is no room for morality in the ordinary, normative sense of that concept; no room for justice in the marketplace. What some economically ignorant people may regard as moral convictions – for example, what may lead some intellectuals to support socialist policies or government intervention – are really beliefs serving economic self-interest. As Stigler notes cynically, "That intellectuals should believe that intellectuals are important in determining the course of history is not difficult to understand."[25] Of course, he exempts those who qualify as scientists in his terms: "The most influential economist, even in the area of public policy, is the economist who makes the most important scientific contributions."[26] But since, according to Stigler and co., there is no scientific basis for discussing morality, intellectuals who explore ethics are influential only as disguised utility maximizers. Their ethical claims carry no conviction similar to that attributed by Stigler to the economist *qua* scientist.

As the position would have it, then, subjectivism is correct: moral judgments involving blame or praise, claims as to what is right and wrong, are unfounded and at best merely show what a person prefers. Even there it is best to pay heed to "revealed preferences", to actual behavior in the marketplace, since that is the most reliable, empirical evidence for what people prefer, for what course of conduct they choose. Most of those Hobbesians who actually discuss the topic of foundations subscribe to a fairly straightforward positivism. Even the more complex Hobbesian views, such as that of David Gauthier in *Morals by Agreement*, rely on a Quinean conventionalist metaphysics. In terms of this view, it is optional what metaphysical system and ontology we select so long as we remain consistent. Accordingly, however, there is nothing ultimately necessary about our moral system; indeed, morals are a system of strategy for survival or utility maximization.

This line of defense is intellectually quite potent. For several hundred years, roughly since the onset of the scientific revolution in the sixteenth century, the philosophical base for morality has been quite uncertain. The one major exception, Immanuel Kant, had to pay a considerable price for reprising the idea of morality as meaning individual human responsibility for doing the demonstrably right thing. Kant had to divide the human individual into a noumenal and phenomenal self; one exposed to moral assessment, the other open only to scientific study. In short, even for Kant, the person the economist studies, the behaving individual in the marketplace, is but a complex and fully determined biological machine.

The economic defense of the free market, which is also referred to as the classical liberal defense, has therefore come to be regarded as *the* scientific defense. And there is no doubt that the mantle of science is a powerful one, at least for those who want to subject the study of human social life to cognitive standards associated with the tradition of materialism and empiricism. This is a powerful bulwark against the intellectual critics regardless of its lack of popular appeal and ultimate theoretical cogency.

Furthermore, even if one wishes to rank political-economic systems by some empirically meaningful standards, there is no question that the marketplace offers at least one thing that is indisputably widely desired: prosperity. Wealth maximization is clearly something the capitalist system makes possible, since it is the most efficient way to organize a human community. And while people may fret a great deal about morality, friendship, justice, generosity and compassion, all these are ultimately sentimental issues. What counts, according to this position, is that capitalism is the engine of production.

A related major consideration in defense of the neo-Hobbesian viewpoint is that the efforts to establish and manage alternative, planned or regulated, political economies have met with colossal failure. The market system may be criticized everywhere, but it is still the place that delivers the goods, and ordinary people acknowledge this when they choose the USA in preference to most other systems of social organization when they emigrate. That is why there is so much talk of reform in the Soviet Union, the People's Republic of China, Hungary, Poland and elsewhere in Eastern Europe, and why, even in the more socialist oriented Western nations, such as the UK and France, there has been so much attention paid to what is called privatization, the transfer of various tasks from the government to the private sector.

It is clear, then, that the neo-classical alternative is still quite potent. Its appeal may be directed more towards the pragmatic side of our lives, where we are mostly concerned with our economic welfare. But because we are clearly concerned with our economic welfare, there is certainly something to the economists' rebuttal to Hobbes's critics.

Nevertheless, some serious flaws remain in the paradigm. The kind of response to Marx made by Conway and many others will not do. Two problems with the Conway response are worth mentioning. Firstly, it is futile to maintain, at least to the unconverted, that in economic exchange "both parties are better off for having engaged in it". If A trades his ounce of cocaine for B's ounce of crack, is it not more credible to claim that neither party benefited? At most, and even this is rather tortuous, both believe they have benefited. Often no such belief accompanies destructive trade, as, for example, in impulse buying. Secondly, Marx was concerned not so much with economic value as with what is the objective value of that which has economic value. In other words, he was concerned with political economy. Mere demand does not seem to do the trick, since persons often demand what is, in fact, very bad – even for themselves.

Let me also mention two other basic problems with the neo-Hobbesian line, as it emerges from the replies to its critics. Firstly, even as a science it is less an empirical theory than a tautological doctrine. Consider the meaning of "utility maximization" or "private interest" within the position. We are told, by Milton Friedman for example, that

> The interests of which I speak are not simply narrow self-regarding interests. On the contrary, they include the whole range of values that men hold dear and for which they are willing to spend their fortunes and sacrifice their lives.[27]

Yet if that is the case, how are we to distinguish between behavior that is self-interested and behavior that is not? If utility maximization involves all possible human actions – even, as some argue, the actions of genes[28] – what do we learn from being informed that we are all utility maximizers? Indeed, what is to be understood by the claim that a free market, capitalist system is more able to give us prosperity than some alternative? It amounts to a tautology: the fact of it being a free system – that is, one that does not permit the coercion of one person by another, although no normative sense can be given to the idea of coercion – automatically ensures it, by definition, of being the most productive or prosperous system. Free behavior that is utility maximizing. In short, this view holds that we all do what we do, when we are not forced to do something else. OK. But what are we doing under such circumstances, and why is that such a good thing? Why should we prefer the system that has this result, and why should we prefer it to, maybe even defend it from, alternative systems?

Secondly, to the extent that the economic defenders of free market capitalism make a good point, they make it by implicitly relying on a frame of reference that they otherwise do not embrace. They talk of capitalism serving our self-interest. It may well do this, but not because by "self-interest" we mean any concern a person may have. It is a plausible claim because there are clearly greater opportunities in a free market system than in alternatives to it to discover what actually does make one's life better as a human being and an individual. And indeed, the system makes the enhancement of that life more likely, especially in so far as this enhancement depends on the personal efforts of the agent. So, yes, one's self-interest may be better pursued under a free market system than in systems that deprive one of the authority to run one's life. That, at least, is the plausible claim made in support of the capitalism that is supposed to flow from neo-Hobbesian individualism.

But we cannot make full sense of this claim in neo-Hobbesian terms. By this view, whether one purchases narcotics or vitamins one is necessarily enhancing one's self-interest. Even committing crimes is *always* a case of utility maximization.[29] So even where the economic defense of capitalism makes the best sense, a different, objective conception of human values and interests from that provided by the neo-Hobbesian view must be smuggled in.

Furthermore, the general paradigm of what being scientific amounts to, and the attendant adoption of the empiricist epistemology and reductive materialist metaphysics, can be and certainly has been prominently called into question. The demise of philosophical positivism came because of insurmountable problems with keeping that system coherent. In the natural or hard sciences, empiricism and materialism do not hold out much promise: theoretical entities, for which no unambiguous empirical groundings are available, permeate physics, astronomy, chemistry and biology.

Finally, as I have suggested, whatever its intellectual plausibility, the neo-Hobbesian approach will not play well even with the bulk of the educated lay public. Most of us are too well aware of cruelty, hardship, unfairness, injustice, callousness and lack of generosity. We are, of course, equally aware of decency, benevolence, kindness, industriousness, productivity and courage. Both vices and virtues are too evident to us in human life for us blithely to accept the morally barren viewpoint the neo-Hobbesians offer about the nature of reality. We will rather put some of the blame for these troubles on those denying all this, such as the champions of the free market economy and their institution!

Marxism, the most comprehensive alternative to the classical liberal line, has flaws, some seemingly fatal. Yet I would argue that we will choose it if our only alternative is quantitative individualism. We are probably like the person near death from thirst in the Sahara desert who comes upon a water hole and reads, "Poisonous water, do not drink." This fellow knows that without water death is certain, but some poisons have been survived. So why not give the bad drink a chance?

We should explore, in consequence of the above, whether there is an alternative to quantitative individualism that successfully avoids these criticisms and serves as a morally sensitive foundation for the free market system. I plan to spend the rest of this work doing so. However, I need to make clear that there is much more to proving conclusively the superiority of a system of political economy than can be done in one volume. My main objective is to show that there is an alternative to neo-Hobbesian individualism that can hold its own against the critics where the neo-Hobbesian view does badly. Whether that is sufficient to defeat the contenders from other corners is a different issue.

NOTES

1. Norton, *Personal Destinies*, p. 42. This point is stressed forcefully in Arblaster, *The Rise and Decline of Western Liberalism*. It needs to be noted that, although Hobbes's doctrine is probably the most prominent internally consistent secular grounding of individualism, it is by no means the only system on which the liberal individualist vision has been grounded. The liberalism we find expressed or at least supplemented in the works of Grotius, Pufendorf, the Physiocrats, Tracy, Say, Bastiat, de Molinari and Auberon Herbert by no means owes much to Hobbes and the reductive materialist or physicalist tradition. Yet the reason Hobbes is significant is that the support for free market capitalism now lies in the hands of the economists and here he clearly is the main philosophical progenitor.
2. Tawney, *Religion and the Rise of Capitalism*.
3. Marx, *Grundrisse*, trans. by M. Nicholas.
4. The former, since Hobbes seems to have believed in something like categories of the understanding that design the world for us; the latter since he also seems to regard these categories as conventional.
5. Norton, *Personal Destinies*, p. 43.
6. Hayek, "Equality, value, and merit", p. 346.
7. *Ibid.*, p. 350.
8. Friedman, *Capitalism and Freedom*, p. 12.
9. Stigler, "Economics or ethics?" p. 332.
10. For examples of this line of thinking, see Leube and Moore (eds.), *The Essence of Stigler*, particularly, "Why have the socialists been winning?", pp. 337-46. See also Stigler, *The Intellectual and the Marketplace*, *The Economist as*

Preacher, and Other Essays (in particular, "Do economists matter?" pp. 57–67), and "The Adam Smith Lecture: the effect of government on economic efficiency" pp. 7–13. (In this last piece Stigler argues that all governmental policies are utility maximizing for the country!) See for basic components of a similar thesis, Ekelund and Tollison, *Mercantilism as a Rent-Seeking Society*.

The essence of this type of explanation of human affairs is that we are all necessarily rationally motivated to seek advantages in whatever ways we can and the human world is simply the result of these efforts plus nonhuman natural events. For the pioneering work on this particular theme, see Buchanan, Tollison and Tullock (eds.), *Toward a Theory of the Rent-Seeking Society*.

11. See McKenzie, *The Limits of Economics Science*, pp. 31ff. See also Gray, "The economic approach to human behavior", pp. 46ff.
12. Marx, *Selected Writings*, p. 53.
13. Bellah et al., *Habits of the Heart*. For an even more radical thesis, one that maintains that the individual self never existed and is a pure as well as regrettable invention of the eighteenth century, see Lyons, *The Invention of the Self*. The charge that Hume invented the self is odd since he seems to have denied that it is anything but a series of experiences. Descartes might be better credited with this "invention", when he gave primacy to the conscious self in the cogito. All in all, however, the self, as ordinarily affirmed by all persons now and then – i.e. the deciding, choosing, wanting, desiring, thinking and criticizing agent that one often is – seems to have made its appearance throughout recorded history.
14. Some particularly biting criticisms may be found in Bell and Kristol (eds.), *Capitalism Today*. See, for a good example, Kristol, " 'When virtue has lost all her loveliness': some reflections on capitalism and 'The Free Society' ", pp. 13–26. For a more sweeping criticism of the neo-classical economic approach to understanding human affairs, especially law, see Baker, "The ideology of the economic analysis of law".
15. Jaffa, "A conversation with Harry V. Jaffa at Rosary College", p. 11.
16. Rachels, "Two arguments against ethical egoism".
17. Rawls, *A Theory of Justice*, p. 488.
18. *Ibid.*
19. Marx, *Selected Writings*, p. 185.
20. Marx, *Grundrisse*, ed. by D. McLellan, p. 49.
21. That tradition takes private property rights to be negative rights, prohibitions on the use of force against one's person or belongings (achieved through labor or free trade). There are some who hold that property rights are positive, entitling one to be provided with goods.
22. Conway, *A Farewell to Marx*, p. 50.
23. Sowell, *Marxism*.
24. See, for example, Topitch, "How enlightened is 'dialectical reason'?"
25. Friedman, *Capitalism and Freedom*, p. 200.
26. *Ibid.*, p. 331. "Please do not read into my low valuation of professional preaching a similarly low valuation of scientific work" (*ibid*). Does this square with Stigler's imperialist thesis that "man is eternally a utility maximizer . . . [e.g.] in his scientific work . . ."? And, in any case, what force can his low valuation of anything have (in his own terms) if all such valuations are subjective and have no objective significance? What is the objective difference between Stigler's view of preaching intellectuals and the intellectuals' own view other than that one is one's, the other the other's? Is there any room for

an objective difference in the kind of position to which Stigler and his followers are (sometimes inadvertently) committed?
27. Leube and Moore (eds.), *The Essence of Stigler*, p. 330.
28. Dawkin, *The Selfish Gene*.
29. Becker, "Crime and punishment". For a more radical application of Beckerian imperialism, see Hemmermesh and Soss, "An economic theory of suicide".

Chapter 2

Economic "Science": An Amoral Discipline?

WHITHER THE ECONOMIST'S REJECTION OF MORALITY?

One reason why I am very concerned with the topic of this work is that the main defense of Western liberalism has come from the social science of economics. If that defense is flawed because the Hobbesian individualism that backs it is untenable, knowledge of the fact is very important. And it is even more important to learn whether this political order may nevertheless still find support in a different philosophy. Can Western liberal capitalism be supported from a different view, one that is less vulnerable to the objections raised against the neo-Hobbesian one?

In Chapter 1 I explained why in general terms the neo-Hobbesian, *homo economicus* defense is very likely to be untenable. Here I wish to develop some of my reasons by reference to certain applications of that framework, particularly to analyzing the workings of government. Let me stress that my purpose is to show the deficiency of the general framework from which the completely free market is being defended by various prominent economists. I make this point so as to prepare the way for advancing a different approach to a similar end: the defense of the wholly free market system. This explains why I do not advance arguments against views that fall between the fully free market and the centrally planned (including democratic or market socialist) economies. It is a separate issue entirely whether for various reasons the welfare state or some similar position between free capitalist and fully statist economies should not, after all, be regarded superior to either, even after I defend capitalism on the basis of what I argue is a superior normative theory.

Milton Friedman, F. A. Hayek, and James Buchanan are contemporary thinkers who advance the classical liberal social vision as the most sensible live option in political economy. And they have tended to rely for their support on the neo-Hobbesian viewpoint, albeit not in identical terms. All three clearly share the view that economics is a value-free social science and that what persons gain from the system that economic analysis supports is a good shot at prosperity in their lives. Friedman is perhaps the most straightforwardly positivist economist. Hayek sees matters a bit differently, but the difference does not matter much for our purposes. Instead of prosperity and liberty, Hayek thinks that the market helps to secure the growth of knowledge because it encourages spontaneity and thus the most efficient spread of information, as well as the development of the most (evolutionarily) fitting institutions in society. Their predecessors, John Locke, Adam Smith and John Stuart Mill, have written most persuasively in support of limited government and the free market. Buchanan also has his unique ideas. But in the end he too is a neo-Hobbesian and finds room for what is called a social contractarian idea of morality only because he assumes all individuals would agree to certain rules of conduct once they emerge from the state of nature. None of these thinkers finds the prospect of natural, objective, nonconventional moral values very promising.

As I noted in my Preface, one of the most theoretically potent charges leveled at defenders of the free market system was issued by Quentin Skinner. Are we, as he claims "very poor guardians of our own liberties"? Do we have a "minimalist view of civil obligation"? Does his lament about the "dangerous privatization" of certain values of Western civilization not make a valid point?[1] What Skinner had in mind is that whether one values the institutions of the free society seems to be left by economists to private taste. And indeed, by that framework there can be no binding obligation for anyone to defend this system. Economic science, the main bulwark against statism in our time, does not show that we ought to defend our own liberties.

If the charge made by Skinner is correct, it has major geopolitical consequences. The situation he describes could be a major threat to the preservation of freedom all over the globe. If the most prominent, formidable defense of the free system cannot make sense of the idea that the system ought to be defended, if it must leave the issue optional, a matter of private preference, the intellectual backbone to the free society is seriously weakened, if not broken. Nor can that kind of system gain the adherents it might from the newly-opened societies of Eastern Europe and Asia.

The main source of liberalism's self-defeatism is its reliance on the *homo economicus* model of human nature. The definition of "human being" employed by liberal economists may differ as to precise content, but most, including members of the Chicago, Austrian and public choice schools, hold to the general idea, as expressed by Dennis Mueller, that "man is an egoistic, rational, utility maximizer".[2]

Some may doubt that this is true of the Austrian school, yet an examination of von Mises's *Human Action* will show that even for the Austrians what motivates people to act is an inner drive to improve their conditions, the need to crush an uneasiness associated with unfulfilled desire. Among public choice theorists, too, James Buchanan can no longer be held responsible for accepting the simple *homo economicus* model we find in, say, Gary Becker's *The Economic Approach to Human Behavior*. But being a Hobbesian, Buchanan would have to explain people entering a social contract by reference to the urge to survive. In all these cases, the economist would claim that being scientific requires that they hold such a value-free, descriptive idea of human nature, one that manages to make no room for genuine choice or free will, or for objective morality.

We have already noted George Stigler's claim that "Man is eternally a utility-maximizer – in his home, in his office (be it public or private), in his church, in his scientific work – in short, everywhere."[3] This idea underlies most neo-classical, scientific economic analysis and is often generalized, just as in Stigler, to apply to all human action, not just to some possibly distinct economic realm. Sometimes it is argued that the idea is merely a useful fiction, an unrealistic but fruitful assumption. Yet in most works no such qualification is advanced for it.

The amorality of the economists' viewpoint is not difficult to apprehend. No basis for moral judgment can be found therein, nor little if any room for the sort of human being that we associate with the idea of moral agency or individual responsibility for actions. Yet there is clearly plenty of evidence for even economists taking morality very seriously, as when they criticize each other, their children or others in their society. While they might subscribe to subjectivism officially, they lay it aside as they criticize other human beings or take the blame for some misdeeds. All in all, then, the idea that there is a moral dimension to human life that rests on more than (even deep-seated) subjective preference should not be so revolting to economists.

Furthermore, there is the plain matter that the very idea of trade or exchange of commodities embodies certain value considerations. For trade to make sense, something must be owned by someone, and ownership is a moral phenomenon. To say "A owns X" means, in part, that "None other than A ought to have a decisive say about what happens to X." This does not mean that none other will have such a say – a thief very well could. But even to understand theft we have to confess some understanding of the moral issue of who ought to have what say over what.

Accordingly, the moral dimension of life touches economics at a very basic level, in the definition of market exchange, of trade. Why should it be so unthinkable, then, that there are additional moral dimensions of human life, some private, familial and fraternal, some social and some political, pertaining to one's role as a citizen in a human community?

It thus seems that even from the economists' viewpoint the amoralism that is contained in the neo-classical paradigm cannot find full or consistent acceptance. There is ample activity economists engage in, even as economists, that has a moral dimension to make this amoralism highly questionable.

THE PUBLIC CHOICE APPROACH

In 1986 Professor James M. Buchanan of George Mason University received the Nobel prize in economics. He was rewarded for his pioneering work in the field that has come to be called public choice theory, an arm of economic analysis that studies the behaviour of politicians and bureaucrats, especially in a representative democracy such as the United States.

Public choice theory is perhaps the most easily accessible of the several efforts to make economics into an imperial discipline, the tools of which enable us to study and understand human social life in general, not simply its economic dimensions. It is an especially noteworthy example of the amoralist stance economists take toward human affairs.

Briefly, in public choice theory we are urged to forget about our moralistic approach to the vocation of a public official, supposedly characterized by disinterested service to the public and the rejection of private gain as a main professional objective. Public choice theory holds that this is a hopeless outlook and that, just as everyone in the marketplace seeks to maximize his or her utilities, so too does the public official. If we conceive of public service accordingly, we will be able to understand its ramifications correctly; for example, we will be able to predict the development of public affairs and policies.

Buchanan developed his theory with cooperation from other economists, most notably Gordon Tullock. (Indeed, later Buchanan and Tullock parted on some issues, including the topic of whether economic analysis is as powerful a tool as the imperialists believe. Buchanan developed doubts about this and now makes use of other disciplines for purposes of understanding social life.) Buchanan's and Tullock's book, *The Calculus of Consent*, pioneered the new application of economics. Since its publication, others have followed, including the scholarly journal of the Center for Study of Public Choice, *Public Choice*, edited by Tullock, which publishes extensive and complex, often quantitative, studies on a great variety of topics of concern to public choice theorists. Buchanan and Tullock have also inspired numerous other economists, philosophers, political scientists and legal theorists to explore various implications of the public choice approach.

Public choice theory is just one offshoot of the economic approach to human behavior (another being the field of law and economics). Essentially, public choice theorists hold that, when people enter government and become "public" servants, they act on the same motives they would if they were agents in the marketplace. "Public" servants are motivated by private interests no less than are men and women in business. As Buchanan puts it:

> Politicians and bureaucrats are seen as ordinary persons, and "politics" is viewed as a set of arrangements, a game if you will, in which many players with quite disparate objectives interact so as to generate a set of outcomes that may not be either internally consistent or efficient.[4]

Public choice theory, Buchanan says, also holds that "The bureaucracy can play off one set of constituents against others, insuring that budgets rise much beyond plausibly efficient limits."[5]

To appreciate adequately why public choice theory delivers its paradoxical conclusions concerning what our public servants actually do, namely further their own private or vested interests, one needs to know the basic postulates of contemporary economic science. Mainstream economics today assumes that we are always behaving so as to maximize our satisfactions or wealth. As another Nobel prize winner in economics, Milton Friedman, expressed the point:

> [E]very individual serves his own private interest. . . . The great Saints of history have served their "private interest" just as the most money grubbing miser has served his interest. The *private interest* is whatever it is that drives an individual.[6]

Or as Gary Becker put it in spelling out the fundamental tenets of his social scientific approach to understanding human affairs:

> The combined assumptions of maximizing behavior, market equilibrium, and stable preferences, used relentlessly and unflinchingly, form the heart of the economic approach as I see it.[7]

What this view means in common parlance is that economic science assumes that we are all driven by our desires. These are ranked in order so that some of us prefer sweet things, fresh air, excitement, music and sports in that order, and others do not. It is such desires to have or do various things that motivate us and there is nothing from the economic point of view that needs to be said about whether these are good things or bad. And in the more extreme scientistic versions of economics, there is nothing anyone can do about what will motivate people. Our motives are simply what explains what we do, period. And if we wish to understand people's behavior, we need to pay attention to the fact that they are motivated by their desires.

Of course, there are various fine nuances in economic theory which are not captured in the above general statements. But the main point is that we must do what we desire to do. And public choice theorists take this view into the special area of understanding the behavior of public officials by asserting, as a corollary of general economic analysis, that we do this not only as shoppers, bankers, merchants, corporate executives, brokers and the like, but also as "public" servants.

REVISING COMMON SENSE

There would be little interest in public choice analysis if it did not serve to modify our nontechnical understanding of how public servants behave. That is why Professor Buchanan was honored with the Nobel prize. He pointed out something that we were not normally aware of – indeed, something that we would very likely have missed without him.

Ordinarily we take it that politicians, bureaucrats, diplomats and other "public" servants are devoted, by a professional commitment or even oath, to the public interest, not to what they privately desire. At least, we take this as their professional responsibility, something they ought to be doing. A public servant is not supposed to be a profit maximizer, one who wants to fully satisfy himself or herself in a competitive market place. Put plainly, such a person is supposed to pursue the public interest.

Yet public choice theorists deny this common assumption. What they say by way of economic analysis may be put in more familiar terms: they believe that people in public positions really try to advance their own lot before anyone else's. Is this really the whole story?

PUBLIC VERSUS PRIVATE SERVICE
IN THE WELFARE STATE

Governments of welfare states get involved in all sorts of activities where the objective is to achieve particular goals that various individuals and small or large groups of citizens seek to achieve. They further the lot of artists (via the various arts councils and endowments), farmers (via subsidies and price support programs), various professions (via licensing requirements), car workers or high-tech industries (via trade policies) and so on. The welfare state is expected by many to make extensive governmental provisions for its people. So even if its officials tried conscientiously to fulfill their duties to their constituency, they would necessarily serve private interests and go astray in the task associated with public service, namely to do only that which serves the public as such. Thus it is not surprising that "public servants" in the welfare state are not able to keep their mind on what the public interest as such happens to be. Virtually no meaningful distinction between the public and the private interest is possible when government promotes the very same kind of ends that are promoted in the private sector.

Indeed, in modern democratic states, as soon as some of the constituents are dissatisfied with how the private sector achieves (or fails to achieve) some given objective, governments are approached with the aim of taking over or supplementing the task. Many examples come to mind but a very apt recent case is day care centers. Although hundreds of private companies and other agencies provide single or working parents with child care facilities, there is constant support from various segments of the public for government expanding its involvement in this activity. From AIDS research to trade restrictions, the bulk of contemporary legislation comes to little more than government helping people with their private or vested interests, misnaming it all as the pursuit of the public interest. There simply appears to be no public interest distinct from the varied private or special interests the government now also serves.

Various programs of the US Federal government are supposed to support undergraduate college students with scholarships. One of these is the Jacob J. Javits National Graduate Fellowship Program. (I have been personally familiar with its operations during the first few years following its inception in 1985.) As in other such programs, individuals from within diverse branches of the educational profession are appointed to oversee and administer this program. Colleges and academic associations devoted to graduate education appeal to these people for a good program, one that really does help deserving graduate students. At the same time, others are asking government to fulfill different and competing goals.

In this case public choice theorists would find a clear application of the assumptions of their view. What happens in cases such as the above conforms perfectly to what public choice theory would predict. Those on the overseeing board eagerly promote the efficient administration and ample funding of the program in question. They select the appropriate panels and panel chiefs, they encourage the supporting staff, in this case from the Department of Education, and they report back to Congress with information and requests for further and more abundant support for the program. They are thereby advancing their interests as educators, as bureaucrats, as members of a special interest group; that is, as utility maximizers.

VESTED VERSUS PUBLIC INTEREST: A MEANINGFUL CONTRAST

But there is another way to describe what is going on here. It may be compatible with public choice theory but it does not cast the situation in the same conceptual light. And it may be important to try to do this because the public choice theory idea is rather pessimistic and may even be vacuous.

If we are all really just trying to gain our own advantage, even when we swear that that is not what we will be doing in our role as politicians or bureaucrats, what is the use of even pointing this out? Those assigned to fix the situation, even at the institutional level (as Buchanan suggests), would really be simply pursuing the same hopeless path as all the other "public" servants. Even public choice theorists must be understood to be making note of the entire problem primarily because doing so serves their economic interest. After all, did Stigler not say that we maximize our utilities as scientists? That could mean that we are willing to promote just those findings that advance our projects.

In cases such as the Javits Program, appointed overseers and administrators take an oath to do a good job. They are asked to report to Congress about how well they are managing to do what members of Congress have decided needs doing. In most of these cases the administrators see that the money they have to administer the program is not enough to do the job as well as they can easily conceive of doing it. After all, if the people take an oath to administer a program, they should do it right, shouldn't they? This is so at least where the task is a serious one and not some casual or playful adventure. In point of fact several of those on the Javits board refused to support others who wanted to ask Congress for greater support for the program. In 1987, when their first report went to the US Congress, there was no mention of the desirability of additional funds, mainly because several board members refused to sanction such an appeal by the traditional approach of transforming a report into a lobbying effort. They simply resisted the effort, risking their own possible removal from the board when their appointment came up for renewal. While this is no earthshaking case, it does serve as an illustration.

As I have just described it, what happens in bureaucracies need not really be a case of politicians and bureaucrats simply wishing to fulfill their desires, nor of being driven by private interest – not quite, although that is clearly part of it. This is especially so when we focus on the staff hired to administer the programs in question; that is, "those persons", as Buchanan describes them, "who actually *supply* the goods and services that are provided via governmental auspices". Even they are quite conceivably only doing their jobs. After all, if police officers, the quintessential public servants (in that they are upholding the law for everyone) ask for more staff, better equipment, etc., surely this can be understood as pursuing the public interest – in this case probably used in its proper, restricted sense of serving people in their capacity as members of a human community who observe certain rules just so as to be participants?

MODIFYING PUBLIC CHOICE THEORY

Some friendly critics now make a point against public choice theory that seems to take into account the above understanding of what goes on in public administration. They seem to be aware that referring merely to the private or vested interest of those involved in carrying out the project fails to do full justice to the situation. They contend that, in order for public choice theory to explain adequately how politicians and bureaucrats behave, one must also consider the belief system that motivates them: whether they are conservatives, liberals, libertarians, socialists or whatever, and whether they have a bona fide commitment to the programs involved or are merely advancing their private agenda in the administration of such a program. They may even have a bona fide public service orientation, albeit one manifested in a somewhat unorthodox manner.

Some who have been studying public choice theory have suggested that an "ideology" variable must be added to the public choice or *homo economicus* model so as to explain what members of the US Congress and other bureaucrats do as they approach their various projects. In particular, Joseph Kalt and Mark Zupan have studied what the US Senate did in the case of coal strip mining. Their statistical analysis shows that the "ideology" variable explains the voting patterns of the Senate on the Surface Mining Control and Reclamation Act (passed in 1977) better than does the public choice model. In short, in addition to considering the desires of the legislators to be re-elected, of the bureaucrats to continue on and expand their jobs and so on, we need also to consider the broader political ideals of public agents.

Economic imperialists reply, however, that adding the ideological variable does no damage to the *homo economicus* model. They will say that the urge to follow an ideology is no less a case of utility maximization than the urge to seek a vacation in the Bahamas or to increase one's income. But this simply makes a shambles of the explanatory value of the *homo economicus* model. Any factor or model that explains anything whatever – for example, self-defeating as well as self-serving conduct – simply explains nothing much! If the model fully explains the bank-robber as well as the banker, what can we learn from the explanation? In no science would this kind of approach be admitted; the melting of the ice explained by the same factor as the freezing of the water, private interest! In fact, when the economists explain anything plausibly enough, there are sure to be found some additional assumptions that make the crucial difference, assumptions that are not part of economics, such as those concerning psychological assessments, ascription of cost estimate (which is an unexplained datum in economics, since for economists cost and benefit are both subjective matters) and treatment of available information. Why do some people prefer X to Y? No answer here. Why do they value rather than disvalue (i.e. regard as cost rather than benefit) some activity, such as labor? How is it that they did not find out about something and are now ignorant?

In order to avoid this vacuousness, the "ideological variable" has to be seen as adding a dimension, namely what kind of conduct human beings take to be proper, what they see as binding on them quite apart from what they may prefer. This is how we can make sense of self-control, restraint, integrity, etc., not by lumping them all together and thereby wiping the human world clean of meaningful distinctions.

Despite this, however, some economists insist on treating such moral and political convictions as nothing more than additional preferences or sources of satisfaction for people. Thus Dwight Lee notes that "Certainly nothing in public choice theory rules out the recognition that self-interested people may want to promote their vision of the good society."[8] This is an extension of the point made by Friedman, quoted in Chapter 1, concerning how "interest" has a very broad scope. It goes hand in hand with Becker's application of economic analysis to such areas of human life as religion, marriage and crime. In this context, then, the concept of "interest" does double duty. On the one hand, it suggests that what public servants are doing is really something other than what we had hoped they would be doing, namely serving a public purpose and not a private one. They are serving their own self- or vested interests. On the other hand, there is nothing odd about what these people are doing, since anything they do qualifies as their self- or vested interest, or their "private interest". Here for "interest" read "concern". Any concern one has qualifies as one's own concern so, thus understood, a martyr can act in his self-interest while sacrificing himself to the welfare of others.

But if this is how public choice theorists understand what public servants do, their view is not at all contrary to common expectations. These persons are doing what is of concern to them, nothing less. And one would certainly hope that this is the case: we would not want people in public life who were not concerned with public projects.

In addition, public choice theorists may wish to argue that, while there is a risk associated with lumping together economic values and moral and political convictions, when one stresses that there is a cost to acting on the latter, the assimilation becomes perfectly justifiable:

> [T]his risk is avoided by making sure that we go beyond simply explaining that people behave ideologically because they want to. The public choice model does go beyond this obvious tautology by predicting that people will behave more in accordance with their ideological convictions when the cost of doing so is low than when the cost is high.[9]

Yet will this help? Does not the term "cost" hide still another element of emptiness in the analysis? What will be the measure of cost, one might ask? The answer has to be, "That is a subjective matter, depending on what people want and do not want." Indeed, for the economist cost is a matter of subjective preference: if I like pain, then suffering it is not very costly, quite the contrary. If I enjoy hard work it is not put on the cost side of the equation, but if I do not then it is. And so if someone finds helping the public for nominal pay or fighting for his or her country rewarding, satisfying, worthwhile, even in the face of rejection by peers or voters, then acting on his or her unpopular convictions will not be very costly. This, once again, reduces to the claim, from the public choice viewpoint, that those who want to defend principles will do so, and those who do not want to will not do so.

None of this denies some of the insights of public choice analysis. For example, people may vote in line with their ideology, with their convictions about morality and justice, much more readily than they will actually act on it in their personal lives. If their ideology goes against what they take to be their personal welfare, they are less likely to give it their support. In other words, for an ordinary citizen it will often seem to cost very little to vote in line with his or her self-denying moral or political convictions. For a bureaucratic or elected official actually to deny himself or herself the benefits that stem from pursuing particular vested interests, such as promoting a bill that will bring business to his or her district and thus satisfy constituents, will not be so inexpensive. Thus, public choice theory predicts, people will follow ideology only when it has little impact on vested interest.

But this insight capitalizes on our prior commonsense understanding of what people value, of what indeed seem to be worthy goals for them to pursue. Financial security, income, re-election, continued employment and so on are all such values. But to the economic theorists there are, strictly speaking, no given or objective values, only the fact that people do value things. Such analysts and analysis cannot, therefore, rely on this background knowledge. For the public choice theory to work, it is necessary that we can explain both bureaucratic stagnation and occasional trend bucking simply by reference to the empty idea that people are utility maximizers or value pursuers. But actually to assume that some given concrete things are of (objective) value would commit the science of economics to the validation of actual value judgments, something quite illegitimate to what is generally understood to be the science of economics.

The problem with public choice theory remains despite the protestations of the faithful. A modified version of the theory would take the idea of the peculiar characteristic of the welfare state very seriously and still provide for dissolving the pattern of interest group politics, inside and outside government, by those who take their moral and political convictions seriously, not merely as trivial preferences or sources of satisfaction. It is this trivialization of moral and political matters, placing them on a par with the choice between vanilla and chocolate ice-cream or golf versus tennis, that undercuts the significance of public choice theory and other economic explanations of non-economic spheres of human affairs.

James Buchanan himself has lately focused his attention on some of the broader, philosophical issues concerning public choice, finding the pure economic explanation of human behavior insufficient. The following passage from Buchanan will shed light on just how his thinking differs from the pure *homo economicus* approach to understanding political behavior:

> [O]nce the body politic begins to get overly concerned about the distribution of the pie under existing property-rights assignments and legal rules, once we begin to think either about the personal gains from law-breaking, privately or publicly, or about the disparities between existing imputations and those estimated to be forthcoming under some idealized anarchy, we are necessarily precluding and forestalling the achievement of potential structural changes that might increase the size of the pie for *all*. Too much concern for [distributive] "justice" acts to insure that "growth" will not take place, and for reasons much more basic than *the familiar economic incentives arguments*.[10]

In other words, focusing on the behavior of public servants within the current political and legal framework is not sufficient for understanding what alternatives face us in conducting public affairs. It can serve to block basic reform which is not itself impossible despite the motivations of public servants.

IDEAS CAN HAVE CONSEQUENCES

The basic reform Buchanan himself alludes to may emerge as part of the viewpoint that public officials themselves could infuse into their conduct in the public realm. If public officials were to become convinced that the promotion of some favored project is indeed not a proper public activity in the first place, then despite what they might do in circumstances which are not governed by this "ideological" consideration, in the private sector, they could come to behave quite differently from how public choice theory itself predicts when understood to propose that public officials advance mostly their own vested interest or personal welfare.

In particular, suppose that a politician or bureaucrat came to understand that, as the government is conceived under the welfare state, its operations must produce the famous tragedy of the commons, the overuse of the public realm (which in this case is public funds or resources). This a genuine tragedy in that something is actually morally amiss, yet given some of the structural features of government it is not possible to remedy matters. Indeed, the program of balancing the budget versus promoting worthwhile goals is just the sort that characterizes this tragedy: everyone conscientiously aims to serve a worthwhile goal, yet in the process a general shortage of support for such goals is created throughout the community.

Once this is understood by public servants, it could turn out that they will discipline themselves to focus on the appropriate reforms, even if they may lose the support of their constituency. There are in our time ample cases of such realignment of public behavior. For example, in the US Congress some representatives have decided to join the call for a balanced budget amendment, even though this may eventually prevent them from being able to fund various projects desired by their constituents. In other cases, candidates show clear preference for ideals and principles, even with the full knowledge that this may prevent their election or re-election. They try to educate the public; as the old fashioned phrase would have it, they try to act in a statesmanlike way.

It is, of course, true enough that those who reach the places of power in political and bureaucratic matters are not very likely to prove the public choice theorists wrong. But this is not necessarily because of their Hobbesian motivation, as public choice theorists maintain. Rather these are the people who started in politics with the conviction that the various projects that governments might have the power to fund ought to be funded by the government, especially if other funding is not readily forthcoming. Those who did not believe this probably did not reach the corridors of power in the first place. Once a political organization or system is so constituted that the possibility of supporting various special interest group projects exists – and this is certainly true of the US system, with its ample legal provisions for the regulation of interstate commerce and for legislating economic, scientific, educational or moral affairs – those who take the best advantage of these opportunities are likely to win support from the voting public. A veritable Hobbesian war among all the special interest groups ensues, not because everyone is blind to principle but because the principle most people have accepted is that government exists to help us out of difficulties. (Even Mancur Olson, who argues largely from an economic perspective, agrees that ideas have consequences, even though it is often only the narrow vested interests of the special interest groups that drive public policy.)

Despite the fact that a program such as the Javits Fellowship serves a valuable purpose that no one can fault, there are some involved in it who believe that it is not the proper function of the government to serve this purpose. This idea may be unusual these days and indeed the people in question on the Javits board were sharply resisted by many of their colleagues and by those supporters and lobbyists who came to "testify" before board meetings of the administrators of the program. Pleas abounded about how other, similar projects, aimed at helping the sciences, are receiving so much more funding. So why not carry forth with this little bit for the humanities? The "ideological" people answered with the following remark: This is where I can do public service and if I had the chance to do it elsewhere, I would. Having this program is objectionable and I will not promote it. I will merely administer it and see to it that it remains the size it was when I joined. If I could do more, I would, to send it into the private sector.

Any resistance may, of course, come from a different understanding of public affairs. So the particular "ideology" that may lead to the reform must be carefully scrutinized, apart from the analysis of public conduct itself. But clearly the viewpoint of the public official, not simply his or her vested interest, has a bearing on the development of public affairs. The reason why this is obscure, and why public choice theory may only now be adjusting itself to the insight, is that the welfare state is structurally ill-equipped to help public officials serve the distinct public interest. It implies, by its scope, that no distinction exists between public and private concerns. Thus everything becomes part of the public interest, even when by common sense it is clear enough that a distinction needs to be recognized.[11]

THE PUBLIC CHOICE TEACHING

Public choice theory was developed by economists who found the government of liberal democratic societies running amuck with tasks and unable to avail themselves of the resources needed to fulfill them. Public choice theory aims to show that this situation stems from the fact that governments are run by self-interested persons. These persons will not look out for the public interest but only for their vested or private interests. Thus government will grow and grow, with no way of being stopped other than, perhaps, a constitutional measure to limit its growth.

Granted, the public choice thesis is descriptive at one level. It has, however, been used as a criticism of the expanding state: the more facets of society come under state jurisdiction or public policy, the more the opportunity exists for those in government to turn the state to their own advantage. And this is generally assumed to be a bad thing.

There is nothing in public choice theory as such to defend the view that the growth of government by vested interest peddling from within is a bad thing. That notion is simply assumed. One may suppose that any system that encourages bankruptcy deserves criticism, but that is merely common sense. There may be reason to go bankrupt if, for example, the goal being sought is worth the effort to try to reach it. Public choice theory's reliance on the commonsense thesis from which its normative component derives turns out, then, to be insufficiently powerful against the frequently advanced contrary normative thesis that sacrifices must be made, that the government must serve all the people in whatever capacities, or at least give that task a good try.

More generally put, the problem with public choice theory further suggests that, while economic analysis is crucial for understanding virtually any area of human behavior, it is not sufficient for such an understanding. There are, for example, politicians who buck trends, who see the fulfillment of their responsibilities to lie with remedying, as far as possible, the consequences of the special interest hustling that dominates the politics of the welfare state. Such politicians might buck the trend in different directions: one might say either leftward or rightward, or in some other direction.

Since in this work I am discussing arguments that advance the case for a more limited government, a system of *laissez-faire* economics, I am concerned with those who buck the trend in that direction. And there are such persons, even if not very many for reasons already discussed. In the United States few, incidentally with the advice of James Buchanan, support the Balanced Budget Amendment movement. Others support appointments to various government bodies knowing that those whom they will appoint are not going to ask for more support for their programs. They will, instead, urge greater and greater restraint so as to solve the broader problem of creeping statism, holding that the special problem the program has been established to solve should be handled by people outside the scope of politics.

Buchanan has reminded us that when government extends beyond its proper scope, it is very hard to limit its expansion. My point is that this lesson can serve different goals, not just the goal Buchanan and many of his colleagues hope to serve with it, that of reducing the scope of state activity. For that, something else is necessary. Only a normative argument will give us that result; not surprisingly, since that result is a norm, urging us to do one thing rather than another, or that one course rather than another is right.

NOTES

1. Quoted in Higgins, "British philosopher says self-interest corrupts Western liberty", p. 17. See also Skinner, *The Foundations of Modern Political Thought*. Skinner's Tanner Lecture was collected in *The Tanner Lectures on Human Values*.
2. *Public Choice*, p. 1.
3. Stigler, "Economics or ethics?", p. 332.
4. Buchanan, "Why governments 'got out of hand' ".
5. *Ibid.*
6. Friedman, "The line we dare not cross", p. 11.
7. Becker, *The Economic Approach to Human Behavior*, p. 5.
8. Lee, "Public choice: the rest of the story", p. 29.
9. *Ibid.*
10. Buchanan, "Boundaries of social contract", p. 27 (emphasis added in last sentence).
11. Yet neither is it sensible to leave it merely to the distinction between the public and private sphere. Within the private sphere – that is, the non-political sphere – there are numerous divisions such as familial, fraternal, professional, community, and other areas of any person's life.

Chapter 3

A Metaphysical Recasting of Economic Science

WHITHER ECONOMICS?

It is necessary now to stave off the leap in logic some might take given the above analysis, urging that economics is entirely misguided, even beside the point. The critics of neo-classical supporters of the free market often make that inference, following their correct point that the economic analysis is incomplete and thus insufficient for yielding adequate understanding of political economic affairs.

Here I wish to argue, rather briefly, that there is a way to see conventional, mainstream *homo economicus* analysis as entirely proper within its scope; that is, when searching for an understanding of market affairs and institutions. I want to argue that economics, if it does not embrace the *homo economicus* idea as a universal claim about the nature of human action but confines it to understanding what motivates economic behavior, is a valuable tool of analysis.

Essentially my argument is that even if economics is placed within the context of a normative framework, such that it is possible to combine it with normative perspective on of human behavior (including ethics, politics, etc.), it can remain substantially intact as it now stands, provided its imperialistic ambitions are abandoned. I argue that, by rejecting determinism and by admitting that human life gives rise to norms of conduct in innumerable spheres, a place is gained for morality or ethics, including normative politics. This makes it possible to evaluate morally what people do, including in the marketplace, though it does not follow that it leads to a justification for making them do the right thing.

Once those persons have chosen to enter markets, however, economists can go to work and figure out the (statistical) implications of that choice for all facets of market behavior. Economists need not morally evaluate such behavior, so for all intents and purposes their field can remain value free, provided we grant that it is generally morally justified to engage in market behavior in the first place, just as it is generally accepted that it is morally justified to engage in the preservation of one's health, the seeking of knowledge, the pursuit of artistic development or enjoyment, and so on. The economist, then, can proceed to study market behavior, even while others might proceed to evaluate it morally at various turns, for example to decide whether some investment should be made as a matter of certain moral principles that may override the generally proper goal of seeking prosperity.

Let me now turn to this admittedly brief but unavoidable consideration of the proper scope of economic science within at least one possible and promising normative perspective on human affairs.

ECONOMICS, A CONDITIONAL SCIENCE

The various ways economists of the neo-classical school attempt to demonstrate the errors of a primarily centrally or collectively administered or regimented ("command"), or perhaps only "nudged", economy will not suffice. The underlying framework, based on the neo-Hobbesian elements we have discussed earlier, will not overcome the normative objections advanced against the free market or capitalist system neo-classical economists seem to favor. At a later point I will discuss the limitations of these refutations of non-market systems but for now let me consider, first in outline form, an alternative approach that would help to support the market system but would avoid the difficulties of the standard neo-classical economic approach.

There are evident problems with the way neo-classical economic theory is employed. We have seen that the uses to which it is put trade on common sense or the tautological character of the analysis. Yet despite the fact that these problems are pointed out to economists, they seem to cling to their framework quite tenaciously. The reason, I am convinced, is that they believe that only this value-free, tautological approach qualifies as scientific. If they gave content to the idea of "self-interest" or "utility maximization", they would get embroiled in the issue of what is really to a person's benefit and what is really to a person's harm. They would become encumbered with the problem of value. Subjective value theory frees them of this and also keeps them from having officially to give up their quasi-empiricist, quasi-positivist epistemology and methodology. The threat of tautology does not seem to phase them either, probably because it brings them close to mathematics, where tautological reasoning is a virtue and produces the kind of certainty of which all scientists used to dream.

I do not want to enter the fine points of this debate. Many have taken it upon themselves to discuss it, often very productively. I want, instead, to explore some broader, philosophical misconceptions about the neo-classical economists' outlook. Firstly, let me note that there is perhaps an explanation for its tenacity that has not been fully explored. I am thinking of the fact, suggested earlier, that the most respectable moral framework in our time is of Kantian origin. And as such this framework has two elements that economists find quite odious. It is dualistic in its underpinnings. Ought is not of this world but of another. Kantian ethics originates somewhere other than in the natural world. Yet, of course, economists are interested in the natural world, not in some noumenal realm. So they stick to the phenomenal, scientific side of Kant, indeed to Hume or the later pragmatists, and stay away from morality.

Then they also find something odious about the substantive morality associated with the prominent Kantian tradition. This tradition tends toward out and out altruism. What is morally right to do is always disinterested, selfless or unselfish, if not outright subservient to the welfare of others. But this view would render human economic behavior *ipso facto* amoral. No one who acted as a commercial agent, as a person engaged in business, in seeking wealth, could be thereby a morally good person, and, indeed, those not so engaged would always be assured of the moral high ground.

Such an ethics or morality can only be upsetting to those who are concerned with how human beings best secure for themselves what is to their well-being. Economics, if it is any kind of discipline at all, is the science or technology of human prosperity. That is why some economists will claim, with tongue in cheek, that they recognize only one virtue: efficiency. If one inquires toward what end we are to be efficient, the answer is, anything we care to pursue. Yet that is not quite right, since no economist really endorses, at least as an ordinary person, a life of destruction, waste, idleness and parasitism. Less do they tend to endorse living on narcotics and alcohol. So efficiency is to be directed towards what we normally take to be prosperity: some benign enough notion of the enhancement of the person's life on earth.

What I argue in this work is that there is a philosophical theory that manages to underpin this commonsense viewpoint. It will, I believe, play better with the economist than the neo-Kantian, self-denying ethics. It will be closer to Adam Smith's idea that morality should be not self-denying, but concerned with the virtues productive of a happy life for human beings. While I cannot defend this view against all possible critics, I think I can show that neo-classical economics would benefit from considering it and perhaps even resting on it its general understanding of human life.

What I wish first of all to suggest is that economics might retain its scientific character without attaching itself to the flawed philosophy of Hobbesian individualism, with its stress on value subjectivism, reductionism, determinism and nominalism concerning human nature. It seems to me that it is a major concern of neo-classical economists to be scientific. Perhaps this is possible without remaining wedded to the neo-Hobbesian outlook.

Put broadly, the basic message of economics should be that when people go to market they want to and try, more or less, to make a deal. By this I mean the following, put in more elaborate terms. There are circumstances in which people prepare themselves to embark on exchanges of goods and services that they take to be of benefit to themselves; and when they seek out these circumstances, they should try to benefit themselves – they should pursue their goals as is most suitable to their own needs and wants – recognizing that others are there for the same purpose and that the chance of success requires mutual recognition of and respect for this fact. Going shopping, playing the stock-market, speculating in commodities, seeking employment, hiring help, producing and creating various goods for sale: all these are instances of the general conditional principle stated above.

The details of the application of the above principle will yield the bulk of economic science and technology (business, marketing, sales, finance, etc.), but our concern here is not with the details. Rather I wish to indicate why a conditional statement embodying the imperialist *homo economicus* conception of human market behavior will achieve the scientific status of economics, without leading to that distortion and vacuousness attained by the categorical version of this "axiomatic" proposition.

Science often proceeds by conditionals. If you mix A with B, you will get C. If the conditions of light are such and such, the coloration on the film will be so and so. Under non-Euclidean conditions, the principles of geometry will come to the following. In each of these and many other cases, science embodies procedures that allow conclusions to rest on conditional truths. I am suggesting that one way to avoid making economics ridiculous in its general claims without destroying its substance is to conceive of it as resting on certain assumptions that have limited applicability in human life.

When Democritus of Abdera (*c.*460–*c.*370 BC) observed that "the same thing is good and true for all men but the pleasant differs from one and another",[1] an observation some regard as one of the earliest recorded distinctively economic insights, he was on to a crucial economic point, though I think even he overstated it. Goodness might have to be identified by reference to how some action, some trait of character or some institution accords with human nature. There is reason to suppose this to be just so. Among other things, we judge to be good for us whatever in general, applicable to all persons, accords with the requirements of being a flourishing human being; that is, makes us a good instance of the general kind designated by "human being". In so far as we are considering ourselves in terms of our humanity, there may well be objective and universal truths as to what is good and evil, right and wrong. If something is true about one of us by virtue of his or her being a human being, it will be true of all the rest of us by virtue of the same fact. That is simply a principle of logic, the principle of substitutability.

But between the objective universally good and the merely pleasant, there could well be goodness that is objective but not universal. Such goodness would pertain to more special yet objective and stable aspects of persons, such as their belonging to a given profession and their roles as parents, friends and citizens, and in the end to their unique individual attributes. These are by no means subjective, yet they are not universal either. (I will return to this central point of the present work over and over again, in connection with various aspects of our discussion.)

Now if goodness in the case of human beings has to do with, for example, how fully or poorly any given person realizes certain capacities, then with proper accounting for individual differences we could find a common standard for judging human conduct pertaining to those capacities. Suppose that what makes us human beings is that we can think and need to do so for living our lives. And say it is also true that life for us is (normally) better than death. This could imply that, for human beings, living rationally with a clear mental focus on the facts of their existence is valuable – a sound approach. For now I will leave this at the level of supposition and suggestion. The main point here is that it is not so problematic to conceive of some general moral truths being generated from some common human traits and capacities. Much more is needed, but two matters would be extremely important: that human beings have the capacity for freely choosing some of what they will do; and that a standard exists to guide our choices.

As to the pleasant, whether one chooses an apple or an orange for one's lunchbox is not ordinarily a matter of right or wrong. There are great differences among us, not only as to the individuals we are, apart from being human beings, but also as to our subjective tastes. The suggestion implicit in calling these matters pleasant is that the element of objectivity is missing and that the pleasant is a matter of subjective determination.

That suggestion makes sense *vis-à-vis* our tastes, but not in regard to various other matters open to choice for us, such as what careers to pursue, whom to marry and whether to defend human liberty or advocate some other value as of primary importance. Indeed, do economists really wish to argue that whether one accepts the teachings of one school of economists or another is just a matter of preference and that no objective guidelines can be invoked in that decision? Stigler, as we have seen, tried a hopeless move on this.

Simply because something is not universally good – that is, good for all persons to do or have – does not mean that it is not objectively good, that its value cannot be determined by objective standards. Now there are clearly many good things that are not universally good: two aspirins for my headache may be suitable, but yours would go away with one or, even better, by taking some other medication. For me a size 44 jacket may be very proper, but for you, smaller than I, such a garment would be quite wrong. An operation will serve me well, given *my* back troubles, yet for you it would be best simply to rest for a couple of weeks so as to get rid of *your* back problems. For one person it is right that he or she be firm with his or her children, while for another it would be best to approach discipline with more flexibility. One individual ought to invest in long-term securities, while another should be willing to speculate and take risks.

These and millions of other common judgments are not universalizable. They are person and/or role relative, as some call them in philosophy. But they are not subjective either, as the economist has mistakenly regarded them, not merely of importance because someone has so decided. Rather they are objective, based on facts about the individual that pertain to that individual as such, not to him or her as a human being. Or they may rest on some special attributes shared among some but clearly not all human beings.

Furthermore, we commonly treat persons as being at least partially responsible for what they do, as well as for the suitability of their actions. Most of us clearly concern ourselves with what a person ought to do. We worry about parental misconduct, governmental corruption, the behavior of the President of Austria in the Second World War and so on. We are constantly interested in holding persons responsible, both in matters that may be very private and in spheres of progressively greater general concern. We take it that they were free to do what they did not do, that they could have made a different choice from the one they did make.

But it has been supposed by many scientifically minded persons that, if this approach were accepted as having intellectual merit, scientific study and analysis of human affairs would be impossible. As B. F. Skinner puts it:

> The hypothesis that man is not free is essential to the application of scientific method to the study of human behavior. The free inner man who is held responsible for the behavior of the external biological organism is only a prescientific substitute for the kinds of causes which are discovered in the course of a scientific analysis.[2]

And, as noted, this same view is either explicit or implicit in imperialist neo-classical economic theories.

But this view is quite mistaken. That is so even apart from the fact that the theories are a violation of the canons of science itself, canons that do not permit simple extrapolation from one area of (e.g. inanimate) existence to others, except as clues to research. It is not science itself but a certain metaphysical position that is involved here. A reductionist metaphysics would, of course, require that everything in nature be treated as if it were governed by the same laws. That in turn suggests that free choice must be a myth, not even conceivable as part of (human) reality. But if we reject the reductionism that came out of the eagerness to guide all of our inquiries along lines that proved successful in some areas, such as classical mechanics, then the extrapolation must be seen as non-binding. And if human beings can choose some of their behavior, then a scientific study of human affairs would require taking that fact into account.

That human beings are free to choose some of their conduct is inferable from several factors. For one, it would not be possible to make clear sense of science, and the search for truth, without so regarding human behavior. For if our actions were all fully out of our control, the idea of scientific objectivity would vanish and we would just arrive at our beliefs as a matter of necessity. We would believe what we had to believe and disbelieve what we had to disbelieve, and it would not be possible to take an independent stance to learn whether we were right.

Furthermore, certain fine points about even arguing for determinism would indicate that determinism is false. Arguments aim to convince, to communicate that someone should accept a conclusion. But there is no room for consideration of what should or should not be done if what we do must be done or is compelled by forces outside us or embedded in our genes.

It is also simply obvious that much of what we do is chosen by us. Self-awareness, like any other, is open to error, yet there are many cases where error is out of the question and it is clear that our conduct was determined by us, that we chose what we did.

Finally, there are scientific theories in psychophysics, itself a complex and respected science, that advance the free will hypothesis as of greater explanatory power than its denial. I have in mind the views of Nobel laureate Roger W. Sperry, who argues that the brain of a normal human being is so structured that, given its psychophysical constitution and context, each person with that brain is capable of self-governance, of self-determination.[3]

But perhaps the idea of free will or self-determination will be shunned on grounds that, if it were true, man would turn out to be some kind of freak in nature. That is, one might think that any being that has the power of self-determination or self-governance – as distinct from being powered, as it were, by forces either that are acting on it from the environment or that it had built into it, for example genetically – is so odd that it is frankly incredible that it should exist, somewhat as to most of us ghosts are an incredible supposition.

But that itself is a mere prejudice. Why should it be impossible for something in nature to choose freely? What is it about nature that prohibits that? Nothing. Nothing in metaphysics requires that all entities exhibit the same type of behavior, that, for example, they all behave by being moved by the same kinds of force that move, say, pebbles or rats. Self-causation or determination is by no means a contradiction in nature unless one already assumes the reductive materialist metaphysics we discussed in connection with Hobbes in Chapter 1.

Free will, admittedly, may not simply be assumed to exist. But in the case of human affairs there is ample reason to believe that it determines much of human behavior. Firstly people see themselves as choosing some of what they do. They differentiate between such cases and others that merely happen to them. This is evidence from personal experience and it is mere prejudice totally to discount it. Secondly, it makes no sense to deny free will if we are to distinguish between independent and prejudiced scientific and related (e.g. judicial) judgment. The determinist holds that we all believe what we have to believe, with no personal responsibility in the matter. Thirdly, this backfires against determinism because the determinist now has to admit that he or she also was compelled to believe in his or her views, thus rendering those views in no way superior to ones others hold since they are all believed in by chance. Fourthly, as noted before, science itself seems to give some support to the free will idea now, once the reductivism of the seventeenth, eighteenth and nineteenth centuries has failed to serve as a sufficient cosmological hypothesis. Finally, the enormous variety of human affairs seems also to be better explained by reference to self-determinism than by the type of determinism that attributes all human behavior to impersonal causes.

If thus the free will idea is at least plausible, reasonable and possibly correct – and this I cannot fully demonstrate in a work that aims mainly to compare different defenses of the free society, not to demonstrate the ultimate superiority of one of these defenses *vis-à-vis* all competing outlooks[4] – we need by no means give up scientific economics but merely reconceive it. It seems to me that we should look at the matter along the lines of the next section.

EXPLAINING THE SCIENTIFIC AND MORAL NATURE OF ECONOMIC LIFE

Among that which is of value to human beings in their existence in this world is a certain degree of prosperity with respect to the satisfaction of their needs, desires and wants. Persons will need to eat, to provide shelter for themselves, to clothe themselves, to entertain themselves, to travel to friends and work, and so forth, in order to flourish in life. In general, persons will want prosperity as one of the values available in their lives. This is not the only value they will want, but it is certainly one important value.

In the vicinity of other people some of these things can be achieved by human beings through the benefit of what others know, their skill and so on. In this effort markets can develop, and do indeed evolve, as history demonstrates. When persons embark on trying to obtain goods and services in the company of other people they will most likely try to give up as little of what they have already in the effort to obtain other things. This is quite sensible and prudent. If they already have something, presumably they wanted to have it at some time, and if they continue to keep it, presumably they still want it to some degree. So they would not be very sensible to treat these things lightly, to squander them. They wish to use these things, possessions, wealth and so forth, frugally in their efforts to obtain other things they want at least when they trade with strangers to whom they owe no more than ordinary human respect.

So assuming that persons will want to go to market, which as we have seen is a reasonable assumption, we can also assume that when they are there they will want to make good deals. This provides us with a fundamental characterization of human market behavior, out of which, with care and precision, we can infer all sorts of details, depending on the complexity of the markets we are concerned with. The proposition that in markets people aim primarily for prosperity, for doing better than they have before in terms of possessing goods and services, including liquid assets, can be the axiom of economics. It can be as rigorously put as one would need to put it, and as systematic and potent scientifically as the tools of formal analysis and empirical research can make it.

What is a market? A sphere of human interactions where men and women offer their goods and services in exchange for ones they would rather have, provided certain terms are met. Markets arise from men and women now and then considering one another as sources of little more than the satisfaction of their mutual desire for prosperity, for material wealth and advancement.

What is remarkable about so viewing economics is that there is nothing in this picture that conflicts with taking a normative view of human life. One can consider, for example, whether people ought to enter markets in the first place. Clearly, there can definitely be some values that should be pursued apart from and even prior to prosperity, even in preference to prosperity. For instance, protection of the rights to life, liberty and property should probably be pursued prior to prosperity, inasmuch as the most effective pursuit of prosperity, namely that which ensues in markets, requires the security of these rights. There can be no trade without liberty to act and property to offer. A market presupposes the value of these rights; for there to be a market system they must be treated as inalienable, since all of its features presuppose it. The suggestion, sometimes advanced in economics, that one can trade away one's rights is confused: then one would have to have the right to trade away the rights in question, *ad infinitum*. (This does not mean that there cannot be values that are objectively more significant than the social-political value of human rights. But that is something different from rights being subject to trade-offs based on their market value, their price.)

And then there is perhaps the value of personal integrity, which is more important to human beings as such than a minimal level of prosperity. Friendship, loyalty, love and the rest might be features of human life that are more important than prosperity, let alone great wealth, although here one would need to explore individual circumstances and note that for different cases different judgment would apply. We can rank basic values as well as the more particular, special and individualized ones involved in trade.

Saying all this does not imply that these values should or could be achieved at the expense of the right to liberty involved in free market pursuits; quite the contrary. If social life itself, including economics, requires respect for the right to life, liberty and property, then the pursuit of values in a social context other than prosperity or profit also would require respect for these rights. What is the good of loyalty which is coerced? What kind of friendship can tolerate compulsion? How could God be honored from fear and force instead of free choice?

No, there is nothing necessarily in conflict between the pursuits carried out in the market and other pursuits. But the achievement of profit, wealth and so forth might be at the cost of breaching some principle of morality, for instance by lying, betrayal or self-abasement. On these occasions it would be true in most cases that one should not sell out, not because there is some greater economic value to be attained by not selling out, as some who wish to give room to morality in economic analysis put it. Rather, one should not sell out because the selling – or breach – of one's moral integrity is itself morally wrong. It can be done, no doubt. But it should not be. Still, when it is done, it can be studied in terms of economic categories. But that does not prove that such matters can all be fully understood in economic terms. One can also study human beings by focusing entirely on the physiological composition of their bodies. Biological researchers do this, but we do not suppose that thereby they are gaining a full understanding of human life. To forget that a human being is a person as one embarks on these limited studies of human existence can lead, for example, to toleration of experimenting on someone without his or her consent or to the treatment of marriage as if it involved only economic considerations.

The point is that there are many values the pursuit of which is mostly an economic matter. The buying of tires and shirts and haircuts is a matter studied quite properly largely in economic terms. Concerning these particular items and services, there really are probably no universal judgments of value that would be correct – which is different from being objectively true, meaning that they could be shown to be true with reference to the individuals in question. These concerns are tied up with our individuality, with tastes and preferences, not with general moral principles of human conduct.

As I have already noted, even though the bulk of economic values is not universal and has bearing on individuals who value them, it is not true that the value of some item, say a gold watch or a size 11½ leather shoe, might not have objective value for some particular person. In short, the item could be good for the person, all things considered, even if she did not want it or wanted it less than something else, something that might not be good for her. Given that a person has embarked on life, it could well be that taking this medicine tonight is of objective value to him. Given that we have decided to live, we might very well benefit from certain items such as gloves, cars, bread, dresses and courses in economics. Indeed, just because, from the point of view of comparative economic value (price), items and services sold on the market are not of universal worth, it does not follow that some particular item or kind of item will not have some very definite objective worth to someone. That economists are not concerned with it does not justify their declaring the idea of objective standards of worth invalid.

Let me just reiterate how vital the issue of objectivity versus subjectivity can be. Something can be worthwhile to someone objectively, even if that person fails to recognize this. As a plausible example, one that should be pertinent especially to those who advance the value-free approach to economic analysis but who also professionally value that approach over others, consider someone who is taking economics courses from Milton Friedman, George Stigler or James Buchanan. Doing this could be of considerable educational, as distinct from subjective economic, value. It would contribute to the person's understanding of political economy. Yet, if he or she fails to recognize this fact and forgoes taking the courses, the value would also be forgone. As a feature of the objectivity of such a value, let us further consider that others might be able to ascertain that the potential pupil would (objectively) benefit from the lessons and that they recognize the loss when the lessons are not taken.

The same might be said, as noted earlier about innumerable other values that persons might – as well as could fail to – pursue. It is clear that for some persons it is of value to stop smoking, while for others it is not. For some it is of value to find a good health insurance program, while for others an alternative would be better. For certain persons with somewhat hidden talents that need initial encouragement it is clearly of value to receive special treatment from their employers, while for others this would be superfluous. Generally, moral points may be valid in many different, simple or complex, context where economists also do work.

We could continue endlessly with examples that make clear enough sense in ordinary terms. Different individuals can benefit from different courses of conduct, including in their free market commercial endeavours. Some, however, fail to realize this so they lose out on some values, even neglect them. The values, in turn, could be of varying magnitude. Some fail to develop honesty as part of their character, which can seriously undermine the quality of their entire life; others fail to seek out good car insurance and simply grab the first policy they become aware of, or neglect getting any at all. And in all such cases others, normally persons who know the individual involved well enough to tell what range of options was available to him or her, might know all this, at least as well as one can know such matters.

Here is a clear case where critics of the fully free market such as John Kenneth Galbraith are on solid ground as they talk of certain kinds of market failure: the possibility, that is, that in the free marketplace some values will not be produced. The lack of sufficient demand for those values does not demonstrate, as the subjective value theorists hold, that they are not values. It shows only, at least in certain cases, that they may well have been neglected. When the *homo economicus* defense is offered that the only values or preferences are those exhibited in the free marketplace, only a half truth is pointed out. Certainly, it would be no remedy to force the values on people in a sense that would deprive whatever is at issue of its value because it would not be chosen by the agent. But there is the forgotten matter, forgotten at least by the economists, that sometimes people "demand", seek out in the marketplace, the wrong thing or service; sometimes they do not demand something that they would benefit from more than from the alternative they actually select.

In a recent exchange with me, Milton Friedman expressed his view that this attitude lacks humility. In Friedman's words, "the value that seems to me most important and most neglected in the kind of approach here . . . is the value of humility."[5] That is to say, it is arrogant to assume that one knows what is good for others. Yet that seems to me to be quite beside the point. Of course, any claim to knowledge, ethical, scientific or religious, implies such a failing, if it be considered a failing. Any good parent, doctor or financial advisor, not to mention any good friend, is in the position to show such lack of humility when he or she offers a judgment as to what a child, patient or client ought or ought not to do. This is mere common sense, required by anyone who embarks on a critical view of any aspect of his or her culture. Naturally, we need to consider whether this common sense can utlimately prevail in the face of critical challenge. I will return to this in Chapter 4.

One additional reason that this point about objectivity is frequently misunderstood is that people confuse "objective" with "intrinsic". They are correct to argue that nothing is intrinsically of value: a chair or an oil corporation has no value in itself, each must be of value to someone. As Ayn Rand notes:

> It is in regard to a free market that the distinction between an intrinsic, subjective, and objective view of values is particularly important to understand. The market value of a product is *not* an intrinsic value, not a "value in itself" hanging in a vacuum. A free market never loses sight of the question: Of value *to whom?* And within the broad field of objectivity, the market value of a product does not reflect its *philosophically objective* value, but only its *socially objective* value.[6]

On the market we find the economic value of something, which is a measure of how much (social) demand there is for it. "Thus", as Rand puts it, "a manufacturer of lipstick may well make a greater fortune than a manufacturer of microscopes – even though it can be rationally demonstrated that microscopes are scientifically more valuable than lipstick. But – valuable *to whom?*" This must not be confused with the erroneous metaeconomic notion that values are subjective, established only by the desires of those who trade. Certainly, some of what people demand in markets is nothing more than an expression of their hastily formed desires, but that is not all there can be to demand:

> If the stenographer spends all her money on cosmetics and has none left to pay for the use of a microscope (for a visit to the doctor) *when she needs it*, she learns a better method of budgeting her income; the free market serves as her teacher: she has no way to penalize others for her mistakes.[7]

But if her desire were necessarily subjective, it would make no sense even to call it a mistake for her to have spent so much on cosmetics that she could no longer obtain what she needed more. Then all we could say is that at one point in time she desired cosmetics, while at a later point in time she needed the microscope. Indeed, all the hand-wringing about having splurged, spent recklessly, loaded up on useless merchandise, having failed to consider one's (objective) priorities, would have to be regarded as nonsense; just as feeling guilty would have to be if none of us could ever have done anything other than what we in fact did.

We are well aware, however, that at times we can state confidently enough that a relative or a friend would definitely benefit from buying some item, even though the person will refuse to buy it. We can sometimes explain to people why they should (not) buy something, and witness a stubborn response. But from the subjectivist viewpoint this way of understanding the situation makes no sense at all: we simply have different subjective perceptions as to what is desirable. Yet surely someone's choice could be a bad one, all things considered, just as the choice to consider a given theorem of economics to be important or trivial could be a bad one. A given skirt might really be bad for Suzzie, yet she just will not recognize this. Or şome kind of health program might be very beneficial to George, even though he is wasting his money on a fad diet.

It might be replied here that, in the end, even the choice to carry on with one's human life, possibly the ultimate source of objective values, is merely an arbitrary one. Most folks want to live, some do not. We cannot establish the rightness of the former and the wrongness of the latter. So we are left with a hypothetical standard of value in any case, which is tantamount to subjectivism.

This objection fails to appreciate the context of value concerns. Value concerns arise only in the context of life, never in the context of death. Death could not be of value to anything because valuing beings are necessarily live beings. Dead beings, as far as we can make sense of it in rational, practical terms, do nothing, including choose to value something in relation to their death. It is only in connection with life that values make sense in the first place, so this is not a hypothetical but an objective, although not an intrinsic, account of values after all.

THE SCOPE OF ECONOMICS

These kinds of observations are not matters to be explored within the science of economics itself. They are at most metaeconomic notions. They may enable us to place economics within the rest of the scientific disciplines and concerns. What the economist wants to know qua economist is why certain events occur in markets, what principles govern various events in markets and so on, and on this issue the matter of the value of certain items for particular people or even special groups of them, has no bearing. All that needs to be noted is that markets exist because people place value on various goods and services that they can obtain from others who have done the same and are willing to trade. To go on from this to try to characterize the placing of value on things, to try to explain why or how or in what ontological respect something is of value to people has no bearing on economics as such. That task is beside the point of economics once the field has been identified as being concerned with trade.

But this does not mean that others, or that even economists in different roles, may not have a perfectly legitimate concern with placing economic values within the broader context of values in human life. Here is where one can argue about these matters with not just philosophers but those economists who wish to explore the prospects of exporting their models to other than familiar economic dimensions of human life. Here is where it is clear that methodological issues, contrary to the views of some in the field of economic metatheorizing, matter considerably.[8]

The value judgments the economist is interested in are those that people actually act on in the market. That people might make the wrong value judgment is of no interest to economists as economists, although an economist who leaves his or her study and returns home to find the children listening to some awful noise they call music might lament the popularity of some rock group and the price they can charge for their wares. And as an economist, a person might study the market of paintings one way, while as a connoisseur of the arts he or she might be appalled with the choice of the current consumers of paintings. There is no reason why, although from an economic point of view the value of Jackson Pollock's works is considerable, from the aesthetic point of view it might not be much less. It is silly to assume that, because the economist is interested only in the market value of a painting, this is the only value it could have. Again I ask you to recall that, while a pianist's hand might be looked on as just so many bare fingers, a complex limb, that would be very narrow from the point of view of the performing arts. But saying this does not at all suggest that that point of view introduces something necessarily relative or subjective into the perspective. For example, it leaves open the issue of whether the arts are of objective value to human beings or even whether there are objective standards of artistic excellence.

VALUES AND LIBERTY

One thing that many economists have been, while they have denied it, is implicit advocates of the free market. At least they have regarded what they are studying as a morally acceptable human institution – unlike, for example, one might view concentration camps. If an engineer, exploring the most efficient operations of such camps, were to claim that he is engaged in a value-neutral endeavor, he would certainly be denounced.

In actual practice it is not possible to be entirely value free in any of the human sciences. Economics takes for granted the value of prosperity; that is it assumes that it is morally justifiable to pursue prosperity, even if it leaves open whether on some particular occasion that is what someone ought to do. Economists accept "profit seeking" both in terms of its bearing on most individual lives and from the point of view of the wealth of nations, communities and societies. There would be no economics without an interest in prosperity, without acceptance of the fact that on many occasions it is quite right that people try to satisfy their needs, wants and desires.

Scarcity is of no significance if nothing is wanted. Because there are wants, scarcity is important. So is productivity. These are attitudes, actions and circumstances over which human beings can have some control, and so norms are applicable to thinking about them. But this does not mean that, if the system of economic activities rests on some general endorsement of some values, such as prosperity or desire satisfaction, the principles of the circumstances and activities involved cannot be studied impartially or scientifically.

Thus, for example, some claim that individual profit seeking is wrong; only for the sake of collective wealth should there be production, saving, use and so forth. However much of this may be wrong, many economists have been concerned not with the wrongness of the point, but with some alleged incoherence of it, as when some refer to considerations of basic rights as "music", not science, suggesting that such matters are about as near to dealing with truth as the playing of music is. It is as if saying that the notion that persons should not seek their personal welfare but should promote the public welfare could not even make sense, is meaningless and could not possibly be true. But why? Firstly, because we are all supposed to be pursuing our welfare necessarily; saints and capitalists alike are seeking their private interests. Secondly, because values are subjective and everything should be assessed from the agent's point of view; psychological egoism and value subjectivism preclude the intelligibility of normative ideas entirely, we are told.

But we have already seen that this is all wrong. We do not all promote our own interest; that is, we do not all act to benefit ourselves. If only we did, we would be closer to the beasts who automatically or instinctually do the "right thing", that which facilitates their living on this earth. (It was Hobbes who believed that in the state of nature, prior to the establishment of civil society with its legal conventions, all human beings automatically do what is right. At least, that is what he meant by claiming that we all have the natural right to do what we will! Hobbes, as we have already noted, was a determinist, believing that human beings behave according to the laws of matter and have no choice about what they will do.)

It may be difficult to nail down just what is the correct standard for distinguishing between our interest, our own benefit, that of others, and something that benefits no one. But certainly most of us recognize the distinction in ordinary circumstances. A thoughtful friend will be able to tell when I act self-destructively, even as I stubbornly refuse to see his point. And if I am helpful to another, even at my own expense, that too is clearly recognizable. That the knowledge is tied to particular or individual cases is no reason to reject it as knowledge.

It is not a good reason for doubting all of this that philosophers argue about the matter all the time. Philosophers argue about everything all the time; that is their vocation, as it were. They are committed to question, to seek weaknesses in our convictions. They may be said to have taken a professional oath of office never to leave anything unquestioned. Despite this, they cannot argue away reality, however complicated it may be to get it right or even to know what getting it right would amount to. At least I would maintain this as my input into the perpetual disputation!

Some judgments of value, as I have been arguing, could very well be right, even right for us all. Now one notable objection to this from many who advance the *homo economicus* free market position is that, if we know what is right, then we may clearly make others comply. In other words, many economists are objecting not as much to the possibility of knowing the good, as to what they believe is a threat to the right to freedom implicit in that possibility. The concern is with the belief that there is an intimate connection between knowing what is right and good and the desire to impose what one knows (about right and good) on others. Free market economists see an authoritarianism looming beneath the claim to moral knowledge, one that threatens the very idea of freedom they intimately associate with the marketplace.

Suppose that my purchase of some item is wrong. Suppose that I am wasting my own money by going to silly movies and that I should, instead, invest in books. Or suppose that some of us fret too much about cars or electronic gadgets to the neglect of environmental causes or health food. This is quite possible, and is certainly not ruled out by scientific economics. But based on considerations that have nothing to do with economics, economists often believe that the very idea here is a threat to free markets, to free trade, to the free society itself.

Quite often whenever it has been proposed that people should do this or that, spend time on work instead of play, purchase art instead of entertainment, such suggestions have been followed by rules, decrees, laws or other authoritative pronouncements to enforce them. But a sensible conception of human morality does not imply anything like the use of force regarding the achievement of values, the promotion of good things. On purely logical grounds the inference is wrong: from "A knows that B ought to do X" it simply does not follow that "A ought to compel B to do

X". There is a missing premise, namely "Whenever it is known by A that B ought to do X, A may (or ought to) compel B to do X." This is a difficult premise to prove, to say the least.

The reason the above seems not to be how many economists see matters relates to the idea of intrinsic goodness. Thus, first of all, if one believes that values consist in the existence of some state of affairs, regardless of the means by which it was brought about, then value judgments could at least imply occasional use of force and thus threats to voluntary trade. If the survival of a rare species of fish is a good in itself, then when people choose not to take care of them, it can seem all right to force them to do so. Since many conceive of values in such intrinsic fashion, as if some state of affairs were inherently good and commanded promotion regardless of the means, human liberty has been threatened by value judgments *per se*.

Secondly, one way that seems effective in combating the imposition of values is to claim that no one can know them, that they are personal or arbitrary preferences as to what we want, not what anyone should do. Skepticism about moral knowledge is thought to be a bulwark against authoritarianism. But it is not. If we do not know what is right, we do not know what is wrong either, including whether imposing our wishes on others is wrong. Perhaps we can deflate the claim of knowing the good by skeptical arguments, but this is far from denying legitimacy to the effort of imposing some desire. Why does that matter? Why should we go only with good reasons? Is there something especially good about having good reason for our actions? But then skepticism is itself defeated:

> To claim that there is such a thing as knowledge, or knowledge of such and such a kind, is not to claim . . . the right to impose one's opinion on others or to suppose that the possession of knowledge would confer such a right. If any theory in the epistemology of morals does give colour to dogmatism and the exercise of tyrannical authority it is a subjective theory, according to which nothing is objectively wrong, and hence the exercise of tyranny is not objectively wrong.[9]

In other words, contrary to the view that moral skepticism fends off tyranny or authoritarianism, it opens wide the door to it since there is no moral objection one can raise against such policies.

Thirdly, and this I mentioned earlier, it is simply hopeless to contend and expect others to accept that all values are subjective. In every era we find causes flourishing. Today it is women's liberation, social justice for blacks or national independence in Eastern Europe; yesterday it was patriotism, and before it may have been honor or thrift. Human beings are wedded to making choices and having to guide this process by reference to some norms or standards which at least aim, now and then, at being sound, correct, not arbitrary. On its own, this does not mean that we succeed in finding true, objective standards, but it does mean that we are pretty much convinced, judging by much of what we do and say, that they might be found if only we work hard enough. If some area of social life exists or flourishes in an intellectual framework that denies this possibility, it is often so much worse for that area, in our case the free market. In short, deny values to save freedom, and you deny freedom, not values.

The best rebuttal to those who advocate coercive imposition of values and thus seek to eliminate the preconditions of free markets is to demonstrate that these preconditions are necessary for and conducive to the human good. And they clearly are not because we can mean just anything by "the human good" but because what we should mean by it is indeed enhanced by the type of freedom involved in market exchange.

Let me sketch the classical individualist theory of value and moral goodness, which I shall deal with at greater length in Chapter 4. This is necessary so as to proceed with some hope of being understood in the rest of this chapter concerning how economics might be reformed to accommodate both values and science.

The distinctively human good is tied, first of all, to our capacity for choice. The human good is necessarily a chosen good. Morality is impossible without people choosing what they will do.[10] If they are coerced, this cannot make them better human beings, even if, along Skinnerian lines, it might make them behave more suitably for some purposes. The promotion of any purpose at the expense of human good is itself an evil. And this means that it is evil for a particular human being to act that way because for any particular human being it is good not to have his or her tasks in life taken over by others, except in extraordinary, emergency circumstances.[11] So coercive pursuits cannot ever be morally good and cannot ever justify the abolition of the market, at least in any meaningful sense of the term "morally good".

WHITHER MARKET FAILURES?

None of this means that whatever happens in the free market is always morally praiseworthy, morally right, furthers the human good, or the like. Market failures, as the jargon of normative economics refers to freely conducted bad deeds in the market,[12] can and do occur. But to attempt to remedy them by interfering with the freedom of market participants is to compound the market failure with the even more likely political failure, such as strikes by public sector unions, capture of the regulators, development of shortages, and problems pointed out by the public choice theorists.[13] For it is a political failure to abridge human liberty.

It is here that I wish to suggest, *pace* Quentin Skinner, that the defense of one's free society may be shown to be morally justified from an individualist, liberal perspective, contrary to what value-free economic analysis must maintain. As human beings who have a moral task in life, we should preserve those conditions that make moral choices meaningful, that preserve our moral sovereignty or human dignity. A free society, with its market system, is really the best candidate for this task. It is a very humane system indeed, since it sees human beings as choosing agents, while not denying that they can make bad choices aplenty. This system is not utopian and does not demand that some political means be instituted to remedy all the failings of mortal men and women. Rather it tries to preserve certain necessary borders among people so that whether they unite or keep to themselves is yet another matter of moral choice, not dictatorial rule.

Looked at in this way, albeit briefly, one can see a distinct moral dimension as well as a most crucial role for scientific economics. The free society ought to be defended, just as so many economists are already defending it in their various, though not always intellectually optimal, fashions. This is something we can know from what we know about human nature and the responsibility of everyone to be a moral agent.

The individualist conception of human virtue is the main bulwark against threats to the marketplace, to free trade. And this conception is a complex one, every bit as complex as the main challenger, namely Marxism. It locates ultimate reality in actual entities, not abstractions, such as humanity, as Marxism does. Human individuals are real, actual beings, unlike humanity or the species, or even the community. So the good must be conceived of by reference to human individuality, that is, actual people.

There is an affinity between this view and Marxism because by reference to human individuality some universal and objective values can be identified. But they are not the ones Marxism claims to have found. The reason for this is that while Marxism takes humanity or society as the ultimate point of reference for values and value judgments, the individualist perspective takes actual individual human beings as this ultimate reference point. As Marx states it, "The human essence is the true collectivity of man."[14] In contrast, the tradition of political liberty argues that the human essence is the true human individuality of every person. And it also holds individual human beings ultimately responsible for the pursuit of the values so identified, not society and its cadre, the politburo. The Marxists have transformed a category of being into an individual entity; they have made the collection of human beings into one large human being whose emancipation they seek and will coercively foster.

If you look at humanity as an individual to be promoted, whose values are to be secured, then it makes sense enough that some parts of the large human being, namely some individual persons like you and me, may be sacrificed for purposes of its promotion. After all, you and I would think nothing of cutting into our arms so as to stop some greater damage to ourselves. But we see this as using ourselves as we judge fit. We often endure pain so as to promote health and welfare. However, if we are all parts of one large person, then we are individually subject to the collective rule of mankind, which in practical terms means the rule of wise and enlightened leaders who, according to Marxism, could only be communists.

Although this position is wrong, and its practical implementation is now virtually suspended, it is not without meaning and it would be pointless to insist that it is meaningless. Indeed, such insistence would be counterproductive, seen for the smokescreen that it is, namely to hide a lack of a better alternative. The economists' insistence that objective values along Marxist or other statist lines are impossible must ultimately backfire. It must lead to the conclusion that the free market itself could not be of objective value to us.

Since, however, the neo-classical stance is not the only alternative to Marxist and other forms of collectivism, we are not in such bad shape as it may seem. Actually, economists make it possible for critics of the kind of free society economic analysis postulates to keep fighting strawmen instead of formidable adversaries. Virtually every attack on the freedom of the market I have read and heard in academic circles, from the right via Irving Kristol or from the left via Herbert Marcuse, give Milton Friedman or F. A. Hayek as their central adversaries and do intellectual battle against these advocates of the free society. And the main reason is that these adversaries are quite vulnerable through their unrealistic belief in moral skepticism as a bulwark against tyranny.

A SLIGHT ADJUSTMENT OF ECONOMIC VALUE THEORY

I have tried here to carry out the first few steps of a modest reconstruction of economic value theory. I attempted to indicate, in plain terms, that science does not require that human behavior be viewed along deterministic lines or that values be rejected. I suggested in general terms how there can be a sensible conception of reality with free choice and values given ample room. Then I tried to show that economics can retain its scientific character without assuming that it must explain all human behavior or provide the final analysis of all varieties of human affairs and institutions. I suggested that this could be done by assuming that in markets – that is, in some of their interactions, such as for purposes of obtaining material benefits from each other – human beings want to behave cost effectively; they want to obtain what they desire for as little cost as possible. This conditional claim can provide economics with its basic axiom.

Now that we have found it at least plausible that the science of economics can remain substantially what it is, even without the dubious subjective theory of value, it will be helpful to explore whether something other than a subjective theory of value is possible, one that at the same time does not bode ill for the free market economic system. It is another question, one that is important, whether such a normative individualist or egoist theory, with free market implications, can carry its own weight against alternative normative theories. Obviously I would argue that it can, and I have argued that in several other places.[15] But here what is needed is a normative alternative to the *homo economicus,* value-free defense of the free market system. In the next chapter I take up the task of laying the basis for such an alternative normative approach.

NOTES

1. Quoted in Gordon, *Economics Analysis Before Adam Smith,* p. 15.
2. Skinner, *Science and Human Behavior,* p. 447.
3. Sperry, "Mental phenomena as causal determinants in brain function".
4. For more extensive development, see Machan, *The Pseudo-Science of B. F. Skinner* and *Individuals and Their Rights.*
5. The exchange is in Walker, *Freedom, Democracy and Economic Welfare,* pp. 365ff.
6. Rand, *Capitalism,* p. 24.
7. *Ibid.,* p. 25.
8. For such a sentiment see McCloskey, *The Rhetoric of Economics.*
9. Bambrough, *Moral Skepticism and Moral Knowledge,* p. 43.
10. There is much here the defense of which would require extensive argumentation. It will suffice for now to observe that the closeness of moral goodness or evil, the peculiarly human kind of goodness or badness, to free choice is recognized most readily by the critics, such as B. F. Skinner, whose *Beyond Freedom and Dignity* acknowledges that, when we deny freedom, we are undermining the very possibility of dignity, the sense of human capacity that is presupposed in all moral theories.
11. For a discussion of when disregarding rights – i.e. the freedom of persons to act on their own initiative – is permissible, see Mack, "Egoism and rights" and Machan, "Prima facie versus natural (human) rights". Whenever the basic value(s) or moral principle(s) in terms of which other values or principles, such as natural human rights, are themselves justified is at serious risk without the disregard of those rights, then it is morally permissible to disregard those rights.

12. Of course, the non-normative characterization of market failures focuses only on some alleged cases of market activity that are not Pareto optimal, e.g. competition in utilities. I am concerned with the charge that markets are often inhospitable to worthwhile human endeavors, e.g. to libraries, postal services in small communities, or the broadcasting of classical music and theater.
13. Despite my disagreement with extrapolation and economic imperialism, I am not disparaging the use of economic models in context when politics, for example, has become virtually transformed into a (corrupt) marketplace, a kind of special interest war of all against all.
14. Marx, *Selected Writings*, p. 126.
15. See, for example, Machan, *Individuals and Their Rights* and *Marxism*.

Chapter 4

Classical (Qualitative) Individualism

GROUNDING CLASSICAL INDIVIDUALISM

Individualism is often criticized precisely for its philosophical – metaphysical, ontological, metaethical – underpinnings, and sometimes for its lack thereof. If one intends to rebuild individualism so that it can help us deal with the innumerable problems of human social life, it is necessary to provide it with a foundation. Such a robust outlook may also withstand the criticism that seems to have undone neo-Hobbesian individualism.

I present here the outline of a metaphysics of what I wish to call classical individualism.[1] First, however, I want to make some mention of certain epistemological themes. Together these remarks should furnish me with some of the underpinnings necessary to discuss the more immediately germane topic of the foundations of individualist political economy. Throughout the rest of this work I will have occasion to return to certain features of the basic ideas in these areas, as the need arises to solve various problems by reference to them. It is when we encounter serious difficulties and concerns that the fundamentals of a position come in handy. By reference to them we may be able to assess whether the position is rich enough to help us manage complex issues.

SOME EPISTEMOLOGICAL CONCERNS

As to some of the basic issues in the theory of knowledge, it should be noted here that much contemporary criticism is leveled at the very idea of providing a political outlook with philosophical, not to mention metaphysical, foundations. The point of foundationalism is that the way to defend some proposition is to show that it has some firm base. The paradigm instance of such a foundation is Descartes's supposedly self-evident and absolutely certain judgment, "I think (or am conscious)." From it we were supposed to be able to build up our store of knowledge in all fields, and this knowledge would gain its standing as absolute certainty from the certainty that attended the foundation stone on which it rested. Foundationalism is not popular within the contemporary philosophical community. Yet, even without entering the fray of this dispute, it is worth saying that much of the criticism of foundationalism is aimed at the pretensions that many foundationalists advanced for their system; for example, that what they have identified as the foundations are in fact timeless, incorrigible, self-evident, eternal, unchanging truths.

I make no such claims for the foundations I wish to discuss. I maintain only that from the vantage point of a reasonable investigator there are some principles that appear not to be dispensible and refutable. Unless a refutation is available, we need not give them up as knowledge. We need not yield to the specious rebuttal, "But isn't it conceivable that you might be wrong?" Of course, but that is a criticism only if one aims at the Cartesian kind of knowledge, absolute, eternal, irrefutable certainty.

In short, it is possible to show that some truths are axiomatic, that they are necessary even for an attempt to deny them. I have argued this elsewhere and merely note it here.[2] It is possible, of course, that I could be mistaken. I mean this only in the sense that there is no guarantee against error or, again, that there might be reason in the future to revise the statement of the truth in question.

I am not here advancing a full philosophical defense of the position I have been proposing as a better alternative to the neo-Hobbesian individualism used to defend Western liberal politics. Such a defense must go very deep in order for it to come near to being conclusive, assuming that it is sound. But I do wish to mention that in epistemology I find neither the empiricist nor the rationalist (positivist or a priorist, as applied to economics) theory convincing. Both seem to me to give too much weight to the perceptual model of knowledge, where knowers are passive and knowledge is received by them. As I see it, knowledge has to be garnered by an active, conscious agent, utilizing all the faculties of awareness to their maximum efficiency. I also take it that what is known is different from knowledge itself. Thus a fact known may be expressed in a statement that is true, but this truth is not the same as the fact. Furthermore, the relationship between the fact and the truth must allow that the fact could come to be known in greater detail, in more advanced terms within a given field and so on. Yet, just because knowledge understood in this way is revisable, as argued by J. L. Austin[3] and Ayn Rand,[4] it does not follow that it is not knowledge. (I elaborate this point elsewhere, maintaining that, because it is not appreciated, there is much confusion as to whether moral knowledge is possible.[5])

One of my difficulties with handling matters in this discussion is that neo-classical economics rests on many assumptions about knowledge and reality. For example, it assumes the correctness of a somewhat loose epistemological empiricism and metaphysical materialism. This view holds that knowledge can only involve statements or theories that are wholly verifiable by (sensory) experience, that only that is taken to (be able to) exist that is measurable, quantifiable in terms of familiar units (preferably developed within the natural sciences). In turn I defend a pluralist view in both epistemology and metaphysics. This amounts to the contention, put rather simplistically here, that we may know by various means, including the senses, inferences from data they provide, successful explanatory postulates, introspective understanding, intellectual reflection and whatever other approach can be subjected to meaningful (though not necessarily only empirical) tests and scrutiny. Furthermore, what exists may involve a great variety of types and kinds of being, some studied via the science of physics, some through chemistry, botany, biology, psychology, sociology, ethics, politics, aesthetics and the various subbranches of these. Reality, in short, is not one but innumerable different substances, each studied by means developed within the field that has focused on it.

This may seem to leave matters too indeterminate, but that is a misperception. It is not the case that anything goes, as is claimed by Paul Feyerabend for example. But neither is it possible to tell beforehand, to predict now, what will qualify as means of learning about reality and the results of that learning. The reductionism that is so pervasively assumed within neo-classical economics is presumptuous: it forecloses avenues of discovery and rules out of court entire disciplines, simply because these do not promise to conform to the sometimes obsolete versions of standards drawn from the physical sciences and then, often quite uneasily, adapted to economics.

All this could use extensive discussion, and strictly speaking there is no way to avoid that. But there are always limits and in this work I do not attend to much of what I have covered elsewhere. Instead I aim here to make a plausible case for the classical or qualitative alternative to neo-Hobbesian individualism. In a way this work may be regarded as an entry into a "family" dispute. The classical liberal family of ideas and thinkers have experienced much success as well as some setbacks, and my aim here is to advance the classical liberal idea by providing it with what I hope to be better foundations than it has enjoyed thus far.

This may strike some as rather arrogant; indeed, conservatives have put on record their dismay with classical liberalism based on the fact that proponents of the latter view tend to believe in the ability of the individual to answer basic questions, ones that conservatives believe are really only answerable by focusing on the messages of tradition, custom and habit.[6] Why these are not to be regarded as the product of the thinking of individuals in earlier times, and thus clearly implicitly affirming our own efforts in the direction of answering questions, I am unable fully to appreciate. At any rate I agree that I have the temerity to discuss these issues.

Even without going into the matter in full detail, however, something of an alternative framework needs to be sketched for establishing even the plausibility of the non-reductionist approach and for opening the door to rational normative explorations. That is what I embark upon in the next section, namely to lay some plausible foundations for a normative, qualitative individualism. This will certainly not forever clinch the case, but it may kindle some supportive thought in the suggested normative direction.

METAPHYSICS OF QUALITATIVE INDIVIDUALISM

The central elements of the metaphysics I am concerned with relate to what I call ontological pluralism. This view holds that there are innumerable irreducibly distinct types of being in reality. (They are irreducible at any given time, even though they may have evolved or emerged in part from different beings. For example, the human mind is not fully reducible to nerve cells and nerve fibers, although it clearly depends for its full functioning on the materials of which it is composed.[7])

Albeit varied, the beings that comprise reality are united by certain basic principles, such as the law of identity and noncontradiction. But as to what kind of substances there may be, that is a matter of discovery, not of metaphysics. So ontological pluralism is qualified by formal monism: the existence of no being can be a contradiction to the existence of any other. (This partly accounts for the insistence on the idea of the unity of the sciences, that truths about various features of nature must not contradict one another. But some mistake this to require ontological monism, the fundamental sameness of everything.) And while at first thought such a unity might be just what appears to be contradicted by certain aspects of contemporary (quantum) physics – for example, the equally useful yet contradictory "truths" about light – there is reason to think that on closer examination a different conclusion should be drawn. There are several areas of physics where complete theories are lacking and, because of the need for some workable (but by no means fully established) hypothesis, the field appears to be in partial disarray. If, however, it is admitted that the sciences often work with incompletely established theories, some of which yield sufficient illumination about some subject matter to carry out workable experiments and to develop useful technologies, then what appears to be lack of unity now need not be taken as evidence of lack of unity of principle. Indeed, most general theoreticians seek such unity and regard the suggestion that none exists in principle rather incomprehensible. Even chaos theorists, for example, aim to unite the various strands of cosmology by means of their curious postulates.

While the monistic/pluralistic view cannot be proven here, it is useful to indicate that common sense clearly supports it. Thus, it is reductionism that would appear to require demonstration. Surely a squirrel is different from a symphony and a soap bubble from a frog; or a day from a deer and a tree from a rose bush; or again a woman from a man, a child from an adult and an ant from a pebble? More generally put, differences abound in nature. Certainly we usually act in recognition of this fact. And surely, also, some unity is taken for granted in all this? For example, no theory is deemed adequate if it contains contradictions, and no witness in a court of law is regarded credible who asks the court to accept contradictory testimony.

The differences noted by the pluralist are said by some to be merely nominal. They argue that we have made them up, not individually but in unison, over long periods of time, and that this is what has led to our taking them to be obvious. Yet that view is very difficult to sustain: at least the statement of the difference is different from something else, namely the denial of it. If that too is a nominal difference, then anything is true and nothing is false. On its face, then, the ontological pluralist idea is not implausible. And in the end large theories must be evaluated on the basis of how plausibly they account for the world all of us share and can study for ourselves.

I think the pluralist ontology implies a far richer universe than its reductionist alternative that underlies the Hobbesian individualist outlook. If pluralism is sound, one result could well be that there are some entities in reality that are capable of existing well or badly. Here again common sense supports the idea: we certainly assume that arguments, for example, are good or bad, not all of equal quality. More generally, all living things might be of the sort to which values are connected. Since their life may end, how they live is measured, roughly, by whether they carry on successfully in terms of their nature, as what they are.

This in turn could have an impact on our conception of human existence. It is possible that, among nature's multifaceted types of entity human beings are a distinct class, set off as different by real attributes that introduce a value realm into nature. To evaluate their lives would require learning what kind of beings they are and whether this or that individual human being is more or less successful in carrying on with his or her life. The details depend, of course, on the answer to many questions, some very general, some specific to an individual and some ranging from one end to the other on the continuum from the general to the particular. For example, a person who is a student of the piano may be judged in part in terms of how well she does at that task, in part in terms of how reasonably she acts and in part in terms of whether she is fulfilling her own unique potentials.

Of course, some "talents" and potentialities will not be treated as a basis for evaluation. A talent for being a hired assassin, if acted on, would undermine one's ability to act in line with standards that emerge from one's human nature, such as respect for others' natural rights. Thus it ought not be developed. Normally, one does not have talents for such specific matters but for various skills that may be cultivated for good or for ill, as judged by reference to broad standards of conduct.

All living beings can exist well or badly: there are better and worse specimens of trees, fish, bees, flies and horses. And what each does can contribute more or less to its success. As far as we know, however, only human beings can help to bring it about, of their own initiative or choice, that they behave well or badly, at least in crucial respects. Each human being has the capacity to initiate his or her own qualitative individuation as a matter of what he or she chooses to do. In short, each person (not crucially incapacitated) has free will. This is both metaphysically possible and the best assessment of human nature.[8] In other words, a human being is a moral agent; he or she can be *morally* good or evil. Whether or not he or she will be one or the other is necessarily a matter of individual achievement or failure.[9]

Within this framework, standards of moral goodness and evil are, in turn, objective. They are groundable on facts of nature, namely what a thing must be or do to be or become as fully as possible the kind of thing it is. This gives us standards of what makes it a better or worse version of the kind of thing it is. And in the case of human beings, who choose to act either in accordance or in defiance of their nature, the standards amount to moral standards, ones each person has the responsibility to invoke in his or her life. The objectivity may well rest on both a person's humanity and a person's individuality; that is, on what and who someone is. (Of course, other factors can impinge on what a person has chosen to become, a cook, airline pilot, medical doctor. All these provide a grounding for determining what a person ought to do.) These standards are not, as the economic (Hobbesian) individualist imagines subjective, conventional or arbitrary. They are natural, objective.

From within this framework it is possible and meaningful to raise the question of what makes someone a good human being – that is, an excellent manifestation of the individual person he or she is – and what makes for morally good conduct, actions or institutions. This is how a standard of moral evaluation is possible: those who achieve, as a matter of their own choice, the highest potential of their humanity and individuality are good persons. Those who fail at this task are progressively less good.

Within this framework, individuals may be comprehensible as self-determined manifestations of familiar yet uniquely combined attributes: habits, patterns of conduct, aspirations, etc. It is their unique instrumentality in determining who and what, and what combination of these two aspects, they will be that renders their real ontological situation aptly identified as qualitatively individual. That is, the individual they turn out to be will, in part, be a function of the quality of choices they have made *vis-à-vis* their unique circumstances in life, as well as *vis-à-vis* their common human attributes. (I covered some of this in Chapter 2 where I discussed the difference between and similarity of the subjective value of neo-classical economics and the individual but objective value theory of classical individualism.)

I have already noted that it is the pluralistic character of reality that provides part of the metaphysical underpinnings of individualism as conceived here. But monistic, or unifying, constituents of reality also contribute to that foundation. These latter are the fundamental, axiomatic principles of being, such as the law of identity and the law of noncontradiction. Why are these laws axiomatic? Because any thinking presupposes them; even the use of words does so. Aristotle's defense of them is still undefeated.[10] (In commonsense terms, contradictions cannot be parts of existence. In science a contradiction is the clearest sign of trouble, which is true for any of the sciences, whatever their subject. And that is for the simple reason that any being must be what it is; nature will not suffer contradictions.[11])

In one respect, then, namely as regards formal integrity, nature conforms to the monistic insight about sameness. But as far as its substance, or actual, active content, is concerned, reality is multifaceted, a potentially endless plurality of types, relations and modalities. We are, of course, aware of just this sort of plurality, yet we are also conscious, in even the simplest perception, of the monistic element. We are open to finding yet unknown minerals, viruses, astronomical bodies or subatomic particles. But we balk at contradictions in all fields; unless, that is, we are arguing about this very issue or making some point.[12]

Furthermore, no ontological reductionist mission has ever been fully accomplished, although there are innumerable IOUs on record. From East to West, philosophers are always making some promise about how reality will be shown to be one thing – God, pure self, matter in motion or mind – or two – mind and matter – or some other fixed number; but what we do know of clearly, just from being normally aware of reality, is that great variety is the status quo. The view that there is no limit to the possibility of different ontological domains seems, then, to have a kind of presumptive soundness to it. But to prove all this would be impossible here. All I can do is to indicate why some evident facts make the best sense when looked at from the above metaphysical framework.

For example, it seems that we have to admit of a variety of causal principles. They are found in various fields of concern, in quantum physics, mechanics, biology, meteorology, psychology and political science, and in ordinary accounts of why people do this and that. That human beings possess causal capacity, for example to activate their own thinking (the doctrine of free will), fits within the metaphysical framework that sees the kinds of cause as dependent on the kinds of thing involved in the event. Our way of explaining various events in nature, when not hindered by the insistence that we reduce everything to mechanical causation, would seem to bear out part of this point. Human beings can be first causes.[13]

A certain way of conceiving of the mind–body relationship, namely as involving not the link of two basically different types of being but the unison or interdependence of several aspects or modes of being (physical, chemical, electrical, physiological, conscious and self-conscious, to give a possible list), seems also to support the present metaphysical framework.[14] Put generally, while there may be sporadic unsatisfactory parts to the body of evidence, all in all it stacks up better than what is presented in support of, say, reductive materialism, dialectical materialism, supernaturalism, idealism and other competing metaphysical hypotheses. The cumulative support for the monist–pluralist metaphysical framework, from considerations of coherence, common sense, parsimony, openness to new possibilities, practicality and overall simplicity, seems to make it more plausible than one might assume. It seems, in any case, much better grounded than reductive materialism, which, along with nominalism in epistemology, is the philosophical home of quantitative individualism.

Most importantly for our purposes, within this metaphysics an individualist, or egoist, conception of justice could well turn out to be sound. If there are individuals who cause their own actions, and if these actions have the potential to be good as a matter of self fulfillment or full flourishing for a person as a human being, then these individuals will possess a moral dimension to their nature. And this dimension, when applied to social or public affairs, yields a promising conception of justice. It lacks the full (otherwordly and thus impossible!) idealism associated with Plato and Christianity, but it also avoids the moral barrenness we find in the Hobbesian or *homo economicus* conception of human life.

Indeed, natural rights doctrine, as developed from John Locke and subsequently by libertarian political theorists, accomplishes the conceptualization of justice along normative individualist lines. It does this by identifying the nature of each human being as that of an individual capable of rational choice and requiring the utilization of reason for virtually any significant task in the guidance of his or her life. This, in turn, requires the kind of political community for human beings in which their human individuality may flourish properly; that is, a community that upholds each (adult) person's sovereignty. This is accomplished by means of implementation of the doctrine of natural individual human rights, starting with the right to life and all that this implies: the rights to liberty, property and the pursuit of happiness, as well as more subsidiary or special rights, such as the right to freedom of expression, association and religious worship. Justice in such a political society is conceived as strict adherence to public policies guided, firstly, by the goal of protecting individual rights and, secondly, by the process of not violating those rights even as they are being protected, which are approximated by the civil rights we hear so much about in connection with the administration of justice in, for instance, the USA.

Hobbesian individualism fails to achieve this result because it is determinist and nominalist. Qualitative or classical individualism, however, locates individual responsibility at the heart of human nature, namely free choice – a fundamental capacity of a rational being. This also locates the ultimate standard for morally good conduct: human rationality or, as Aristotle called it, right reason. In plain terms, this means that the highest virtue for human beings is to initiate clear thinking about their lives in this world, to guide their actions towards success in life by careful consideration of their lives. In turn, the natural rights doctrine initially placed on record by John Locke goes on to generate from these foundations a conception of political virtue – justice – although Locke himself did not quite achieve that mission.

Political and legal justice within this framework implies that for each person some "moral space", or sphere of exclusive jurisdiction, be secured within the legal system. Within this exclusive, though within the general theory indeterminately "sized", sphere he or she is able to exercise moral choice. Since moral choice is just that, a choice – and not, as in the mechanistic framework of economic science, merely a selection process that may be quite automatic, in the way that computers make selections given their built-in programs – there is no guarantee that it will turn out right. Thus a just system cannot be utopia or guaranteed perfection. It can merely make virtue legally or institutionally possible for members of a community. That, as well as the infinite diversity of objective human excellences, accounts for why the free marketplace gives the appearance of being neutral with respect to the issue of justice. In a free market many decisions may not turn out to be morally proper yet may not be prohibited.

Nevertheless, there is a dimension of justice in free markets. Producers do tend to receive economic rewards in proportion to what they manage to do to satisfy consumers. This may not satisfy the ideal of guaranteed perfect justice. The market process does not guarantee that people will respond properly to all the good or bad qualities of each other as they engage in free trade; indeed, "free" trade means that there is neither legal banning of bad nor legal mandate of good trade, even though one can conceptualize some cases of such trade and spot where corrective action might be possible. But the free market process may come as close to approximating justice as it is reasonable to expect within the narrow sphere of commerce. The baker making bread and the rock musician playing rock music provide us with what we would like from them, all things considered, and we repay in kind. We are not responding to these individuals by construing them in their totality; only as they are of interest to us. But within those limits the relationship is largely appropriate, just. If we stole the bread from the baker or sneaked into the rock concert without paying, we would be treating these individuals unjustly. We would disregard their terms of our interacting with them. And if they delivered stale bread where they offered fresh bread for sale, or a bad or mediocre performance, not to mention a missed date, they would treat us unjustly.

As an institution the free market is far more just than alternative systems since, firstly, it is necessary for the possibility of justice within commercial endeavors and, secondly, it often approximates just exchange within that sphere, although it is admittedly not the whole of human justice. The free market, furthermore, makes it institutionally possible for men and women to strive for justice when their market affairs do not sufficiently approximate that ideal. That is why boycotts, strikes and demonstrations, quite apart from the just processes of positive law itself, often accompany even the relatively free markets of contemporary Western societies.

We will return to some of these issues in later sections of this work. But now I wish to confront some standard objections to individualism. I begin by connecting what I have been discussing above with further elements of political individualism. Then I shall show why giving up on quantitative individualism does not usher in the larger than minimal state, as some normative individualists have claimed.

ANTI-INDIVIDUALISM ANSWERED

The central objection to individualism, one from which numerous others derive, has already been noted. It is the Marxist point that individuality is a transitory condition in mankind's history – or, rather, prehistory –

somewhat as adolescence is but a stage on the way towards maturity in the life of every human being. Marx, from his earliest writings, embraced the idea of humanity as a kind of concrete universal, an "organic whole".[15] He did this in a complicated Hegelian sense in which what we generally regard as human history is a journey towards the dialectical development of this concrete universal.[16] For Marx, to reach full emancipation individuals eventually "must take the abstract citizen back into [themselves] . . . and become species-being[s]".[17] When that happens, in communism, the "egoistic and independent" individual will not represent the concrete substance of humanity. That is why such beings at this time suffer the condition of alienation; that is, estrangement from, indeed antagonism towards, their essence.

Outside Marx there are, of course, less vehement anti-individualists such as Jaffa, whom we have mentioned before, who maintains, allegedly following Aristotle, that

> the fundamental unit [of political life and community] is not the "individual" but the family. And morality comes to sight as those things which enable the family to survive, and of course to develop, which in turn enables the family eventually to take their roles as citizens.[18]

It may be thought indulgent to discuss these considerations, but within conservative circles, where the free market also receives extensive criticism, they definitely seem to matter most, as, for example, in George Will's *Statecraft as Soulcraft*. Here it seems that the human family, not humanity or the state, is the concrete universal. Not burdened by the fearsome revolutionary package we find in Marx, this is a more appealing collectivist outlook to Western liberal democratic minds. Yet it is no less firmly anti-individualistic. Underlying this conservative thesis we find the view that "for Aristotle, as for Plato, rationality is the power to recognize a universal order", so that "Aristotle cannot account for a rational consciousness that is ultimately unique". And, supposedly, neither can Aristotle, "any more than Plato does, recognize as knowledge the perception of a particularity rather than a universal".[19] In short, because a rational understanding of reality must involve classifications, and since individuals are inherently unclassifiable as individuals, such a view as Aristotle's has no room for individuals.

Let us now look at these points critically. Firstly, the Marxian notion of humanity as an organic whole – in our time given some credence by the biological speculations of Lewis Thomas, who regards the earth as one cell of which human beings, among other living beings, are constituent parts[20] – seems to me to be crucially flawed in several respects. One important aspect of the lives of individual human beings, namely their rational capacity, is not accountable for without reference to individuality. Their particular cerebral cortex is not collective. This central individual element of a person explains the possibility of initiated, free choice, the very power that by Marx's own account differentiates some human beings from others in whether and how they will exercise it. (Marx, it will be remembered, ascribes to some individuals, presumably to himself, the achievement of having come to understand social history as a matter of their own scientific discipline, thus extricating themselves from the bulk of (pre) humanity's state of captivity; that is, class consciousness.[21])

As Roger W. Sperry, a psychophysicist, has argued, it is the individual person's unique brain, and the resulting mentality of individual human beings, that makes initiated, free choice possible. And this power of initiated, free choice is exactly what is necessarily presupposed in any coherent account of rationality and, indeed, organized knowledge. It renders intelligible the conceptual level of consciousness that makes possible human knowledge, science and the differentiation, on justified grounds, between truth and falsehood, right and wrong, and, ultimately, good and evil.[22]

It appears, then, that Marx embraces an unwarranted substance monism whereby individuality is impossible. He accepts that everyone in the central respect of his or her identity is one with all the rest, namely a species-being. This seems sensible enough in contrast to Hobbesian individualism. But in terms of the account of individuality suggested here, neither alternative is to be preferred as a basic account of human nature.

It is very risky to make sketchy remarks about the Marxian metaphysics since Marx hardly lends himself to the straightforward interpretation on this score. Before I proceed with the defense of qualitative individualism, let me turn to considering whether one is really justified in interpreting Aristotle as a metaphysical anti-individualist. Is his political anti-individualism so clear cut and warranted from within his own frame of reference? This is important since almost everyone, especially critics of classical liberalism and modernity, considers Aristotle a good guide to what is politically important. His political thinking simply has to be taken into account, especially when we are stressing the issue of human rationality and virtue for purposes of understanding human community life.

From the point of view of his epistemology alone, it may be difficult for Aristotle to give a full account of individuality. Yet if metaphysical arguments are a kind of epistemological process – that is, one variety of seeking to know with the real possibility of success – Aristotle may in fact have given such an account, albeit in a somewhat roundabout way. I will not attempt to trace out the story but will merely point to one way that it might be told along lines which would favor my own assessment. Emerson Buchanan[23] states the thesis well in the beginning of the work which convinced me that Aristotle has ample room for individuals within his metaphysics:

Since "to be" means "to exist," τὸ τί ἦν εἶναι means "what it is for each thing to exist," and designates a mode of being or existing. Consequently, in identifying *ousia* (Being) with τὸ τί ἦν εἶναι, Aristotle is asserting that the fundamental reality on which everything else depends is the existence of individuals, each existing according to the mode proper to its species. Moreover, if τὸ τί ἦν εἶναι is taken literally, a basis is provided for distinguishing the essence, conceived as the mode of being of each thing, from the properties and attributes of the thing.[24]

In addition, even from the explicitly epistemological viewpoint an Aristotelian account of "a rational consciousness that is ultimately unique" is possible, at least if we allow something that David Norton introduces us to, namely personal knowledge. This is the account of the person given us by the person from "within" in possession of the unique information which, once individuality is made metaphysically comprehensible, will serve as one form of rational account dealing with individuality. The problem is that some take all knowledge, and thus all understanding which can lead to explanation, as propositional, and thus as necessarily classificatory. When one knows something, what one knows is always that A is B; that, for instance, Charley is a human being.

Does, then, an Aristotelian (though not perhaps strictly speaking Aristotle's own) metaphysics leave room for individuals as primary beings; and would it be possible to integrate this prospect with the possibility of identifying individuals *qua* individuals of some kind? Both are viable.

I have already indicated where individualist metaphysics seems to fit with Aristotle. The epistemological support would come from the idea that knowledge need not always be propositional – classificatory, putting one thing with another, deducing A from B – but could also involve direct perception. If direct perceptual knowledge is bona fide knowledge, then individuality is knowable, right in the midst of a rationally categorizable world!

I will shortly discuss the more political anti-individualism often attributed to Aristotle and, by implication, to any view which rests on various Aristotelian contentions. For now, however, I wish to reiterate some of the metaphysical points which the above discussion seems to me to warrant.

It would seem that the denial of individuality, especially qualitative individuality, is shortsighted. It gives short shrift to the ontological possibility of, for example, self-generated development. Just as many reductionists find the idea of initiated action or free will to be anti-natural, because their account presupposes what might be called a one dimensional conception of the law of causality,[25] so those who elevate universality to a position of metaphysical dominance would deny the significance and even the possibility of real, objective individuality. Those who embrace such individuality seem to be pushed towards accepting some fundamentally mysterious element of reality.[26]

The pluralistic-monistic thesis I have sketched remedies matters here by making individuality compatible with an overall coherent account of existence. Such diverse individuality is the substance of existence, and it opens up the need for a division of labor in the disciplines of study, in the sciences. It makes sense of the fact that different methods need to be used in the different fields, since their subject matter is significantly different.

Two more questions arise, one from within metaphysics, the other pertaining to Aristotelian politics. Firstly, are the individuating aspects of human beings – one's being the unique human individual one is – necessary or accidental? This is important because if the answer is the latter then it is not so important, for example, whether a human being *qua* an individual fares well. What matters is whether one fares well in one's status as a member of the species – as Marx would put it, as a species-being – or, following Jaffa, of the family.

But I argue that the individuating aspects of human beings are necessary. It is not possible to be a bona fide human being without also being an individuated, self-determined being. This, following the points advanced by Sperry and Buchanan, is involved in what it means to be – that is, the very nature of – a human being; in the necessarily self-determined character of the life of every human being. Anyone's particular circumstances not merely differentiate that person numerically but also impose on that person a unique pattern of possible self-development. This may or may not be realized, as a matter of the choices of the individual person or some outside intrusion. But if those choices are made without intrusion, they would lead to yet further unique possibilities, all the way to the end of one's life. To ignore these individuating aspects of human life would be to ignore something crucial in what it is to be human.

Secondly, if the account Buchanan gives of Aristotle's metaphysics is correct, some alterations might have to be made in the sort of characterization of Aristotelian politics we found stressed by Jaffa as well as by other conservative critics of individualism. Accordingly, the goodness of the *polis* (as distinct from the justice of the *polis*) might turn out to be inseparable from the goodness of those who comprise it. Thus the goodness of the *polis* is a function of the fullest combined self-realization of individuals as individuals embarking on organized community life. This would seem to be the result of the sort of account of Aristotelian ethics we find in W. F. R. Hardie's works.[27]

There is also some possible confusion within Aristotle's politics regarding how we should understand the precise scope of governmental or legal power. The idea of *polis* seems to mean both human community and state (or government). So when Aristotle argues that the *polis* is responsible for fostering the moral improvement of its members, the case seems to hinge on the earlier establishment of the view that a good deal of moral development in human beings must be supported by the community.[28] Aristotle himself takes it that he has shown that government needs to exert coercion so as to foster the virtues. But this does not follow.

Furthermore, Aristotle's account of the moral virtues as requiring the volition of the agent, at least in adulthood, would appear to make his state paternalism somewhat problematic. If to be a morally good human being one must *choose* to act according to the virtues, what room does this leave for the government regimenting the citizenry towards their moral excellence? At the most a certain degree of coaxing, via good example by the officials of the legal system, would be suitable, accompanied by what today we like to call social pressure, such as rebuke, chiding, ostracism and boycott.[29]

So it seems that, *pace* conservatives and others, from within Aristotle's various philosophical reflections there may emerge several strands of thought which support a form of individualism. This classical individualism, in turn, seems to avoid the Hobbesian trappings so many critics find rightly objectionable. Why this form of individualism does not depart from the crucial features of political individualism and libertarianism – that is, from the Lockean classical liberal political tradition – remains to be discussed.

POLITICAL INDIVIDUALISM RECOVERED

David L. Norton, who is otherwise a great friend of individualism, thinks that "the fact of human growth entails continuous redistribution" not covered by "exchanges and gift-giving".[30] Thus Norton wishes to reply to Robert Nozick, who once opposed coercive redistribution.

However, nothing in Nozick's writing limits the scope of voluntary redistribution to cases of exchange and gift giving. There is ample room, indeed more room than there is in a larger than minimal state,[31] for redistribution motivated by the choice to satisfy moral responsibilities and commitments, as well as other moral demands on one, among them those stemming from love and friendship. These latter are not all cases for gift giving. But Norton fails to consider this and goes on:

> Here arises the function of the state as a standing agency of redistribution. This function is required by justice, and extends the legitimate influence of the state beyond the limits set by Nozick. . . . If we recognize that personal individuality is an outcome which requires to be brought about by individuals themselves, we will understand that it requires to be cultivated and supported

by social institutions, the responsibility for which rests with civil society. . . . Because individuation and autonomy are emergents, they require institutional support for their nurture. If, as individualism contends, civil society exists to foster the worthiest individuals possible, then its imposed regulations will give way in the end to the self-regulation of individuals according to principles deriving from their own intrinsic ends.[32]

Before proceeding let me note that the cultivation and support by social institutions that Norton talks about may both be responsibilities of "civil society", but civil society designates much more of social life than does "government". Moreover, government's role in fostering the worthiest individuals possible may well be fulfilled by just the sort of peace-keeping, rights-protecting activities that Nozick and I would regard as the indispensable and unique function of government. Firstly, there are social institutions, such as the family, neighborhood, school, church, fraternal societies, clubs and professional associations, that cultivate and support individuals in their pursuit of their intrinsic ends. Secondly, what is required from the government is that scrupulous attention be paid to maintaining the conditions which serve to guard against violence, fraud and corruption as much as possible, and that in the process of thwarting crime the government itself conduct itself morally. That, as far as individualism is concerned, is a trying enough job, implying a wide array of special responsibilities suited for carrying out the process most effectively in order to pursue justice justly or in line with due process of justice.

It seems to me that Norton shares what has been called by one scholar a confusion in Aristotle, namely between community (or society) and government (or the state). He is correct to note that Nozick's implicit or at least possible subjectivism – which Norton calls quantitative individualism – "fosters the very extravagances of egoism which, as Tawney shows, reduced classical British 'individualism' to absurdity, spawning statism and collectivism as countermeasures".[33] Yet Norton opens the door wide to measures that would undercut his own general support for individualism. He invites a rather extensive and, I would maintain, unrestrainable state mechanism when he claims that provisions are due to persons via government redistribution. Public schools, child care, health care for the poorer children of society, welfare for orphans and so on would (and do) all spawn further state measures, such as regulatory bodies, state sponsored school texts and hospitals. There is a clear danger of the slippery slope in all this, with the mechanism of due process of law relying heavily on precedent to seek guidance in the development and evolution of the laws of the community.

Furthermore, in leaving such doors open, Norton invites the countermeasure or backlash of subjectivism, whereby someone like Milton

Friedman hopes to disabuse anyone of the idea that he or she knows what is good for others, hoping thereby to nip interventionism in the bud.[34] That will not do, I agree. But nor is it needed. The cultivation, for example, of self-regulation in a child is the responsibility of parents or next of kin – the community – not of those strangers whose pursuit of their ends precluded child raising and focused on other achievements. When parental responsibilities are neglected, of course, litigation can be a remedy and a disincentive. This does not, however, warrant any expansion of state power, merely the sharpening of the state's judicial function.

It would be unjust to impose on individuals burdens others have assumed in their wise or unwise ways of living. To put it differently, how society supports itself outside of making room for individual self-development, including child raising, is a matter of the moral virtues of the individuals choosing to practice them. Whether society makes the maximum room for individuals taking that responsibility upon themselves is a matter for statecraft or politics. The greatest hazard from others to self-regulation is the use of physical force or its threat, something which the state is uniquely equipped to try to thwart. To import these tools into the area of "self"-regulation itself is, however, to defeat that very purpose. Paternalism towards adults is anti-humanism.

In this chapter I have tried to bring out some features of individualism not widely linked with the position. These are that individualism, of a certain kind, is compatible with realism and with the objectivity of universals or the natures of things; that metaphysical pluralism and monism can be reconciled. This will make room for what common sense makes us aware of, namely the multifaceted nature of reality and its possibilities; that with this background, qualitative individuality, for moral beings, is metaphysically possible, as revealed by the reality of free will and the doctrine of personal destinies; and that this kind of robust individualism makes room exactly for the minimal state as a just political organization.

The moral significance of the viewpoint, aside from what has already been mentioned, includes what is perhaps commonplace but not unworthy of repetition. Success in life comes not from using force, restrictions, regimentation or regulation towards others, but from an active goodwill on the part of individuals. That goodwill sets their reason into motion, thus maintaining active, focused minds. Those minds, in turn, will have the best chance to learn the facts, if they are left unimpeded by others. Knowledge of facts will then have the best chance of providing the rational guidance that is so indispensable for human excellence; facts that nevertheless vary a great deal in light of the very individuality of objective ends and the means through which such success might be attained.

Individualism is usually attacked because it is regarded as incompatible with the ideal of human community, with the naturalness of persons finding themselves members of communities. That is indeed the way *homo economicus* conceives of the individual person, although sometimes only for special analytic purposes. Still, this form of individualism has loomed large as a bulwark against collectivism. And since it is not a successful general theory of human nature, it has not fared well in that mission. While the classical or normative individualism I have outlined above no longer embraces the atomism of human individuality, there is something about this view that unites it with radical individualism, albeit for different reasons. This is that human beings are equal moral sovereigns. Even some of what is natural for them, such as community solidarity, fellow-feeling and camaraderie, is treated as a matter of choice, not of coercion by other individuals. This is not because this classical individualist approach shares the Hobbesian view's subjectivism and nominalism but because it recognizes that human individuals attain the human way of excellence only if they act on their own initiative in morally relevant matters. So those who think that by debunking individualism *per se* they will deal a deathblow to the ideal of personal and political sovereignty are mistaken. There is a more mature form of individualism than those advanced at the philosophical birth of the doctrine.

In the end I want to express a suspicion, one that does not figure in the argument of this chapter. It may shed some understanding on the motivation behind the insistence that collectivism is the true reality, or, as Marx put it, that "The human essence is the true collectivity of man." If we have no self, if we are not individuals with rightful sovereign powers, then the rational alternative is that we are parts of a larger whole; family nation or humanity. But decisions will still have to be made by some persons; it is human minds that issue them, not human collectives. Is it not just possible that some of the motivation behind all this debunking of individualism stems from a desire for power over others? Power itself may be used properly, for example in fending off threats to what is good. So many who seek the power to order society may find it helpful to couch this in terms with which they can live guiltlessly. And collectivism provides those terms.

There is also the desire many may feel to be able to dispense quickly and institutionally with the task of persuasion, argument and gaining permission from us all when it comes to decisions as to how we will live our lives. This too may provide a motivation against individualism. Individuals do at times make very bad decisions, and it would be wonderful if they did not do this. Some seem to have a deep-seated impatience with this. And, in all earnestness, they may be tempted to give their emotional disposition a metaphysical gloss. No doubt, this suspicion may be turned around: perhaps some of use are so eager not to conform, not to yield to the dictates of widely recognized moral standards, that we wish to build this into a philosophy rather than accept it as a mere perverse desire. That, however, is not why I regard the individualist alternative as morally sound.

In the end, it will have to be decided by thinking it through quite thoroughly and reaching some agreement, not by cutting it all short via some state edict. And that itself seems to me to be a point in favor of individualism – the recognition that, at least in theoretical disputes argumentation alone, gaining voluntary assent based on good reasons ought to carry the day.

NOTES

1. See Machan, *Individuals and Their Rights*, ch. 2, and "A new individualist basis of the free market". The phrase "qualitative individualism" comes from Norton, "Individualism and productive justice". See his more fully developed discussion of this view in *Personal Destinies*.
2. Machan, "C. S. Peirce and absolute truth".
3. Austin, "Other minds".
4. Rand, *Introduction to Objectivist Epistemology*.
5. Machan, "Epistemology and moral knowledge".
6. Ehrenfeld, *The Arrogance of Humanism*.
7. Sperry, *Science and Moral Priority*.
8. For more on this, see Machan, *The Moral Case for the Free Market Economy*.
9. Moral goodness, as a distinct kind of goodness, is that kind which must be attained as a matter of the choices of the agent. A good deal of so-called moral philosophy rests, therefore, on a confusion: see Machan, "Ethics vs. coercion".
10. Rasmussen, "Aristotle and the defense of the law of contradiction".
11. Aristotle, *Metaphysics* 3. 1006b 18-24.
12. Consider the theater of the absurd movement, some of the wilder points associated with Existentialism and certain contentions advanced about the kind of thinking engaged in by native American spiritual leaders.
13. Sperry, *Science and Moral Priority*.
14. Bissell, "Dual-aspect theory of agency".
15. Marx, *Writings of the Young Marx on Philosophy and Society*, p. 39. See also Marx, *Grundrisse*, trans. by M. Nicolas.
16. Since there are now roughly 300 different versions of the master's true view, there is not much that one can do but turn to Marx himself and see if the rendition being offered squares with what he said. This is argued at greater length in Machan, *Marxism*.
17. Marx, *Selected Writings*, p. 56.
18. Jaffa, "A conversation with Harry V. Jaffa at Rosary College", p. 9.
19. Letwin, "Romantic love and Christianity", p. 135.
20. Thomas, *The Lives of a Cell*.
21. Marx, *Grundrisse*, trans. by D. McLellan, pp. 33ff. Marx here describes the proper methodology of political economy, one he will be using as distinct from

the one used by Adam Smith and David Ricardo which produced "the insipid illusions" (McLellan translation) or "unimaginative conceits" of the eighteenth century. Marx believes that "The same men who establish their social relations in conformity with their material productivity, produce also principles, ideas, and categories in conformity with their social relations. Thus these ideas, these categories, are as little eternal as the relations they express. They are historical and transitory products", *Selected Writings*, p. 202. One may suppose that no such socioeconomic factors led Marx to formulate views which also come to being no more than "little eternal".
22. Sperry, "Changing concepts of consciousness and free will", "Mind, brain, and humanist values" and *Science and Moral Priority*. See also Ripley, "Sperry's concept of consciousness". For the beginnings of the general scientific viewpoint in support of this outlook, see Morgan, *Emergent Evolution*. Some of these points are developed in Machan, *The Pseudo-Science of B. F. Skinner*.
23. Buchanan, *Aristotle's Theory of Being*. For a detailed defense of metaphysical individualism, see Gracia, *Individuality*.
24. *Ibid.*, p. 2.
25. The best Aristotelian account of this issue can be found in Joseph, *An Introduction to Logic*. See also Fisk, *Nature and Necessity*. Fisk discusses the problems with the Humean view of causality and necessity.
26. Those few individualists who support a relatively free market, reject the *homo economicus* line of analysis, endorse a moral perspective on social life and also deny the objectivity not only of moral principles but also of reality draw their intellectual material mostly from a certain reading of David Hume. Michael Oakeshott is one of those (see his *On Human Conduct*), as is, even more so, Shirley Robin Letwin (see her "The achievements of Friedrich A. Hayek"). For an intriguing statement of her views, see Letwin, *The Gentleman in Trollope*.
27. Hardie, "The final good in Aristotle's *Ethics*".
28. Miller, "The state and community in Aristotle's *Politics*".
29. See Hunt, "Some advantages of social control: an individualist defense".
30. Norton, "Individualism and productive justice", p. 123.
31. For some reasons why a more than minimal state thwarts morality, see Machan, "Human dignity and the law".
32. Norton, "Individualism and productive justice", pp. 123-4.
33. Norton, *Personal Destinies*, p. 42.
34. See Friedman, "An interview with Milton Friedman".

Chapter 5

Why Capitalism?

PULLING THE STRANDS TOGETHER

Once we have understood that besides the Hobbesian, neo-classical economic individualism we also have an alternative and better individualist position, namely the classical or qualitative version, it is important to consider why such a philosophical ethical view leads to capitalism in the political economic realm. That is what I wish to discuss here, to show that classical individualism is indeed a solid foundation for the capitalist economy. Elsewhere I argue the truth of this classical individualism and my task here does not fully require that.[1]

Basically my argument goes in the following way. By the classical individualist position we see that every adult person is a moral agent, with the task to make of his or her life a good human life. This task, however, requires that each person be a sovereign agent in a significant sphere of his or her conduct. Putting it backwards, being under the command of others robs a person of the prospect of fulfilling his or her moral task.

Now, when one lives in the vicinity of others, one has prospects both for self-enhancement as well as self-destruction in consequence of that proximity. Of course, persons can destroy themselves independently of others or suffer misfortune, even in others' vicinity. By this independence I mean that they need not dump their destructive conduct on others; others can escape by ceasing their association with the self-destructive person or group (as in a marriage or a corporate venture). If one fails to cease such an association, that is again a choice that must be left free for persons. In such cases, we may be tempted to blame only the party who has initiated some bad policy, yet those remaining associated with that party are also to be blamed for what happened to them in consequence of their failure to withdraw.

As an example of this, let's take the case of smoking, which seems clearly to be harmful to the smoker's health. Manufacturers, sellers, and advertisers are often held responsible for the damage suffered by smokers. In turn, those near to the smoker by their own choice – say by frequenting a "smoking permitted" establishment - hold smokers responsible. In cases of children, and some rare, helpless adults, such a shedding of blame may be justified, but in most cases it reveals only that individual human responsibility has been denied, that persons are deemed helpless in the face of "pressures" put on them by, for example, advertisers.

Yet although many cases of alleged coercion are nothing of the sort, it must also be noted that other persons often have the opportunity to hinder one's achievement of one's moral tasks. Given this fact and its realization, one ought to devise means by which the benefits of the community are preserved while the hindrances are avoided. This is where the idea of government will have found its moral support in a classical individualist viewpoint. The government's role is to preserve peace and each person's sphere of sovereign authority. The practical implementation of this will involve the implementation of the principles of the rights to life, liberty and property. The last, which gives rise to capitalism, is simply the practical or concrete application of the former. To do what one chooses to do, one needs to have a sphere of control extending from oneself, including all aspects of oneself under potential voluntary guidance, to what one has appropriated for oneself from nature without limiting others to carry out a similar mission.

This is a somewhat revised version of the Lockean defense of natural human individual rights. The argument construes it a rational or moral act for human beings to avoid the state of nature while at the same time preventing any tyranny or untoward intrusion in the state of civil society. Unlike the Lockean position, however, this view rests on a more substantial ethical theory, namely on classical individualism or egoism. I did not develop the full case here since I have done that elsewhere, but I needed to summarize the case so we can see that classical rather than Hobbesian individualism better supports and preserves the free society.

A general statement of the central theme of this book is that a moral argument for the free market system is available and is needed to supplement, and sometimes even to counteract, what economists have to say in support of capitalism. The moral defense of a political economic system must rest on the best ethical system that human beings can discover. And my position is that classical individualism or egoism is such a system and that it supports the free society.

MORALS, COERCION AND NATURAL RIGHTS

From knowing the moral nature of human beings, that as rational animals they ought to choose to conduct themselves according to standards of right, it is evident, among other things, that everyone ought to choose to act rightly. Without being free from others one cannot do so. Ought implies can: when one has the responsibility to do something, it must be an option for one to choose to do it. It cannot be something that others accomplish for a person. That is what the Lockean theory of natural rights stresses.

Natural rights are the basic principles by which all members of society can respect the requirements of morality in the context of human community life. There is nothing mysterious about natural rights when so understood. They are the proper parameters of morally relevant conduct within the context of community life.

Such rights derive from the moral nature of individuals; that is, any individual's moral responsibility to be as good as possible at living his or her human life. They are the principles by which certain dimensions of autonomy are required in the company of other people. They are general rights, not "bundles" of or narrowly conceived rights, for example the right to lift one's finger, the right to step to the left, the right to speak about politics, the right to make love to a member of the opposite sex, the right to privacy and the right to worship. (This is how many utilitarians, such as Robert Bork, view rights). Only when translated into case law do the general human rights we possess break into such detailed instances of the general principle that spells out the basic requirements of human social life as such.

A human community renders it imperative that these rights be respected and protected by the inhabitants. Without such respect and protection a community would fail to honor the nature of human life itself. To the extent that these rights are violated or abridged, human life as such is not being fully honored in a society. This is what is meant when people note that human rights violations undermine a political system's legitimacy.

What gives rise to these rights is the fact that everyone in society must have a sphere of personal jurisdiction or, to use Nozick's phrase, moral space. If the rights to life, liberty and property – the absence of others' coercion of or aggression upon us as natural living, self-determined beings – are not secured within society, it is to that extent unsuitable to human living; it is an unjust society. The absence of *de facto* and *de jure* observance of these rights renders a community unfit for a full, promising human life, although that may still make it fit for human survival at some tolerable level. (Even in the absence of institutional protection of such rights they might well be widely observed and respected, but it is, of course, probably true that such observance and respect will be more vulnerable where the legal system fails to support them.)

PRIVATE PROPERTY RIGHTS AND MORALITY

The system of private property rights, derived as it is from the principle of the right to life (since life must be lived in the context of nature, of which property is composed), secures for us, among other things, our sphere of personal moral authority. That system is the practical, concrete implementation of the general doctrine of natural individual human rights. How else could one act on one's own initiative if one had no sphere of jurisdiction?[2] One would have to act by permission. So either a *de facto* or both that and a *de jure* recognition of private property rights enhances the moral quality of human social life.

It bears noting here that in a small (intimate) community the *de jure* element might be omitted because of the clear availability of constant and widespread personal vigilance as to the entire community's respect for the principle of private property rights. This is why in certain experimental communities, such as monastic orders and kibbutzim, no *de jure* recognition of private property rights exists while general respect for such rights, even under a different name, can easily be observed. But in large societies, where commercial interaction predominantly involves strangers, persons not on intimate terms with each other, the *de jure* element – that is, the law of property, derived from the basic constitutional and common law system – preserves the *de facto* part.

That is what makes capitalism, which relies for its operations on the recognition and protection of these property rights, a morally sound and superior system, compared to fascism, communism, socialism and so on. Not only is this system productive, though that is an obviously worthwhile aspect of it; not only does it allow us to gain knowledge so as to flourish, although that too is a very good thing; not only can science prosper in its midst more than in alternative systems, yet that too is a great benefit of the system. What counts the most, what is centrally significant about this political economic system, is that it enables individuals to live a morally dignified life, to be in maximum command of their own existence in whatever conditions of existence they happen to be born into. Poor or rich, beautiful or ugly, talented or of meager prospects, men and women in all their variety are equal in the one respect that is crucial in society: they are all rights possessors and may not be used for others' purposes without their explicit or at least implicit consent.[3]

Everyone, then, must embark on the task of living a morally good and successful life without coercing, regimenting, ruling or enslaving any others. Individual rights to life, liberty and property do indeed presuppose the moral responsibility for each individual to embark on life only with those others who are willing to join in the journey.

Does this mean we ought not to interact with persons who are hapless or unfortunate? We should interact with them only if, firstly, they allow us to and, secondly, it achieves a goal that does not defeat our own proper ends and flourishing in this world. This leaves ample room for generosity and charity. But it also imposes some limits: for example, one ought not to waste time reforming those who refuse the help. Of course, just because this is what we ought to do, it does not follow that we may disallow or legally ban actions that involve interacting with others in a useless fashion. What is morally required is not always to be legally mandated, and what is morally to be avoided may not always be legally forbidden. Most understand this when it comes to freedom of religion and the press but do not generalize it to other human activities.

The reason for the existence of private property rights is that human beings are complex natural beings and that in the task of making choices in their lives they act on the natural world around them. The right to property is simply to indicate that, in order to have moral space, they must have "room" in which to operate, a sphere of jurisdiction, if only in their own lives, skills, talents, ideas, etc. They must have their own sphere of authority within the natural world. Other persons must be able to learn the extent of this sphere so they can take care not to intrude on their fellows' sovereignty, however limited or extensive it might be. (And this sphere of personal authority can change as one's conduct is successfully directed towards expanding it. Property rights secure one's authority to engage in this expansion, or, alternatively, in squandering what one has, including talents or skills.)

Not to create any misunderstanding, this position does not mean that the natural right to private property involves any kind of entitlement to have goods and services provided for one by others. That would place some into servitude to others, make them into partial slaves. In fact, others have the task in life to make something of themselves, as a matter of their own choice and effort.

What the right to private property means is that one has the authority to take actions which could eventually result in securing for oneself whatever is appropriate for one's individual life. The property involved is not limited only to land or physical space. Thus one's skills, labor, poem, computer program, musical arrangement or economics text can constitute private property. So can a logo, a design or a name, or whatever may be produced and obtained by human beings without violating anyone's rights. One need not give some physicalist or materialist specification of what the right to private property secures, although such things are quite often the most evident candidates for the designation.

The right to private property is the foundation of a market economy, which secures for anyone the authority to set terms of trade. One has the authority to say, "This is mine; and so I have the say over what will happen to it and others must ask my permission concerning their interaction with what is mine." The right to private property is a practical, potentially elaborate specification (once developed into property law) of one's general right to life that derives from one's moral responsibility to make the most of one's human life. Life is a natural phenomenon and the right to it requires expression that can be applied to living in the natural world, with regard to natural processes, objects, concerns, aims, goals, needs, wants and so on.

Without the right to private property, the right to one's life is an empty gesture, a mere permission by those who in fact control property, including persons and their labor – for example, under communism and any other nonvoluntarily established collectivist or authoritarian system. The relationship between a system wherein private property rights are upheld and one in which they are mimicked is similar to the relationship between the wilds and a rather elaborate wild animal park. Some animals in the latter may get the impression that they live unbounded and sometimes they may even fare better, but in the last analysis they are really captives.

DIVERSITY, COMPETITION IN PEACE

The rights to life and to private property, and thus the corresponding free market system, need to be respected in order for people to lead very different lives in peace. Some think that one problem with a free society based on individual rights is just such diversity, assuming that morally decent lives are rather uniform in content and style. But the different lives of millions of individuals can be both equally good and varied. People can pursue diverse goals, embark on different careers, take up different hobbies and cultivate different styles, yet not vary in the overall moral quality of their lives.

Of course, at the same time, some of these lives will be morally odious, some mediocre and some a mixed bag. Yet, the individualist conception of what renders the lives of different persons morally good, mediocre or a failure does not entail the doctrine that everyone requires the fulfillment of uniform needs. For example, it may well be that safe and secure living, insurance for old age security, provisions for unemployment and so on would suit many people. Yet perfectly legitimately it may not suit them all, so that any public policy that imposes any of these on all would violate the sovereignty of these perhaps somewhat unusual citizens.

I should mention how the familiar public goods problem bears on the discussion here. The legal system and its attendant defense from possible domestic or foreign attacks is not the same kind of "provision". It is in fact just the kind of public good for which one dwells in civil society, as Locke pointed out. Those who choose to be in a society, then, explicitly or tacitly consent to such provisions.[4] But they do not consent to those that are not required for the provision of justice, for the protection of their individual rights.

Wherever laws obscure the borders around people – that is, do not protect and maintain private property rights – someone's misconduct or unwanted behavior may be dumped or discarded on others. One's actions in a system that lacks the specification of everyone's sphere of personal jurisdiction, sometimes developed in a complex fashion to include a myriad of possible types of property, may have negative externalities but without a system of property rights we would not even be able to tell whether they are, strictly speaking, externalities at all. What would they be external to? The very idea of externality presupposes the possibility of distinguishing between a realm within which some party has legitimate jurisdiction and one over which he or she lacks this.

What is generally known as dumping, for example pollution, presupposes at least the conceptualization of a realm of individual sovereignty or private property rights. In a system that respects these it is more likely that such problems as the tragedy of the commons will be overcome, since extending the principles to new spheres – as they were, somewhat obscurely, to the electromagnetic spectrum in the United States in the 1920s – is a viable prospect. (Where they cannot be extended, it is preferable that some kind of total prohibition should be implemented, following the principles of quarantine in the containment of serious contagious deseases. This would uphold the priority of respect for individual rights as against the idea of the need to achieve some utilitarian public purpose via, say, social cost-benefit analysis.)

Since this work is concerned mainly with the general line of argument available to give support to free market capitalism, I am not here concerned with the details of the legal framework, including the complexities of property law. It should be obvious that when the myriad of problems of contemporary culture, including industrial production and waste disposal, come face to face with the general framework being presented here, many unanticipated twists and turns of law will have to be expected. Nevertheless, this is true for any system, capitalism, the welfare state, socialism, fascism or whatever. All such systems aim to combine some measure of rational predictability, justice and the fact of constant change in human life. In the last analysis, to judge conclusively the comparative merits of the various systems one would need to see how well they handled various practical problems. Yet even without delving into those details in the fashion of the specialized journal articles and research studies, one can explore how likely it is that one broad framework, such as free market capitalism based on classical individualism, will adequately meet the challenge that any general political framework is designed to meet.

At this point let me return to the issue of dumping – pollution. In the context of a collectivist system, the problem of dumping or externalities makes no sense. If human beings were, as Marx and others believe, simply parts of a larger whole, there could only be a shifting of burdens from one part of the whole to another, as one shifts a heavy bag from one arm to the other, or shifts from one foot to another, or again utilizes some bone from a little used portion of the body to reinforce some other part of it for medical reasons. It would be a matter of collective priorities and the issue of illegitimate dumping would vanish.

Unless we know whether we are essentially individuals or essentially parts of a larger collective, we cannot determine what kind of political and economic order is right for us. Marx knew that if "the human essence is [everyone's] true collectivity"[5] then communism is the right system for us. But he was wrong to think that that is the human essence, or that it would become the human essence in the future.

THE JUSTICE OF THE MARKET SYSTEM AS SUCH

A rights oriented society, with its economic capitalism, makes possible the recognition of minor or major individual differences in achievements. Here again the economist is wrong to claim that the market system is a value-free institution. Although I have already touched on this in Chapter 2, I should like to consider the point with reference to a particularly notable claim to the effect that capitalism is unrelated to justice.

F. A. Hayek says that there is no room for justice in a market economy because justice means doing for people what they deserve and very often in the market you obviously do not do for people what they deserve.[6] Thus if a pornography merchant gets rich, he or she may not deserve this wealth because, after all, selling pornography is detestable. This is so even if it is done in a free market system. The same goes for selling heroin or even a defective car. It is generally immoral to contribute knowingly to drug addiction or careless transportation of people. Yet the pusher or used car merchant is being rewarded, at least economically. Clearly market transactions are not necessarily virtuous or just. They could be, but they need not be.

However, it is wrong to judge the free market by reference to select instances of its operations. The same applies here as regards a judicial system favored by civil libertarians. They will let some culpable people go free rather than violate anyone's civil rights. Does the system promote human morality and other values better than do alternatives? The answer would have to be yes, despite the fact that freedom always entails the possibility of evil. Anything aimed at eradicating that possibility is an illusion, a utopia.

In point of fact, the market rewards, often justly albeit very selectively, those activities that constitute a significant contribution and production, not destruction. If I am a baker who makes some very good rolls and by selling them becomes reasonably well off, yet I am also a negligent parent, then, yes, I am being rewarded for a small portion of my life despite my failure in another sphere. Such market-confined justice is clearly not sufficient to recognize a person's life-worth. But as far as establishing economic justice is concerned, that is all that is necessary. I did, after all, make a good roll! If I and others benefit from my economic actions, that suffices for justice here.

Thus, while the free market does not secure all facets of justice, still it does best at serving the commercial and economic facets of it. Contrary to Hayek's too ready concession, some of our market conduct is indeed justly appraised – rewarded or punished, more or less – even though the bulk of it may be ignored within the market process. The question, though, is again whether as a political economy the system of market processes serves justice better than do other systems, the welfare state, socialism, communism, fascism and so on. The answer is that, all in all, it does.

SOME SORE POINTS OF CAPITALISM

Abuse of private property

Karl Marx argues against the right to private property that "the right of man to property, is the right to enjoy his possessions and dispose of the same arbitrarily without regard for other men, independently from society, the right of selfishness".[7] This is substantially correct. The basic property right to anything from one's voice to a factory no doubt authorizes one to destroy these. This is the essential focus of Marx's remark. With the right to private property, one may not be prevented from disposing of what one owns, even if one does this arbitrarily, for no good reason whatsoever. So, yes, an implication of having rights is the authority to do the wrong thing. For example, the right of free speech includes the authority to say bad, offensive, reprehensible or profane things. Yellow journalism or pornographic literature is lamentable. Still, it is authorized by the right to speak and publish freely.

But Marx focuses only on the destructive or bizarre ways of using property. When one focuses on basic rights, including that to private property, is it logically defensible to deny them or to offer in refutation of them the mere possibility or even the reality of the occasional, discrete lamentable ways of misusing them? Do we deny a right because all of us do not exercise it in a laudable manner at all times and everywhere? This would certainly render the right of the press or artists or philosophers to publish freely no less susceptible to voidance. Human beings are not only capable of misspending their lives; they are also capable of spending it virtuously, fruitfully, creatively and imaginatively.

As a determinist who also embraces a rather pessimistic (Hobbesian) idea of human nature during the capitalist phase of humanity's development, Marx evades all of the positive aspects in his characterization of the implications of having the right to property. Having the right to property authorizes one to dispose of one's possessions not only arbitrarily but also sensibly, carefully, prudently, generously and productively. But, as I have tried to argue earlier, all this depends on what persons choose to do; it is not determined one way or another! Rights establish borders around people not just, as Marx suggests, because persons want to act crazily, arbitrarily or recklessly, but because they act very differently. Voluntary interdependence is thus preserved within human societies.

Labor at risk

If there is an Achilles heel of capitalism, many believe it is its labor market. Periodic unemployment seems unavoidable under this system. For example, does not a free society do badly – callously, inhumanely, ruthlessly, without compassion – when it comes to dealing with workers who lose their jobs due to changing market conditions, competition with foreigners or plant relocation?

Whenever people change their preferences, from small to big cars, from typewriters to computers, from pet rocks (a recent American craze) to Michael Jackson gloves; whenever in a free market innovators create novel processes to produce food, shelter, transportation or entertainment in different, more efficient ways; in short, whenever we make changes of any kind, certain adjustments may well need to be made by those involved in the commerce of the past.

Of course, sometimes change is brought about in ways that are plainly unjust. Here the law may be utilized to remedy matters, for example through restrictions on trade with countries that permit dealing in stolen merchandise, treaties prohibiting such trade and so forth. (I am not concerned here with exploring which of these measures is or is not fully consistent with international free trade, which is, of course, the proper global extension of the principle of private property rights. Arguably "dumping" should not be prohibited if it does not involve violation of rights. Even in domestic private business a firm may dump. No one may prohibit customers from benefiting from such possibly uneconomical conduct.)

But even in perfectly free markets, workers are seen as occupying a position of serious disadvantage. Those owning businesses, including corporate executives and the stockholders, are seen either as being wealthy enough to last out transition periods, or as not having a great proportion of their wealth dependent upon one firm's or even one industry's economic welfare. Workers, however, in car or steel plants seem to depend fully on the solvency of their company. If such plants are closed, the shareholders may take a small loss relative to their total income or pension funds, but the workers appear to depend on the plant for their very livelihood. Its closing is a devastating event for them.

Karl Marx, the most severe critic of capitalism, prophesied that such unavoidable, inevitable upheavals in the labor market would spell doom for the system. The growing number of unsettled workers would become fed up with capitalism and vote for more and more government intervention, so that eventually the system would change from capitalist to socialist.

At times, it might have seemed that such a revolution was under way. Labor unions grew, gained political power and sought just the sort of government intervention Marx imagined. Nevertheless, the growth of unionism need not support the Marxian view of history; the explanation for it could be that workers came to realize that certain ways of operating – that is, in unison – made better sense within the context of a capitalist system. (One must admit that, at the outset of the industrial revolution, many workers started from a decidedly unfair position, namely carrying the burden of being without property despite their unjust deprivation of such property in the earlier feudal and mercantilist eras. This is somewhat analogous to the burden suffered by American blacks who for a considerable time after their legal emancipation continued to carry the burden of the enslavement of their ancestors.)

Unionization has not been a uniform process throughout its development in Western industrial systems. Individualism and fractionalism are evident throughout, and at the present this has resulted in the considerable diminution of the power of organized labor. The working class, so called, does not seem to be the class Marx had supposed it to be, united by one underlying common objective interest.

None of this obviates the point that labor faces relatively greater risks in a free market society. We need to remember, however, that speaking of labor is somewhat like speaking of bachelors or people wearing warm clothing: there is great mobility into and out of the category in question. Moreover, in some cases the mobility required of labor might be fully justified in that it is simply the condition of modern life for most people. In some cases market trends may require settling for lower wages in new jobs, for retraining, for lower living standards. But there is also another avenue for reducing labor's risk.

Lowering risks in the labor market

Marx believed, along with some non-Marxist economists, that capitalism depends on wage labor. Marx saw it this way since he believed that capital accumulation occurred as a result of worker exploitation. But he was wrong on this last point. And he was also wrong that wage labor is a necessary condition for the existence of capitalism: both skilled and unskilled workers could form business firms and contract out their work, as lawyers and doctors do.

Much of this has been misrepresented by Marxists as well as by the activists who listened to them. They promulgated a viewpoint that made workers appear only as victims. The capitalist, in turn, was seen as the enemy, a different species of human being entirely, one who just looked to exploit the workers, never mind what happened to them in the process. From this antagonistic coexistence in the marketplace, workers had very little to gain. A few could extricate themselves and become small capitalists, but the bulk remained in the workforce. Even partial escape from total victimization seemed to require the formation of massive labor organizations protected from competitive and market forces by the government. By pooling workers' political strength, labor set out to strike some better bargains.

Yet this really did not do a great deal of good because as soon as wages rise collectively, independent of higher demand or more efficient productivity, the ripple effect is that prices, on the average, will be very likely also to rise. The workers who organize may receive some job security – partly artificial since, when they lose their political clout, unions simply cannot keep protecting their members – but not a significantly more abundant life.

What was substantially suppressed in this view of the relationship between capitalists and laborers is that this is not the only alternative to the working person's situation. It is easy to think of a far more profitable approach, namely the forming of labor corporations, partnerships, firms and so on, and the utilization of private insurance to cover the contingency of unemployment on those rare occasions when it cannot be avoided. Many workers could establish their own business, even if others, such as younger people, might prefer the wage-earning arrangement and thus run the risk of periodic dislocation. Certainly, the incorporation of labor is familiar in such areas as law, medicine, banking and education.

Basically what is necessary is raising and/or borrowing some capital, just as in any other business, and managing the service, labor, in line with its demand in the market. Of course there are risks, but for those who wish for a risk free economic world there really is no way out. At least in this setup the worker is not "at the mercy" of others, namely employers. Rather, workers can manage their own labor corporations, go out on jobs, sign up on retainer, have pension programs within their own firms, reinvest and set up retraining centers which keep an eye on the everchanging marketplace. Furthermore, it is also possible to improve on the current experimentation in some industries with employee ownership schemes. These are often difficult to develop since workers do not always want to become owners, to take on the kinds of project that are involved in the ownership and management of profit-making businesses.

The adversarial, antagonistic relationship between capitalist and workers could disappear. Instead, we would witness the emergence of a greater and greater proliferation of subcontracting and jobbing. If Ford needed to produce a car, it could obtain the services of the American Autolaborers Corporation, which would supply the skills. The contract would specify what the job is worth to both parties, and payment would be made accordingly, not as an hourly wage. The status of the laborer would also change from employee to business professional.

Despite immense practical difficulties, existing unions could transfer themselves into such useful and productive organizations. Some of these alternatives would require government legislation. Still, new institutional arrangements can start out as new ideas. Perhaps we should promote this one and help re-establish progress towards a more consistent capitalism, the real engine of economic progress.

Should business be regulated?

Another frequent criticism of market processes is that without government regulation, without some planning, there will be too many neglected concerns in a society. We simply cannot leave everything of importance to the market. Three such criticisms follow, with brief rebuttals to round things off. Certainly, a free market usually enables people to do the best that can be done. Free markets encourage maximum efficiency, as well as responsible conduct that encourages the production of goods and services which are of value to the community.

On the other hand, some exceptions are said to exist to all this beneficence of free markets. As to efficiency – that is, allocating resources least wastefully – the free market sometimes fails to achieve it. The point was made by a champion of the market system, John Stuart Mill.[8] A case of alleged inefficiency of markets is the production of utility services. If there were free competition in such production, we would have much duplication, with different companies putting up telephone, electricity and water lines side by side. So it is important for government to restrict competition and thus to correct market failures.

Another aspect of this market failure, identified by John Kenneth Galbraith,[9] involves market misjudgment as to what is important. This too is supposed to be remedied through the political process. Markets often do not respond to real needs, such as for medical care, libraries, safety measures at work, health provisions and fairness in employment and trade. Therefore governments should remedy the market failures by heeding the citizens' (political, not commercial) call for various regulatory measures: zoning ordinances, architectural standards, safety standards, health codes, minimum wage laws, affirmative action and all those regulations aiming at improving society.

A second source of justification for government regulation of business is the belief that government is established to secure for us the protection of our rights, and that there are many positive rights not widely acknowledged which go unprotected in a free market. How do we know there are these rights? Different sources for identifying them have been provided. Some, such as Alan Gewirth,[10] rely on a Kantian deduction of both freedom and welfare rights from the very nature of human action; some, such as John Rawls[11] and Henry Shue,[12] make use of intuitive moral knowledge; and some such as Steven Kelman,[13] use a theory of benevolent paternalism. Some thinkers, such as A. I. Melden,[14] employ a revised Lockean approach.

The substantive position of all these thinkers is that employees are due protection of their health and safety, provisions for social security, fair wages and so on. Consumers, no less, should be warned of health problems with the goods and services they receive. In short, it is the right of all those who deal in the marketplace to receive considerate treatment. It should not be left merely to personal caution, consumer watchdog agencies or the goodwill of traders. Rather, each person has a right against others when it comes to being provided with such care and consideration. Government, having been established to protect our rights, should, in turn, protect these neglected rights. Government regulatory activities are the proper means by which this proper role of government should be carried out.

The last argument for government regulation we will have space to consider actually accepts the considerable power of the free market to remedy its mistakes. But it points to one area where this power is ineffective, namely public pollution: uninternalizable negative externalities. Kenneth J. Arrow,[15] has spoken about the need for regulation here for reasons of judicial inefficiency. His case goes roughly as follows. Usually one who dumps wastes on the territory or person of another can be sued and fined. Or the permission of the potential victim of such dumping can be obtained and payment for the harm can be made. But in a wide variety of cases of dumping, this is not a simple or even possible approach. Pouring soot into the atmosphere or chemical waste into lakes may cause harm to victims who cannot be identified.

Now since emission into public realms involves such judicial inefficiency – culprit and victim cannot be brought into contact – regulation is appropriate when the activity which can lead to public pollution is deemed to be important enough. This general idea derives from the utilitarian value theory that some things important to the public at large must be done even if individuals or minorities get hurt. So long as general supervision of such hurt is available – that is, so long as a social cost-benefit analysis guides government regulation – the public pollution is morally permissible.

All these arguments can be elaborated upon, but let me outline responses to them that favor deregulation and thus provide support for free, unregulated, capitalist market processes.

Government regulation rebutted

As to the market failure of inefficiency, we may ask whether establishing a number of monopolies, say in public utilities, really secures efficiency in the long run and at what expense. For example, striking is more crippling in the case of a public utility than in a competitive enterprise. To prevent inefficiency, strikes must also be prohibited. But that in turn infringes on a vital freedom of workers. So the market failure is being "remedied" by way of producing a serious political failure. It would be morally better to accept the inefficiencies, since in any human political system it is unreasonable to expect perfect economic efficiency.

We need to recall here that, while many economists do promise superior efficiency from the free market and hold that to be its main selling point, this is not necessarily the most basic reason for accepting it as the best political economic alternative. I have been arguing all along that that argument assumes that efficiency is all. It is arguably more important to secure the protection of individual rights, including the right to withdraw one's labor when one believes this will serve a purpose one has freely chosen to pursue.

One might respond to this that binding arbitration is a valid option for workers in publicly owned or monopolistic industries. Yet if a field of work is restricted by law to one form of the employment relationship, that is certainly unjustly discriminatory. Why should workers in the telephone, railway or electricity industries have to accept only one way of settling labor disputes, while workers in non-monopolized industries have options which emerge within a competitive market?

Concerning market failures in producing vital but commercially unfeasible goods and services a similar problem arises. Government remedies embody their own share of hazards. Political failures are even more insidious than market failures, especially in a welfare state. I have indicated earlier that this, at least, has been amply demonstrated by James Buchanan and his colleagues at the Center for the Study of Public Choice, George Mason University. Enacting bad redistributionist laws has widespread undesirable consequences which are difficult to remedy. (And it is difficult to tell when state redistribution is not bad, since for it to be good one would have to know a great deal more than any planning authority could come to know, for example about the valid purposes of individuals who are subject to the redistributionist schemes.)

Furthermore, bureaucracies, once established, are virtually impossible to undo. Regulators are virtually impossible to sue, even when they have a strong influence on manufacturing, transportation and other commercial processes. For instance, in airline travel in the United States no one even considers suing the Federal Aviation Administration following an airline crash, despite the fact that the FFA is responsible for ascertaining the safety of aircraft. The errors of government regulators are not usually treated as being open to legal remedy.

Naturally, once it is assumed that government should grant a monopoly or take over some industry, the argument for introducing government regulation is hardly assailable. But that is not, strictly speaking, government regulation but rather government administration, most directly observable regarding highway administration and maintenance. Whether government ought to be involved in the running of the various services and tasks it takes on in various societies is a separate issue. Within the framework of public administration that is compatible with the principles of the fully free market, only a few "public goods" qualify for such administration; these are mostly tasks connected with the protection, maintenance and promotion of the basic rights of individuals and what is implied by these in the development of a complex legal structure.

The market failure case for government regulation maintains, firstly, that efficiency considerations demand government granting of monopolies or outright transfer of some putative market processes to the jurisdiction of government and, secondly, that the absence of certain services deemed by some (significantly large numbers of) citizens as important – for example, libraries, schools, parks, affirmative action programs, unemployment or social security insurance, and health and safety provisions – ought to be supplied by government at taxpayers' expense. Because the inefficiency is neither the central concern of a free society nor evidently remedied by government intervention, and because such government intervention carries its own set of risks for the society, by some accounts far greater than those posed by the market, government regulation cannot be justified by reference to it. Further, government provision of various worthy programs, services and outright goods involves comparable sacrificing of what people might want to obtain without government foreclosing this opportunity by its taxation policies and imposition of regulation. Add the attendant risks of having governments provide such things in the first place and we can see that there is no conclusive support for regulation from even this version of the market failure thesis.

Now there is no question that government regulation can here and there, now and again, solve some problems that emerge on the free market and might otherwise be left unattended. Certain safety and health measures, no doubt, have saved some workers from injury and even death. But what is at stake is the integrity of a system that is otherwise deemed desirable, at least by reference to the general arguments advanced earlier in this work. In other words, granted the general thesis in support of the individualist, libertarian system out of which the free market idea gains support, making compromises on it for certain exceptional occasions is very risky, if not indeed fatal. In legal systems where precedents function to support and gradually to establish trends, it is better to hold out for integrity – to quote the famous television character J. R. Ewing from *Dallas*, "Once you give up integrity, the rest is a piece of cake." This seems to be generally acknowledged even by modern liberal critics of the free market, at least when they consider compromising the principle of the right to freedom of the press, of artistic expression and of political, religious and philosophical associations. It seems that only when we turn to business or commerce does it begin to be permissible to make exceptions to the right to freedom, such as of enterprise, trade and manufacture.

Let me now respond to the argument that government regulation of business defends individual rights. One potent reply is that the doctrine of human rights invoked by defenders of government regulation is very bloated. I have argued[16] that often what are clear cut values to people are wrongly taken to be things to which they have rights. Protecting these "entitlements", however, does violate basic individual rights. Consider the right to a fair wage or health care. For these to be rights, other people would have to be legally compelled to supply the "fair wage" or the health care. But consumers may well choose to pay less for some item than is deemed enough for generating a fair wage. If the "fair wage" were something workers were due by right, then consumers would have to be forced to pay it. This deprives them of their sovereignty over their lives and their belongings. They would not be parties to free trade as required by natural rights theory.

Essentially, then, the rebuttal to the moral argument for government regulation based on human rights considerations holds that the doctrine of rights invoked to defend government regulation is just wrong. A sound doctrine would prohibit such regulation. (But it would also open the road to the establishment of non-governmental regulation, for which the incentive, in the absence of government's willingness to enter the arena, would certainly be present if regulation is already welcome in democratic political systems! It is unlikely that any free rider problems based on the *homo economicus* analysis would undercut this expectation: people are not obsessed with getting away from paying for what they want, even if others might benefit from the purchase.)

The rebuttal to the judicial inefficiency argument for government regulation of commerce mainly involves the idea of prohibition or quarantine. Whenever pollution cannot be absorbed by the polluters – for example, producers of pollution cannot establish technological preventives (to use the economists' way of putting it, methods by which to internalize their negative externalities), cannot be sued by their victims, or cannot pay for injuring others – pollution must be prohibited. In short, a policy of quarantine, not of government regulation, is the proper response to public pollution. The courts, as I argued elsewhere,[17] not legislators via regulators, must remedy the rights violation that pollution involves.

Of course the problem of pollution is complicated. For example, one car in the Los Angeles basin does not produce enough exhaust fumes to harm anyone because these are diluted in what engineers used to call the "infinite sink" of the atmosphere. Likewise, one small factory with a tall stack may well harm no one at all, thanks to dilution of its output. The same goes for liquid pollutants into lakes, rivers or oceans.

Arguably, however, none of this changes the principle of the matter. Once a certain level of emission has been reached, any addition or increase would amount to pollution. And permitting such pollution amounts to accepting it as legally permissible for some persons to cause injury to others, who have not given their consent and who cannot even sue for compensation. A just legal system would prepare itself to deal with these complexities, as it does in other spheres where crime is a real possibility. The failure to do so produces our present destructive pollution problems.

It is useful, in considering this approach, to keep in mind the concept of threshold because much of what is deemed pollution involves waste disposal beyond a certain determinable level that is harmless to people encountering it. Only when this threshold has been exceeded does genuine pollution occur. The solution proposed to avoid the attractiveness of government regulation and remain consistent with the ideal of a free society based on individual rights to life, liberty and property – the legal system of which is obligated to protect against dumping, including pollution – may appear drastic at first. But once it is understood that much of the trouble arises because manufacturers do not choose to operate at full cost and their negative externalities are not impossible to manage internally, only too costly, and that up to a certain level waste disposal into the public realm is harmless, there need not be concern over some drastic industrial setback with the implementation of the quarantine or prohibition approach.

The process of government regulation regarding the use of public realms is commonly guided by social cost–benefit analysis, which is consistent with a utilitarian but inconsistent with a rights conception of political justice. In the US legal system this social cost–benefit approach has been legally sanctioned on grounds that the economic realm is exempt from the provisions of strict constitutional protection of individual rights. (Justice Oliver Wendell Holmes, in his famous dissent in *Lochner* v. *New York* (1905) quipped that "The Fourteenth Amendment does not enact Mr Herbert Spencer's *Social Statics*", which is to say that free enterprise is not demanded by the provisions of the US Constitution.)

If, however, the subsequently influential Holmes thesis is rejected and substantive due process is guided by reference to individual, including private property, rights, then the social cost–benefit approach is effectively blocked. It is not permissible in a system that protects individual rights, and must carry out that protection within the framework of such rights, to ration costs and benefits regardless of culpability or responsibility for the costs and benefits involved.

One reason this rebuttal sounds unacceptable is that those who usually discuss the problem are wedded to the *homo economicus*/utilitarian approach to tackling uninternalizable negative externalities. (Incidentally, "uninternalizable" usually means not "impossible" but only "extremely costly" to internalize!) Adopting the quarantine approach could require scaling down a great deal of production in various branches of industry, such as transportation, at least until non-polluting ways are found and willingly paid for.

Yet while some practices and policies might be of value even to millions, if innocent people are victimized in the process they should be discontinued. Where paint factories dump effluents into rivers, if the rivers are public and cannot be privatized (i.e. bought or rented) then this dumping amounts to impermissible intrusion into the lives of many members of the public. If power grids produce water and air pollution, they will have to explore alternative methods for realizing their main objective, namely the production of power. If cars cost too much to manufacture in a manner that avoids dumping toxic carbon monoxide into the atmosphere, if spray cans inevitably contribute to the erosion of the ozone layer, then these must not be allowed to be utilized as they currently are. It is plain enough that, with adequate prohibitions placed before such manufacturing processes in the first place, no dependence on them would have been created and alternative technologies could have developed. In some instances, perhaps, a course of technological development would have been blocked, but why should that be such a drastic result? Many purposes are blocked because the only way to attain them would involve violating people's rights.

A plain example of this is black slavery. Many benefited, at least now and then, from this public policy. Nevertheless, from a moral point of view that is not decisive. The emphysemic who chooses to do without many of the world's technological wonders should not be forced to suffer the burdens which come from producing these wonders. Nor should such a person be forced to move her domicile; after all, she is guilty of no wrongdoing, so she should not have to carry the burden she has not invited or created. In some cases it might be that these burdens justly fall on such a person, but that is not what usually arises from policies guided by social cost-benefit analysis.

One argument for government regulation of business I have not discussed is that, since states created the institution of corporation, states are responsible for supervising and regulating their offspring. Ralph Nader likes this argument in favor of his divestiture program.[18] But, as Robert Hessen says,[19] the fact that states created corporate commerce is a historical accident; in the Soviet Union states create the press, but not even Nader would argue that therefore the Soviet government has the moral authority to run the Soviet news media! In a free society the citizens, not the state, create economic, scientific, entertainment and other endeavors, although in the feudal and mercantilist past of such a society other processes might have been employed to solve problems.

Some argue that corporations can get so big and powerful that they are virtually "little governments". But one must remember that no business corporation, university, science lab or sports club, however huge in size and wealth, has the legal authority to use force in its endeavors. While they may possess the power to do so, the exercise of the power would be unauthorized and illegal, and, if the business of government were confined to crime prevention, freeing it from the millions of tasks that now fall on its shoulders even in so-called liberal democratic societies, that danger could be handled.

Of course it is arguable, as Karl Marx and many others maintain, that huge corporations will inevitably make governments bend to their will, in which case they will subvert the principles of the free market. But to this we should answer that there is nothing necessary about such a claim. If citizens vigilantly defend the integrity of their legal system and refuse to sanction the corruption of political power, there is no reason why such power should be systematically corrupted, although pockets of corruption could hardly be avoided. The issue in political theory is one of comparing a system not to some dreamed-up ideal but only to other live options. In any theory, even within such formal sciences as geometry or probability theory, it is entirely unreasonable to demand final completion and complete consistency all at once; not so long as there is the possibility of discovering new circumstances, so long as one can imagine yet unheard of but not impossible circumstances that might need to be addressed by theories in the field. The question is always whether a given theory handles the issues better, with greater comprehensiveness, with fewer wrinkles, as it were, than alternative live options.

So as to where government is likely to become increasingly corrupt, in a culture with a free market or in one with socialism, fascism or communism, there is little doubt of the relative moral superiority of the first.

CONCLUSION: CAPITALISM VINDICATED

As the arguments about the allegedly unavoidable plight of labor and about government planning and regulation of business show, any general public policy impeding the free market system, one that rests on the right to private property, does not constitute a legitimate part of a just human community. Some of these arguments express serious doubts and worries, stemming from an incomplete appreciation of what a just human community can aspire to and what capitalism and the constitutional republican form of (libertarian) government that supports it can deliver. But some of the criticisms are clearly based on utopian thinking, on wanting the political institutions of society to solve all variety of problems that human beings face. This faith in the efficacy of force is either misplaced or a façade to hide the desire for power over other human beings.

No argument is ever complete in these matters, certainly not within any reasonable space restrictions, let alone with the limited powers of its author. Yet it seems to me quite plausible now to conclude that even mere government regulation of a substantially private economic system, as distinct from national planning, is in the end a form of petty tyranny. Petty or not, government regulation involves a measure of tyranny over some people for reasons that do not serve to justify such tyranny. Of course, the practice is also usually counterproductive.

It seems evident now that most attempts at abandoning the principles and practices of the free market system land societies in deep economic and social troubles. This may not have prompted the full switch to the free market. Yet it suggests that on the whole the free market alternative is practical. In this chapter I have been arguing that it is also just.

Is it surprising that something lacking moral support will also turn out to be generally unworkable? That is what we should appreciate from the discussions advanced above. The free market embodies the kind of social conditions in which persons are free agents to choose between the various alternatives available to them. The system is effective in securing for human beings not only what they want, but also the opportunity to do what they ought to (want to) do.

NOTES

1. See Machan, *Individuals and Their Rights*.
2. By "action" I mean purposive, intentional or deliberate behavior in the natural world of objects, thoughts, compositions, novels, computer programs, designs, manufacturing plants, rivers, etc. I am not considering the extreme metaphysical idealist idea that our actions might all take place in a purely mental or spiritual sphere. My previous discussions touching on metaphysical and ontological considerations should suffice to give some justification for my doing this.
3. For a discussion of explicit versus implicit (or tacit) consent in the context of political associations, see Machan, *Individuals and Their Rights*, ch. 7.
4. *Ibid.*
5. Marx, *Selected Writings*, p. 126.
6. Hayek, " 'Social' or distributive justice".
7, Marx, *Selected Writings*, p. 53.
8. *Principles of Political Economy*.
9. *The Affluent Society*.
10. *Reason and Morality*.
11. *A Theory of Justice*.
12. *Basic Rights*.
13. "Regulation and paternalism".
14. *Rights and Persons*.
15. "Two cheers for government regulation".
16. Machan, "Wronging rights" and "Should business be regulated?".
17. Machan, "Pollution and political theory".
18. Nader, *et al.*, *Constitutionalizing the Corporation*.
19. *In Defense of the Corporation*.

Chapter 6

The Moral Superiority of Capitalism

THE MAIN DEBATE

In the preceding chapters I have concentrated on arguing that there is a moral case to be made for free market capitalism and that this case is a reasonable one, as well as one more likely to be pertinent than the more barren *homo economicus* argument advanced mostly by neo-classical defenders of the free market. Furthermore, I have tried to show that, with such a moral case in hand, it is possible still to make ample use of economic science as conceived within the neo-classical framework, provided no grand imperialistic ambitions are demanded of the latter. And I have argued, as well, that this moral case enables us to defend against some of the laments that are expressed about the free market system.

What I have not attempted to do is to argue that the moral case for the free market system is actually superior to various cases made for centrally planned or mixed systems: those proposed by Karl Marx, John Rawls, Ronald Dworkin, Alan Gewirth, Russell Kirk, Irving Kristol and so on. One reason for this is that I have made the attempt to do this elsewhere. Another is that the main purpose of this book is to reframe the argument for the free society, not to defend the free society against a legion of critics.

Nevertheless, it will be useful here to spend some time at least indicating why the pure capitalist system is superior to its main contender, Marxist communism. While at present somewhat in retreat in its geopolitical posture, the Marxist alternative has many (albeit revisionist) backers in the Western intellectual community. We could, of course, compare free market capitalism to a number of other alternatives. But as Jean Paul Sartre, the major twentieth-century representative of Existentialism noted, Marxism is *the* going idea in our era. Almost every attack on capitalism, or even Western liberalism (as a somewhat ambiguous contemporary stance), draws on the vocabulary of Marxism. Even defenses of the welfare state require Marxian notions about exploittation, property, human nature, alienation, exchange, participatory democracy, planning, labor and so forth. When capitalism is charged with being wasteful, cruel, reactionary, unjust, dehumanizing or crass, the charges generally have Marxian underpinnings.

So the main debate in our time is between the political economy of individualist capitalism and the historicist view of humanity's development put before us by Karl Marx and indeed still a part of the rhetoric of many regimes around the globe. If capitalism means to be a significant intellectual political alternative in our time, it must confront the Marxian outlook head on. Yet among capitalist thinkers very few today are concerned with Marx. In the past it was somewhat different. Some members of the Austrian school of economics, notably Bohm-Bawerk and von Mises, have addressed Marx's economics. Hayek too has dealt with certain central aspirations of socialists. Marxism had to be contended with by those who found capitalism a promising socioeconomic system, even though such focus tended to be confined to the economic issues. There are many reasons for this, among them that economic scientists happened to be the main defenders of capitalism; this was partly because they understood the system's worthwhile features, partly because their methodology made it easier for them to discount some popular criticisms and partly because the defense of the system of broader (non-positivist) philosophical grounds had to wait for some changes in the broad intellectual atmosphere, such as the demise of scientism, the view that all disciplines must mimic the natural sciences in their methodologies. There is also the point that moral philosophy was much influenced by the work of Immanuel Kant, and that Kant found the one virtue that might underpin capitalism, namely prudence, really morally irrelevant.

THE PARADOX OF LIMITATIONS

There is one interesting explanation for the lack of adequate concern with Marxism among those who have tried to defend the free market economy on normative grounds. This is that the little normative content that has been associated with such a defense - found, for example, in classical liberalism from John Locke to Robert Nozick - has too narrow a focus.

Classical liberals and free market capitalists are committed to allowing only a minimal portion of life to be tied to politics. They want to stress only one political point, namely "Don't tread on me!" or "My life is off limits unless I say otherwise." Expressed somewhat curtly, that is the central capitalist ideal. But this leaves capitalists philosophically united on very little, which is both their strength and weakness. Capitalists, as political theorists, hold that *vis-à-vis* strangers the only thing one must always keep in mind is a negative duty or a prohibition. We need only remember and respect the rights of others; murder, assault and theft, and all the variations of these in their complex legal renditions associated with a rapidly developing technological era, may not be committed. And so long as others do the same, capitalists will be theoretically satisfied.

Yet life involves far more than politics. There is family, the arts, sciences, entertainment, sports, hobbies, friendship and the numerous divisions of these, plus a lot more we think up as we carry on with living. There are problems, challenges, puzzles and mysteries connected with all of these realms. And there are millions of different ways to tackle them, depending on who faces them and under what circumstances.

None of this falls within the purview of the politics of capitalism. This is wonderful because capitalists can refuse to be pretentious. They can remain modest, just as their political outlook requires of them, and they can remain true to their political ideals when they keep all this clearly in mind. But it is also scary because as capitalists they will probably confront Marxism and other systems of thought in a wide variety of ways, thus making themselves vulnerable to the charge of being confused and divided on crucial issues.

MARXISM: TOTALITARIAN IN SPIRIT

Marxism knows it all. One can see this even if one is just watching from the sidelines. Marxists know everything about women's problems, workers' problems, education, drugs, divorce, poverty, technology, psychology, racial conflict and history. Marxism strives to be a total system of thought and action. It is also totalitarian, politicizing everything from the nurturing of one's psyche to the building of one's dwellings and to how to plan an enormous economic community. My concern is not with geopolitical expansionism. I am interested in the propensity of Marxists to take hold of every issue, to ignore completely the ideal of specialization and to make every subject their full possession, however artificial their treatment of it ultimately proves to be.

Firstly, this is all quite natural within Marxism. Marx thought of humanity as an "organic whole". And just as holistic medicine will not permit the separate treatment of various portions of an individual's body, so Marxism will not tolerate looking at sociology or economics or history or psychology or political science as if these could be mastered independently of mastering all the others.

Yet the mastery tends, ultimately, to be prejudicial. It is based on some key formula, in this case the dialectic principle; on some notion which promises to unveil many of the truths of human social life but which also embodies central difficulties, such as determinism, self-referential inconsistency and unwarranted universalism. This is demonstrated by the findings of anthropology, which contradict the ideas Marxism advances regarding the character of early human societies, namely that they were largely collectivist, tribal or communal. The dialectic seems, then, to be counterfactual.

Yet the dialectic does appear to be a formidable approach, one that can impress most of those who are eager to grasp things intellectually. The philosopher's stone has been the hope of the ambitious intellectuals who wanted to find a principle that unites reality's multifaceted nature and consequently yields a single methodology for exploring all of existence. Dialectics is perhaps a more complex but still evident reductivist approach to dealing with a pluralistic real world.

MARXISM SCORES AGAINST MAINSTREAM ECONOMISTS

Marxism is not, as some economists claim, economically naive. Marxism does not pretend to be an economic theory. At most Marxism proposes a political economy, with emphasis on the "political". Then, also, Marxism has solid rebuttals to those who believe that economics can be a pure, value-free science. Marxists can note, as we noted earlier, that economics studies trade, which presupposes that some things are owned. But ownership is not a value-free concept since it means that "None but X (or Y or Z) is authorized to decide what is to be done with the owned item." If this were not presupposed in market analysis, why would it be assumed that without mutually satisfactory terms no exchange will ensue? If the valued item is not really owned, why worry about failure to come to terms? It can simply be acquired without mutually satisfactory terms.

However inadequate it ultimately is, Marxism provides interesting and impressive ammunition against the classical liberal conception of capitalism. And since capitalists agree on very little besides their ideal of negative liberty – which itself is a rather hollow since, unless one accepts a system of natural individual rights or some other doctrine, it does not provide a clear standard for distinguishing liberty from its infringement – many of them find themselves barred from answering Marx.

GOING ON THE MORAL OFFENSIVE

However, there is a way to approach Marxism despite its impressive points and despite the fact that individualism is not totalistic or wholistic. It is to realize that one is not just a citizen or a political animal but a complete human being. And that means that one needs a way of thinking about life which will have something to place in the path of the Marxian Pac-Man. I have been spelling out the crucial elements of this system, and I will utilize them here in opposition to some crucial Marxist ideas.

1. Marx thinks the world develops dialectically, in a threefold process, towards its perfection in the end. That is why Marx prophesies communism as the last stage of humanity's predictable development; the natural maturation of the organism, as it were. But even if the dialectic method could be found here and there, it is quite evidently not all pervasive. In other words, there is not only one principle of growth or development in nature, even in that part of it which is humanity. A pluralistic universe defies reduction via the dialectic. The forms of explanation that will help us make sense of this universe will be varied according to the forms of existence we find in the universe; some existence, no doubt, may yield to dialectical scrutiny, but some will not. In human affairs, in particular, that hope is seriously dimmed by the evident presence of the capacity for free choice. And while general trends may nevertheless be observed, history, economics, politics and other social and human sciences will do better to take into consideration that the central subject of the inquiry makes choices and decisions often, and especially, in defiance of previously noted general patterns.

2. Marx accepts the collectivist idea that humanity is a concrete universal, the being that one should think of as the individual which may be harmed or benefited. He has said plainly enough that "The human essence is the true collectively of man." He adds that "isolation from this essence is out of all proportion more universal, insupportable, terrifying, and full of contradictions than isolation from the political collectivity".[1] This means that the most advanced form of human society not only gathers individuals into a political unity – for example, by way of equal principles of justice or rights – but gathers them into a cohesive cultural body, a "true collectivity". In short, one is happiest when one is but a cell within what Marx calls (in *Grundrisse*[2]) the "organic body", or by another translation the "organic whole", of humanity.

Although Marx takes this notion quite seriously, it is clearly absurd. Consider just one implication of the idea. It flows from treating humanity as one being of which we are a part and the various aspects of which are all interwoven. If everyone really were a member of our collective organic body, a kind of huge family unit, we would be, among other things, emotionally crippled all the time. All the deaths, births, anniversaries, illnesses, weddings, joys and sorrows of all persons would have to be as meaningful to each of us as they are when involving our intimates.

But intimacy is based on individuality and special relations. Collectivity would demand of us to die emotionally so as to be able to survive all of what happens to everyone in the world. If we really tried to live as if humanity were a large family, we could not do it – even granting that Marx expects the human race to reach a new stage of development where a kind of natural altruism would motivate us all. In short, this kind of life, which seems fantastic even with the most generous interpretation, is exactly what Marx demands of the communist person; he or she must regard everyone in humankind as an intimate! And, aside from the above, the human essence involves persons having goals, determining purposes, making decisions, choosing values and so forth; something that only individual persons, not groups, can do. To think otherwise is ridiculous.

Marx seems clearly to carry to the ultimate a conception we find in much of philosophy, East and West, namely the view that humankind is all one: not just that we form a large species of individual members, with much to benefit from interaction, but that there really are no selves and that humankind amounts to one gigantic being. Another version of this view is that the universe is just one large being of which we are a part, perhaps the conscious part.

We can put it differently. Marx, following such other thinkers as Plato, seems to accept the idea that the term "human being" is a name for one entity, that the universal concept by which we mean each separate one of us really means that one transcendent being. The universal concept has become a real, concrete entity for Marx. This is comparable to arguing that the concept of "chair" really stands not for millions of individual chairs but for one large one that the rest comprise.

For Plato this idea may have served as a kind of myth. It was to remind us of the fact that members of the same species really are members of a species, not disparate, totally separate, isolated entities. As we saw, Marx too was reacting to a different extremism which had maintained that we are all independent, isolated atoms. Marx went to the opposite extreme and condemned our individuality to virtual insignificance. He looked upon humankind as a materially real entity of its own, undergoing its individual development. All the collectivist talk about species-being, liberation, human (not individual) emancipation and the like testifies plainly enough to Marx's view that all persons are really part of this large person who is growing up. But, it turns out, this large person has no brain, no eyes, no memory and no imagination; no regrets, sorrows, joys or delights. Humanity has no consciousness. So what Marx took to be the most important aspect of humankind is not really human at all but some imaginary glob of being, even by his own account of it.

For Marx humanity will have grown up when it has reached the dumb state of an ant colony or beehive, carrying on without purpose or thought, just automatically. Marx quite explicitly denied that we at present are human beings: that is the full meaning of his theory of alienation. Only once we are emancipated to become full species-beings will we achieve our full humanity, a humanity that is, at once, the universality or collectivity of all human beings. It is not original of me to suggest that this comes very close to the idea of heavenly bliss within numerous religions, including Christianity. It is the promise of salvation here on earth.

3. But if humanity cannot really be the depository of human nature, what is? Well, it is our human individuality. This is rather different from what we get in the individualism of classical liberalism, but some elements of that radical tradition remain. What the classical liberals got wrong, as we saw earlier, was to think that each of us is individual only in that we each count for one being among many others, somewhat as a chair in an auditorium is an individual chair among many others. We are that and more, namely beings who create much of what is crucial about themselves quite on their own. We are separate not just numerically physically and materially, but morally. We possess individual responsibility for becoming what we will be. That is a major revision, to be added to the individualist tradition discussed earlier in this work.

Thus individuals are vitally important to humanity; they are, indeed, the most important aspect of humanity. And since individuality is diverse, both because of circumstance and because of personal variation in effort and capacity, a society must honor individuality first and foremost, in order to be humanly appropriate, good, fit or excellent.

For Marx the free market exchange economy is a temporary phase of humanity's growth, comparable to the adolescence of an individual person. It is wild, crude and reckless, but it helps build the organism into a powerful machine. Capitalism, Marx held, was the most productive system of human organization. It is also indispensable. That is why the Soviet Union had to, by a Marxist account, conquer other countries and had to have an internationalist expansionist foreign policy – because without capitalism at home and abroad, it had no capacity for survival, let alone for flourishing, in Marx's own theory. As Marx wrote in the preface to the Russian edition of *The Communist Manifesto*, "If the Russian Revolution becomes the signal for a proletarian revolution in the West, so that both complement each other, the present Russian common ownership of land may serve as the starting point for a communist development"[3] It is even arguable that what is happening in most Marxist–socialist countries during the 1980s and 1990s is an attempted realignment to Marxist theory. Once the expansionism did not secure the base for communist development, it may have become necessary, in the eyes of Marxist leaders, to approximate a kind of capitalism in their own societies – *ergo glasnost* and *perestroika*. Without this, as Marx argued, socialism amounts to no more than the socialization of poverty, just what the Soviet Union and Eastern Europe have witnessed lately.

But now, with the individual person back as the centerpiece of value in human community life, what about capitalism? It turns out to be the best system because it can best – though not always and certainly not necessarily – accommodate an individual's highest rational aspirations. That is to say, in a free market capitalist system there is a legal framework to preserve the morally independent, though most often voluntarily cooperative and harmonious, development of each person. This is what is allowed via the principle of private property rights, the coordinating system of the price mechanism of the market, civil liberties, the rights of free expression, thought and religion, and so forth.

4. Much of the force of the Marxian alternative must be given up once it is understood that individuals, not collectives, are the essence of humanity. And in the wake of this realization, the capitalist market is vindicated, morally and scientifically.

This is not to say that the idea of the pre-eminent human individual is not a relatively recent one in human history. As Colin Morris observes, "Western individualism is . . . far from expressing the common experience of humanity. Taking a world view, one might almost regard it as an eccentricity among cultures."[4] Marx himself made much of the fact that

> The further back we go into history, the more the individual, and, therefore, the producing individual seems to depend on and belong to a larger whole: at first it is, quite naturally, the family and the clan, which is but an enlarged family; later on, it is the community growing up in its different forms out of the clash and the amalgamation of claims. It is only in the eighteenth century, in "civil society", that the different forms of social union confront the individual as a mere means to his private ends, as an external necessity.[5]

Certainly there is nothing odd about the recognition individuality, the reality of the distinctive human self of every person, had been suppressed in many epochs throughout human history. There is no great advantage to those who oppress others in permitting the idea of individuality to gain prominence. Moreover, many ideas come to light antecedent to the facts that are meant by them: as Morris puts it in his title,[6] the individual had been discovered, not invented, as Marxists and their allies, such as Alasdair MacIntyre, believe.

The issue of whether human beings are essentially individuals is not itself a historical or a factual question, but perhaps a very basic ontological one. It seems evident, as we have already discussed in Chapter 3, based on the kind of activity that is most central to human life, namely volitional rational consciousness as a guide to behavior, that it is impossible to understand the human situation without granting the essential individuality of every human being. In a sense it is odd that modern philosophy admits of the existence of the human individual, since this philosophy is largely in the grip of mechanistic materialism and can make room only for "quantitative individuality". After all, self-determination in a framework of efficient causal relationships is inconceivable. Kant could make room for the autonomous self only by inventing the noumenal reality, a kind of supernatural realm that transcends mechanistic science. Only after a naturalistic pluralism could be philosophically identified, philosophy having been freed of its positivist/empiricist biases, could we find true individuality.

The human essence, then, is the true individuality of every person. The bourgeois individual is the first occurrence in human history when men and women are not first of all members of a tribe or a clan or even a family, but are recognized for what is most essentially human, namely self-responsibility. Bourgeois men and women belong by nature to no one; they are sovereigns, they are capable of using this sovereignty for good or for ill and they require a political community that pays relentless, sustained attention to this fact.

Does the qualitative individualism here advanced rule out the possibility, even the central desirability, of a sense of community, of fulfilling one's self in large measure by devotion to matters of community concern, or of moral obligations to other persons within the community of which one is a free and independent member? No. Clearly, however, that is not the main focus of the position; it does not mandate such a devotion to community as the primary objective of human life. To pretend that it does would be folly, since it would remove the individualist element at the outset. But once the social aspect of human individual life is acknowledged – and qualitative individualism does not deny our social nature but simply construes it as a matter of a sensible choice rather than a natural (i.e. primary and necessary) characteristic of a human being – it becomes clear that a large part of every person's life, if lived properly, morally, would focus on the welfare of fellow humans, of family, friends, fellow citizens, neighbors, associates, colleagues and so on. The fulfillment of the goal of a good human life includes as a crucial, though not necessarily an exclusive or even primary, feature the fulfillment of a flourishing and benevolent social existence. Indeed, the coming together of free and independent citizens signifies a social life that embodies greater rewards than one that sees men and women as parts of a whole they cannot by nature escape. It is akin to the presumed rewards from marrying out of choice rather from prearrangement.

There is a central reason why Marxism, despite democratic commitments, tends towards one party totalitarianism. This is that human beings are essentially individuals and a public policy guided by a vision of ultimate unison into a global collective will invite much resistance from many. That resistance then must be met with efforts to eradicate the individualist aspirations and tendencies in all human life.

The contention that Marxism implies totalitarianism goes contrary to what so many of Marx's (especially Western) admirers and he himself in his more democratically sounding passages maintain. But it is eminently reasonable to suppose that, without brutal regimentation, the collectivist idea of human nature cannot be made to fit human community life. That collectivist view is the fundamental flaw of Marxism. It infects the entire system, even where it makes some valuable points, for example about the importance of meaningful work.

IS CAPITALISM A FREE ECONOMIC SYSTEM?

When we consider whether a capitalist, libertarian society is free, whether it secures human beings their maximum individual freedom or liberty, serious controversies arise. Some agree that, of course, in capitalism, where our private property rights are respected, we enjoy the greatest freedom. Despite the fact that such a system does not offer the utmost security in life, or equality of wealth or even of opportunity, capitalism certainly does secure for people the maximum freedom.

There are many, however, who dispute this contention. Not only do they criticize capitalism for failing to insure for us well-being and equality of opportunity, but they also hold that capitalism is in fact an enemy of individual freedom. Marx made this point in the nineteenth century, and in our time many have followed his lead. For example, in his posthumously published work *Grundrisse*, Marx notes that

> This kind of [capitalist] individual liberty is . . . at the same time the most complete suppression of all individual liberty and total subjugation of individuality to social conditions which take the form of material forces – and even of all-powerful objects that are independent of the individuals creating them.[7]

He also said:

> [F]reedom . . . can only consist in socialized man, the associated producers, rationally regulating their interchange with Nature, bringing it under their common control, instead of being ruled by it as by the blind forces of Nature; and achieving this with the least expenditure of energy and under conditions most favorable to, and worthy of, their human nature.[8]

Marx is invoking the idea of freedom which ordinary people invoke when they say they wish to be free of worry, trouble, hardship, emotional blocks, bad memories, disease or whatever. From the time of Plato this sense of "human freedom" has been a powerful contender. It refers to our capability of attaining full human flourishing, unhindered by such obstacles as ignorance, illness or sin.

In our day many think of this sense of freedom when they refer to Marxist-Leninist type liberation. Unlike the more libertarian sense of this term, within the American political tradition, liberation here means guiding one towards emancipation. For a brief reminder of the difference, which may be disputed in a more elaborate analysis, compare the liberation of France to the liberation of Poland! And consider the character of Marxist-Leninist liberation movements, which all reject libertarian freedom or liberty as shallow and meaningless because it does not provide enablements for the people; they may, of course, be liberated from oppressors but they are then allegedly unable to make any headway in life without those enablements.

Larry Preston, following in Marx's footsteps, has advanced a similar claim recently, namely that "a capitalist market, understood as a system in which production and distribution are based on the pursuit of private interest through the acquisition and transfer of privately owned property, generally denies freedom to most participants". [9] Preston defends this position by first advancing the following characterization of freedom: "Free decisions and actions are identified as those in which an agent's conscious deliberation has played an essential role." [10] He clarifies this by adding that "The prerequisite of deliberate choice can only be determined with reference to specific activities associated with particular roles." [11] That is to say, before someone attains freedom – via being readied for the task of making a deliberate choice – that person must enjoy certain conditions, prerequisites. No one can be free who is poor or ignorant or unhealthy or uneducated. Furthermore, as regards free economic exchange, "A choice is voluntary (freely made) if the persons who agree to it possess, before they decide, the relevant capacities and conditions for deliberation regarding the proposed transaction." [12] This comes to the thesis that persons must enjoy an equal and strong bargaining position before their economic exchanges can be said truly to be freely undertaken. *Ergo* capitalism, since it doesn't secure equality of conditions for all, is unfree.

While to some Preston's way of characterizing freedom would amount to strong support for personal autonomy and self-determination, on close examination it does not. What the Preston thesis supports, instead, is the view that most people are in dire need of having their conditions of life improved; without that, they will lack freedom in the relevant sense, for example they will not be able to bargain as equals in the marketplace. His view of personal autonomy does not stress not being (unavoidably) intruded upon by other persons and his view of self-determination means that one must be fully readied, with all the prerequisites, in one's effort to succeed in life.

In contrast, within the Anglo-American political tradition freedom has been characterized quite differently. As F. A. Hayek observes:

> The original meaning of the word "freedom" means always the possibility of a person's *acting according to his own decisions* and plans, in contrast to the position of one who was irrevocably subject to the will of another, who by arbitrary decision could coerce him to act or not to act in specific ways. The time-honored phrase by which this freedom has often been described is therefore *independence of the arbitrary will of another*. In this sense "freedom" refers solely to a relation of human beings to other human beings, and the only infringement on it is by coercion by other human beings.[13]

For Marxists and their allies the emphasis has always been on possessing the requisite abilities, including resources and information to act in any way one might wish to act after necessary deliberation, with the hope that this will lead to betterment or progress. In Hayek and the classical liberal tradition, however, the emphasis is placed on a choice being that of the agent, that it be his or her "own" decision. Furthermore, unlike Preston, Hayek does not insist on deliberation having an "essential role" in free choice.

The difference between the two conceptions of freedom seems to be this. Whereas for Preston the sense of autonomy or self-determination that concerns a person's taking action on his or her own initiative alone is neglected, for Hayek it is central; and while Hayek seems to accept decisions of any sort – whimsical, intentional, negligent or deliberate – as possibly free, Preston allows only the kind of choice to be a free one that could be deliberative or self-consciously calculated. In other words, for Preston the conditions of deliberative judgment must obtain for even a non-deliberative choice or decision to be a free one.

Preston holds that "real" freedom is not the libertarian, capitalist sort. His theory, following a very respected tradition, proposes that one can only be really free if one has the prerequisite of being on the right path. The famous biblical insight, "The truth shall make you free" (John 8:32) testifies to the currency of this sense of the term. A person who is imprisoned by temptation, false belief, whim or desire is quite unfree.

Now Preston's idea of freedom does not state explicitly that his understanding of "free to choose" implies that only those are free to choose who in fact choose properly. But that is nevertheless the crucial result of his characterization. This is because the "relevant capacities and conditions for deliberation" would in the last analysis include the individual ability to select wisely from among the alternatives. What else can be meant by "relevant"? The relevance is, supposedly, to the optimal outcome. These "relevant capacities and conditions for deliberation" would have to include the absence of any impediments to reaching such an outcome. But would not wisdom be no less relevant than, say, the absence of poverty? Why this wisdom might be absent in some cases then has no bearing on the question of whether someone is truly free.

Thus it makes no difference to this theory whether it is imposed by other persons or by nature or by the social system in force. No doubt, if a social system protects property rights or health, this also means that those who have no wealth or health or squander it will face the obstacle of poverty or ill health in their effort at successful living. And if one cannot obtain guidance in life free of charge, that too will place one into the class of the unfree. (It is no accident that dissidents in so-called Marxist societies were deemed to be mentally ill: with the requisite guidance fully available to them, it was inexplicable that they would not join the revolution.)

It is worth noting that one might contend that Preston's (and Marx's) conception of freedom subsumes the classical liberal or libertarian conception. To be free in Preston's sense, then, would amount to enjoying the autonomy involved in having one's natural rights to life, liberty and property respected and/or protected, as well as being facilitated with the requirements that make one free in Preston's sense; that is, being fully enabled to make a deliberate, calculated decision.

There is something to this idea, of course. It is not uncommon to find oneself lamenting the loss of one's freedom stemming from conditions of hardship, even while one may value the freedom arising from not being coerced by criminals and/or the government. In some cases when one enjoys the latter freedom, one's mind tends to gravitate towards the former. But it is also reasonable to expect that any political provision of the former kind of liberty undermines the latter kind. In short, if public policy has as its purpose, in part, to secure positive freedom – that is, the right to well-being – then it will often find itself in conflict with its libertarian purpose of protecting negative freedom – that is, the right to liberty.

Now when Preston laments the lack of freedom in capitalism, he can most reasonably be understood as building a case for a public policy that would remedy that condition. What else is the point? We know that in a purely free market some people may lag behind in living standards. That is openly admitted in any theory of the free market; full equality of resources or advantages simply is not construed as either a prerequisite or a goal of the political system. Rather, the goal is to preserve the negative freedom of every individual. It is, of course, also assumed – and I have argued that this is quite reasonable – that with such negative freedom at hand, the positive freedom that Preston and others find desirable, and indeed that free market advocates themselves often consider likely to emerge once their system is in place, will be forthcoming as a result not of public policy but of the aggregate processes of the society; scientific, educational, commercial, artistic, spiritual, medical and all sorts of other endeavors undertaken by people who are not forced by their fellow citizens to serve goals they have not consented to serve.

The problem with Preston and others arguing his Marxist line is not so much that they defend the value of positive freedom, but that they do so in the context of a political mission, striving to foster public policies that directly aim to secure it. In short, they strive to achieve positive liberty at the expense of the right to negative liberty. The central point is that such freedom is politically irrelevant and, as far as it has significance for human social life, the system in which negative freedom is consistently prized will help secure it better than one in which it is directly pursued by public officials. To put it differently, the problem of securing positive freedom is always going to be with us, whether we are near others or all alone on the desert island. The problem of negative liberty, of the right to freedom from the forcible intrusions of others whom we have not ourselves forcibly intruded upon, is uniquely social and thus requires a feasible yet just political solution such as government by the consent of the governed.

It might be argued that, while under the guidance of Marxist thought on this topic there are indeed some harsh (paternalistic, dictatorial, authoritarian) realities, the same hardship obtains under a system guided by capitalist principles. There we find poverty, maldistribution of wealth and so on. Yet there is a difference that should not be obscured by this "moral equivalence" thesis: the harshness flowing from the Marxist guided system are inherent to that system's being guided by Marxist ideas, whereas capitalism does not impose such hardship on anyone. It may not, of course, manage to solve all the problems human beings may face in society. But since that is impossible to do without miracles, it would be unjust to blame that situation on some system that has never claimed, or should never have claimed, that it can produce utopian achievements.

That there may not be any system that could "remedy" this situation is, of course, one of the major problems of characterizing freedom along these lines. But by speaking as if such life circumstances were limitations of liberty, Marx (or Preston) suggests there may be social systems in which no restrictions stand before persons who might at some stage of their lives aspire to success. Marx hints at this when he points to "the absurdity of considering free competition as being the final development of human liberty".[14] Presumably there is a final development.

Another problem with the Marxian idea Preston advances is that a deliberation is a rare process. Most people proceed through their days without deliberation, yet acting intentionally; that is, fleetingly thinking of their objectives and almost automatically using the means to attain them, as when one undertakes to give a lecture on Marxism after having done this for a lengthy teaching career. The intentional character of such actions may be gleaned from the fact that, if some mishap is associated with them, persons who took the actions are held responsible for what they did. (Malpractice suits can be considered in this light.) These then are treated as perfectly free actions when they are not forced on them by others. For Preston, however, they would be unfree actions since they might not have involved even the opportunity for, let alone the presence of, deliberation: the self-conscious, self-monitored mental process characteristic of intellectual activities, such as theorizing about freedom.

Perhaps Preston did not intend "deliberation" to be taken so strictly and he might admit that "intention" suffices. Yet, of course, intentional action often occurs without the availability of elaborate examination of alternatives, without even much knowledge. Indeed, one might argue that most people act intentionally even while they lack much knowledge of what they are about to do. Most exploratory action, adventure, experimentation and, indeed, commerce proceeds along such lines. What seems to make the difference in such actions between free and not free is not the availability of information, but the capacity of the agent to seek such information out, to initiate the conscious process and the actions that would unearth the information he or she may need to improve the chances for eventual successful policies in life.

As a closely related issue, it is also important that, in Preston's and Marx's characterization of freedom and liberty, there is no consideration of the place of free will. Maybe it is implicit in Preston, but it is explicitly denied in much of Marx. It is incompatible with the idea of the dialectical drive that history exerts on all of us and with Marx's own characterization of his "standpoint, from which the evolution of the economic formation of society is viewed as a process of natural history".[15] Preston's own failure to address the issue in his treatment of freedom in capitalism suggests that he too finds it incompatible with his understanding of human affairs. And this is supported, further, by his failure to realize the point made above, namely that those not enabled or equipped to enjoy full freedom might well initiate the kind of conduct in their lives that will provide for them the requisite enablements.

If persons are metaphysically free, possess free will or the power of self-determination, they might or might not elect to inform themselves about the facts that may make a choice a wise one. They may then be regarded as unfree in the Marxist sense. Nevertheless, in the liberal sense of the term "freedom" they are free since they might have placed themselves in a position of being better informed, even though they did not do this.

What is being argued here should not be surprising. It is the terms associated with free market capitalism, despite the incompatibility with the strict *homo economicus* perspective of imperialist scientific economics, that refer to personal initiative, pulling oneself up by one's bootstraps, entrepreneurship, individual responsibility for making one's way in life and so on. And it is the Marxist perspective that stresses the essential helplessness of the workers, the poor, the downtrodden, the exploited masses, even of capitalists and their theorists. The discussion by Preston is merely a more sophisticated, elaborate presentation of this idea, and one that is voiced often enough, in somewhat different terms, by many contemporary neo-Marxists, such as Cohen, Wood, Nielsen, Marshall, Elster and Roemer.[16]

The difference between what is meant by "human freedom" within the two intellectual camps can be more fully appreciated in connection with the women's liberation movement in which two meanings of "liberty" are prominent, though not always noted. Firstly, women's liberation means the absence of restraints imposed by other persons who would keep women under a yoke or treat them as if they were not of age but in constant need of guidance (from males or the state). Secondly, women's liberation means being guided to a higher state of consciousness and human emancipation.

Another way to distinguish the two ideas of liberty, and I have alluded to this before, is to recall the contrasting meaning of "liberation" for the Soviet Union and the United States vis-à-vis the countries of Europe they helped to liberate following the Second World War. The Soviet Union liberated by helping to defeat the Germans and then fully occupying the eastern European countries, while the United States helped to cast off the German forces and then left, which freed these countries to develop themselves.

What sense of the term "freedom", then, is primary? On the one hand, if we are focusing on progress towards human flourishing, human freedom may well mean what has been meant in the tradition of Plato, Rousseau, Hegel, Marx, T. H. Green and many contemporary intellectuals. These thinkers would all join Marx in the view that the liberal/libertarian conception of human freedom is limited and incomplete. To pretend to be concerned with human freedom when one is really interested only in freedom from the aggressive intrusion of others – as so well expressed in that earlier quoted American war cry, "Don't tread on me!" – is to distort an important value in human existence. Even some neo-classical economists prefer to mean by freedom the maximizing of our options, creating a broad range of possibilities. Our freedom, they say, is enhanced with an increase of our wealth.[17]

There is something to this, of course. It is arguable that full human freedom, being unimpeded by various obstacles in life in reaching one's proper goal of self-development, should mean what members of this tradition have meant. Yet, on the other hand, the view that human "freedom" or liberty, in the aforementioned sense, is a political concern, lack of which ought to be dealt with through law and politics, is highly disputable. This view simply fails to credit human individuals with self-initiated effort. It demeans them, treats them as helpless and always in need of guidance from above. It is paternalistic and ultimately self-defeating if we extend it to everyone, including those who advocate and administer totalitarian measures to liberate us.

The ultimate reason behind this drastic and devastating error is that the conception of freedom embraced by the tradition following Plato and today mostly promoted by Marxists presupposes a conception of human nature which is contrary to fact. Marx did not credit human individuals with a basic kind of freedom, namely freedom of the will or the power of self-determination. Nor do Preston and other Marxists, such as Andrew McLaughlin, Charles Taylor and G. A. Cohen. Preston notes that "Capitalist exchanges have become coercive because participants can recognize an alternative situation which would provide them with substantially greater freedom, a situation that the capitalist market prevents them from having."[18] In other words, people are not acting freely under capitalism because by virtue of the structure of the system – that is, its framework of private property rights – they are forgoing options that they might enjoy and that it would be beneficial for them to enjoy.

This treats human beings as helpless, inept creatures who are unable on their own initiative to come to terms with lacking some of what they might want and benefit from in life. They need the state to negotiate better deals for them. Such a conclusion would be warranted in societies where people faced persecution, oppression and liquidation from the state if they tried to remedy their circumstances by individual initiative, including by forming economic alliances. Yet in a society in which no such political limits to liberty are sanctioned, the claim about such helplessness comes to little more than either stressing the exceptions or demeaning human ability.

The "freedom" Preston thinks people might enjoy involves what they could benefit from in their relationship to others, namely greater access to information, better conditions for deliberation and so forth. For example, they might have been better educated, or they might have possessed more wealth. This is, of course, not political freedom but a better standard of living. To obscure the difference is dangerous.

When Marxists, and other critics, say that we lack freedom or liberty under capitalism, they do not make clear that what they have in mind is something we would probably lack far more under any other system, namely the ability and opportunity to make the most of our lives. And that is perhaps because, if put this way, it becomes clear that at least under capitalism everyone has his or her political liberty – freedom from other people's forcible intrusion into one's life – and that in the main this provides most with a good chance of attaining a high standard of living. While capitalism is not preoccupied with the equal distribution of wealth, or rather of poverty, it is a system under which the chance exists for those who make a good try at it to reach considerable economic success. (Nor does capitalism assume that everyone would or even should want this!)

The Marxist position sees persons as we do trees or flowers that grow not from their own determination but because they are spurred on by the natural environment. And if there are deficiencies in this environment, there will be impediments to growth. As Preston puts the point, "We now realize that the exchanges of capitalism generally do not represent agreements in which both (or all) participants are better off if 'better off' is viewed as gaining access to the resources needed to exercise freedom."[19] Once Preston has defined "free choice" as in effect "the best possible choice one could make", it is no wonder that capitalist exchanges are not free.

It may not be obvious that Preston and this entire tradition does mean this by freedom, until it is made clear that the objective is to ensure human perfection, the full emancipation of human beings, not merely their freedom to do what they choose to do, regardless of the outcome. Preston, as others in this tradition, in effect identifies human freedom with human success. Without that identification, human freedom or liberty simply has no value to him. The liberal tradition, however, sees human freedom (from aggression by others) as objectively valuable because it is a constituent part of human moral goodness: without the freedom to choose one's conduct, one is not the agent of whatever good behavior one might engage in. This is not always clearly put in the liberal tradition, yet it *is* part of it.

In the liberal tradition government aims for protecting the human being's role as the agent of his or her own conduct. That is why it stresses individual (negative) liberty and rights. Once persons enjoy this protection, they will then do what they choose, well or badly. Society is not perfect, but it is politically best if it secures for everyone his or her sphere of jurisdiction or personal sovereignty. The rest is in the hands of free individuals. In contrast, for the Preston/Marx position the primary task of good government, of those who understand and have the power to upgrade the species, is to free them from such impediments to growth. This is clearly not accomplished simply by protecting them against the aggressive intrusion of other human beings. No, they need total "liberation", the prevention of all intrusions such as poverty, disease, ignorance, illness and even sin. Thus Preston holds that

> Physical force need not always be either morally objectionable or a denial of freedom. Efforts physically to restrain drug addicts from gaining access to drugs may be done for moral reasons and in the interest of freedom – to enhance the addicts' ability to make deliberate choices.[20]

This is a dubious choice of example for Preston in this context, because even in contemporary near-capitalist societies persons are not granted the right to consume the drugs they choose. But for Preston the scope within which lack of free choice is appropriate is far greater than for those who sanction it in the case of drug abuse. His general thesis would clearly sanction forcing people not only to desist drug abuse but also to stop advocating anti-revolutionary policies, practicing the wrong religion, or reading of bad literature. All these may be morally justified because they may enhance the ability of people to live properly.

Many who have advocated Marxism but have found the Soviet Union politically reprehensible insist that the Soviets distorted Marx and that a proper understanding of this genius will avoid the kinds of policy that have characterized the USSR throughout its brief history. Some of those who hold such views are, nevertheless, wholly disenchanted with capitalism, whether its ideal version or the watered-down type evident in some Western societies. Indeed, some of these same people hold out hope for societies the leadership of which proclaim themselves to be Marxists, such as Cuba and Nicaragua, even when these societies are directly allied with the Soviet Union.

The confusion arises from failing to distinguish between what Marx might have liked and what his views most likely usher in, especially when his vision of the future is not coming about automatically, as a matter of historical necessity. Maybe Marx would have hated Stalin or even Gorbachev; no one knows. But that the policies of many Soviet leaders gain ample support from some of Marx's views, given that those views are basically wrong, cannot reasonably be denied.

Marx may have thought that capitalist societies will turn socialist without much need for violence. But since this has not happened, those who agree with the implicit championing of socialism find it convenient to force socialism upon various countries in the name of Marx. They certainly could not do it in the name of Adam Smith or John Locke. And there certainly are plenty of concepts in the Marxist edifice that give philosophical fuel to the idea of forced socialization. One of these is the conception of freedom or liberty that Marx and his followers embrace. Their idea of freedom may have some grounding in ordinary language. But in one sense that idea is most destructive of freedom, namely the freedom of one individual from the intrusions upon his or her life by another. This is the sense in which it encourages the idea that people must be made to be free, whether they choose this or not.

NOTES

1. Marx, *Selected Writings*, p. 126.
2. *Ibid.*, p. 351. Marx writes: "With a change in distribution, production undergoes a change; as for example in the case of concentration of capital, of a change in the distribution of population in city and country, etc. Finally, the demands of consumption also influence production. A mutual interaction takes place between the various elements. Such is the case with every organic body." Marx goes on here to discuss the relationship between Greek art and modern sensibilities, sensing that, if we treat the Greeks with admiration in their art, this may not permit us to regard them as primitive or infantile in other developments. He rebuts this by calling the Greeks "normal children ... The charm their art has for us does not conflict with the primitive character of the social order from which it had sprung" (p. 360). Such comments are clearly indicative of Marx's view that humanity is a growing, developing organic body, a kind of concrete universal.
3. *Ibid.*, p. 584.
4. Morris, *The Discovery of the Individual 1050-1200*, p. 2.
5. Karl Marx, *Grundrisse*, ed. by D. McLellan, p. 17.
6. *The Discovery of the Individual 1050-1200*.
7. Marx, *Grundrisse*, p. 131.
8. Marx, *Selected Writings*, p. 496.
9. Preston, "Freedom, markets, and voluntary exchange", p. 961. A somewhat oblique answer to Preston's analysis may be found in Roberts and Stephenson, *Marx's Theory of Exchange, Alienation and Crisis*. Roberts and Stephenson show that substituting rational planning for the exchange system introduces tyranny. The choice, then, may be between market exchange, which can involve some "exploitation", meaning the opportunity of some to take advantage of the circumstances of others, and totalitarian rule, which *guarantees* that exploitation will occur, as a permanent and unalterable feature of the system.
   For a lively exchange on the topic of capitalism and freedom, see Machan, "The virtue of freedom in capitalism" and Haworth, "Capitalism, freedom and rhetoric: a reply to Tibor R. Machan".
10. Preston, "Freedom, markets and voluntary exchange", p. 961.
11. *Ibid.*, p. 964.
12. *Ibid.*, p. 964.
13. Hayek, *The Constitution of Liberty*, p. 12. An interesting group of discussions on the concept of liberty or freedom may be found in Howard, (ed.), *On Freedom*. The most recent "classic" on this topic is I. Berlin, *Two Concepts of Liberty*.
14. Marx, *Grundrisse*, p. 131.
15. Marx, *Selected Writings*, p. 417.
16. For some of these renditions, see Machan (ed.), *The Main Debate*.
17. See Stigler, "Wealth and possibly liberty". Cf. Pasour, "Liberty and possibly wealth".
18. Preston, "Freedom, markets, and voluntary exchange", p. 965.
19. *Ibid.*, p. 965.
20. *Ibid.*, p. 965.

Chapter 7

Adding a Moral Component to Anti-Collectivism

SUPPORTING A GOOD BUT UNDEFENDED SYSTEM

Let me illustrate the manner in which the case for the free market economy may be better supported based on the general position advanced thus far. I will consider four different criticisms of centrally or democratically planned systems in which moral considerations are absent. I will then show that, without adding the moral component developed here, those criticisms of planned, unfree economies do not succeed. My aim is not to discuss these arguments in detail but to give a clear indication of the role of the moral component added by classical individualism.

I wish to note right away that not all these arguments are presented by friends of the fully free market system and that not all are aimed at discrediting its diametrical opposite, the fully planned system. However, each argument aims to find fault with certain elements of societies that try to incorporate anti-market policies, such as public policies of extensive redistribution of wealth and public works projects not bearing only on the administration of justice. Each of these criticisms would, if successful, count against the feasibility of a centrally or near-centrally (e.g. democratic socialist or market socialist) administered economic system.

However, the reason it is important to pay heed to the four criticisms is that they may be construed as efforts to admonish political arrangements from a predominantly economic framework. If these criticism do not need additional support from a moral perspective in order for them to carry full weight, then the intellectual value of that moral framework is somewhat undercut.

The four criticisms are: the Mises–Hayek "calculation problem" objection to central planning; the Hayekian doctrine of the unintended consequences of human action; Kenneth J. Arrow's social choice paradox aimed at showing the paradox of forming public policies in a largely democratic society; and Garrett Hardin's "tragedy of the commons". The first argument, advanced by Ludwig von Mises, F. A. Hayek and most recently Don Lavoie, maintains that in a planned economy, which lacks a free market driven price mechanism, economic calculations and coordination are hopelessly inefficient; Hayek also argues that deliberately planned economies lead to consequences that were unanticipated and tend to involve more harm than good. Arrow's social choice paradox counts more specifically against any full-scale liberal democratic system of government, including democratic socialism or economic democracy, because it seems to show that in such a system contradictory decisions will inevitably arise. Finally, the "tragedy of the commons", first noted by Aristotle against Plato's limited communism and more recently by biologist Garrett Hardin, holds that, when people do not have borders indicating clearly enough what is theirs and what is some else's, and are thus left to make use of the commons, an overuse or depletion of resources of the commons occurs beyond that likely in a system of private property.

Calculation and individualism

Why is the calculation – or coordination – problem not a sufficient argument against central planning? Because the notion of the efficient allocation of resources begs a certain question.

The unanswered question in this criticism is "Efficient for what purpose?" The claim that there is a calculation problem assumes, without justification, the importance of coming at least reasonably close to the satisfaction of the aggregate demand of those individuals who comprise an economic system. But many of those who advocate a centrally planned economy very often deny the importance of individual demand. They consider such demand driven economic efficiency as tending towards the frivolous and even decadent. A Marxist, for example, does not regard the exchange economy as in the last analysis an efficient system. That is because it suits too many of our trivial, arbitrary, whimsical individual desires, not our objective needs.

People can want items such as pet rocks, Michael Jackson gloves, pornography, hot tubs, finger nail polish, diamond rings and other similarly frivolous goods. Massive productive activities can ensue solely for the purpose of satisfying these kinds of irrational demand. When those advocating central planning regard these demands as harmful, as bad for those who are demanding them, and thus wish to redirect the productive activity that goes into satisfying these demands, they are not working with a concept of efficiency as understood by those who identify the calculation problem. Rather, they defend their centrally or collectively planned approach on grounds that some theory, such as dialectical materialism, alienation theory or Christian salvationism, informs them about what must be provided for society so that it will flourish. These advocates of planning are very far from being implicit individualists; they are explicit collectivists. Individualism cannot simply be assumed in an argument against them. It is exactly what is at issue, namely whether individualism is a sound social theory: whether to value diverse individual choices or wants.

I am not, of course, claiming that all supporters of a planned or severely regulated economy are explicit anti-individualists. Some, among them those who rely on a kind of neo-Hobbesian theory and derive from it a case for some measure of intervention, may not be. But the point here is addressed not to finely nuanced positions but to the major theoretical counterposition and its general stance on what is important, individuals making choices guided by their own moral convictions (even if these be mistaken), or the planners or the collective doing this for them.

Anti-collectivists who identify the calculation problem think that, unless you satisfy individual demand reasonably closely with admitted occasional "market failures", you have a bad economic system, and anti-individualists who criticize the free marketplace would say it is a bad economic system because it satisfies so much individual demand. So they both agree with the importance of efficiency or workability, but they disagree about what purpose is supposed to be served in terms of which efficiency is to be identified. If, for example, you are a Marxist-Leninist and believe that furthering the revolutionary progress of the proletariat is the most important thing in a society, you will measure effectiveness in terms of whatever most rapidly produces this revolutionary progress of the proletariat. But by neo-classical criteria, efficiency is measured by reference to satisfaction of marginal demand. So, as E. J. Mishan observes, the Mises-Hayek critique

> would be more compelling ... if the declared aim of [e.g.] a Communist regime were that of simulating the free market in order to produce much the same assortment of goods. We should bear in mind, however, that the economic objectives of a Communist government include that of deliberately reducing the amounts of consumer goods which would have been produced in a market economy so as to release resources for a more rapid build-up of basic industries.[1]

The calculation problem argument assumes something that is very much in dispute between free market and socialist advocates: that there is merit, worth, moral or political superiority, in satisfying individual desires.

Now, the main point I have been making here is that, to remedy this failing of the calculation problem, one must justify the system of free exchange. And to do this it is necessary to demonstrate that there is great value in providing for individual demand. It is vital for a political economic system to serve the extremely diverse and changing choices of the individual living under that system. Having shown that one's individuality is essential to one's being a human being, having argued that from metaphysical beginnings it is the entire person, including what is shared with others and what identifies that person as an individual, that is significant, the assumption underlying the Hayekian charge against central planning, or "market socialism", is only completed as a decisive critique by including this normative component. Otherwise it is merely a question-begging protest.

Let us look briefly at one appealing aspect of the planners' objection to free exchange. This is that the market trades in so much trivia. Let us admit that it often does. But is that easy to spot? If it is important to satisfy individual demands, then it may be vital to have a system that can very likely meet even the silly sounding demand for, say, a pet rock by an 85-year-old rock miner who, if you buy him a gift of a pet rock, will have a pleasant nostalgic experience. If that seems too far-fetched, and it need not be, given evident human diversity, one might consider the writer who penned an OpEd piece for the *New York Times* on 24 February, 1989, maintaining that cigarette smoking for her was a vital and beneficial part of life, never mind the few years by which this might shorten it. (She had given up for several years and found herself mentally paralyzed.)

Those who advocate a centrally planned or at least guided economy will appreciate these types of case. They find certain kinds of consumption repugnant to them and that is that (C. Everette Koop, a recent Surgeon General of the USA, has made it a piece of public policy to make America smoke free by 1990!) The bureaucrat is looking at universal human characteristics – "basic needs", as the neo-Marxists call them – that should be satisfied. The joy from a unique gift, a pack of good cigarettes, a yacht or a trip to Europe may be dismissed as a quirk of individual, idiosyncratic desires. A market system manages to satisfy these quirks, these individual desires, and the satisfaction of them is justified if you recognize individuals as being important in their individuality, not only as members of the species, in their "species-being" alone.

The major difference between capitalists and, especially, Marxist socialists is that the former implicitly, but in my defense very explicitly, acknowledge the significance of satisfying individual goals and purposes as an important ingredient of the moral life. They testify to the moral importance of individual human happiness. Even when the presence of many misjudgments in a free market are admitted by individualists, they implicitly recognize that these are part of the life of any moral agent who must be left on his or her own to make such judgments as are of moral significance.

A Marxist socialist idea of human life ignores many individual desires as irrelevant or trivial and concentrates on some overarching human conditions alone, matters relating to us as part of a species. Unfortunately, the scientistic, value-free approach to political economy taken by neo-classical and even Austrian economists who defend the market dismisses the needed normative component of the critique of central planning. If one can justify from a very deep philosophical level the taking seriously of the individual as an individual, then the calculation problem critique is telling indeed.

The doctrine of unintended consequences

Prompted largely by Nobel prize-winning economist F. A. Hayek – who himself has resurrected a thesis widely propounded during the eighteenth and nineteenth centuries by Adam Ferguson, Adam Smith and others concerned with how individual actions often lead to broad results that no one had in mind when embarking on those individual actions – many classical liberals, free market advocates and libertarians now make reference to the unintended consequences of human action, especially of government policies. The thesis is that, whenever people set out to do something, there are various unintended consequences that result, some of them desirable, others odious. They do not design the results, yet they come about and turn out to be significant.

This thesis is then utilized by classical liberals and others to argue that collective or central planning of the economy is necessarily going to backfire; even if the intentions of the planners are decent, unlike those of malevolent dictators whom many socialists and other authoritarians denounce, the plan is doomed. Alternatively, many of the unplanned, so-called anarchic actions of human beings, ones that supporters of planning such as Karl Marx lament, yield many fine results. This too should incline us towards the free market.

For example, it is supposed to be an unintended consequence of everyone employing his or her particular knowledge of market factors in the process of production and consumption that an efficient system of communication results, one that makes it possible for consumers and producers to communicate without having intended to do so. On the negative side, it is an unintended consequence of raising the minimum wage that unemployment of unskilled workers increases. Or again, it is an unintended consequence of people being engaged in buying and selling that a common medium of exchange, namely money, is created. And it is an unintended consequence of virtually any kind of prohibition that whatever is prohibited will emerge as part of the underground economy and that people will undertake its production, distribution and consumption even if it results in some measure of serious criminal activity, such as non-legal enforcement of "contracts".

But do we capture accurately enough what is going on here if we characterize it in the fashion Hayek and his followers (as well as his predecessors) suggest? No doubt, those who produce and consume do not intend for there to emerge a large network of communication. Furthermore, those who intend to raise the minimum wage do not have in mind to create more unemployment. Those who want to prohibit alcohol or drug consumption do not want also to drive it underground. So clearly there is something going on to which the thesis of unintended consequences helps us pay attention.

Yet this is only part of the story. The thesis in question is actually also employed for purposes of showing the inadequacy of human reason. Hayek, in particular, has made a good deal of the fact that when people design something, or plan it, they are unable to anticipate some of the crucial matters that will occur. For instance, in discussing the price system, Hayek notes that

> if it were the results of deliberate human design, and if the people guided by the price changes understood that their decisions have significance far beyond their immediate aim, this mechanism would have been acclaimed as one of the greatest triumphs of the human mind. Its misfortune is the double one that it is not the produce of human design and that the people guided by it usually do not know why they are made to do what they do. But those who clamor for "conscious directions" – and who cannot believe that anything which has evolved without design (and even without our understanding it) should solve problems which we should not be able to solve consciously – should remember this: The problem is precisely how to extend the span of our utilization of resources beyond the span of the control of any one mind; and, therefore, how to dispense with the need of conscious control and how to provide inducements which will make the individuals do the desirable things without anyone having to tell them what to do.[2]

The unintended consequence thesis purports to present us with a kind of mechanism by which broad institutional results are achieved without anyone designing the mechanism or planning the results. It is also supposed to give us an adequate ("invisible hand") explanation for some important human institutions. (Some have even argued that morality is the result of such a mechanism and thus has little to do with foundations and justifications. This line of analysis about morality follows in the footsteps of David Hume's reflections on the topic.)

The mechanism involved is as follows: if you intend and implement X (your explicit goal), it will be followed by Y (something that did not occur to you at all). This sounds like a natural (evolutionary) law. Hayek's language above suggests that this is what we are being offered, since people are "made to do what they do". It is out of their hands, their "conscious control".

In at least one area where the thesis is invoked, something else enters the situation that should be considered important. Often the purported mechanism applies to public policies with which many people in society disagree. In a relatively free society such as that of the USA, it is one thing to legislate some program, but another to control what people might do in response to it. Sure, Congress can raise the minimum wage. But can Congress restrain those who are affected by this from doing a number of things to avoid the impact of that legislation? No. These persons will, in turn, very much intend to avoid the unwanted impact of the law, never mind that that is something members of Congress obviously did not have in mind. The unintended consequences of such legislation are in fact intended, but not by those who drafted and enacted the law. They are the consequences intended by those who are experiencing the impact of the law.

There are few important unintended consequences of human action when all those involved and affected are in agreement with the goals sought. Certainly the results may often be unwelcome, as in environmental pollution. But here again the problem is that the results bear on the properties and lives of people who have not been consulted and whose consent was unobtainable or unsought.

Now, it is arguable that the legislators who enacted an unwanted, intrusive law but did not desire some of the consequences that resulted from other people's reactions to it are still responsible for the results. This might be viewed along lines of the doctrine of strict liability. If I leave a wobbly step on my staircase unrepaired and a guest visiting me breaks his neck, I did not desire that this should happen. Yet I am responsible. What I did intend was to forgo dealing with the bad step. I did not specifically or deliberately intend for anyone to break his neck from this neglect. Still, I ought to have foreseen the probability of such an occurrence. What I intended did, in fact, produce the (probability of the) result.

Similarly, when Congress votes for a higher minimum wage, admittedly it does not explicitly intend that unskilled workers become unemployed. But those who voted for the law ought to have realized that, when the wage is forced higher, fewer people will be able to gain employment. They ought to have thought of this; it is common sense. The same can be said about the far more global and intrusive plans of socialist and other authoritarian systems where central boards or even democratic assemblies try to devise and implement a grand economic plan.

But what about desirable yet so-called unintended consequences of human action? Consider, once again, the efficiency of the price system. Granted, we tend to talk of such matters in broad terms, especially when we are engaged in macroeconomic or political economic discussions. We are then focusing on general principles and broad institutions. But we could easily focus, as well, on the decisions of people who are acting prudently. And we could distinguish these from decisions that are made in a sloppy fashion. We could be talking about flourishing and faltering businesses and even individual households. It is these that give rise to an efficient market mechanism; as well as to market failures, by which I mean normatively lamentable phenomena in markets, such as too much spending on trivia and too little spending on vital goods and services.

By characterizing the process as one of experiencing the unintended consequences of human action, two distortions occur. Firstly, it is assumed that no portion or feature of the consequences is intended by anyone. But even in the creation of the unintended but very efficient price system, each individual person does intend to convey some information; for example, that he or she desires some given good on certain terms, or that he or she is willing to make something provided, again, that certain terms are met. Secondly, it is suggested that no one is responsible for the "unintended" results; they are, somehow, accidental. But just as in the criminal law we hold people responsible for murder even if it is the "unintended consequence" of pacifying a reluctant victim of a robbery, so in politics we ought to keep in mind that the "unintended consequences" of harmful laws are the responsibility of those who intended those laws. They ought to have known what is (most probably) going to happen. And we can also praise people for the so-called unintended consequences, although we will have to rest with general or statistical observations that reflect the good or bad judgment of millions of individuals.

It seems to me that one reason that Hayek and others are fond of the doctrine of unintended consequences is that it precludes any commitment to values. But in fact that is a myth. As critics of free market economics often point out, there is a value judgment implicit in the preference for the market mechanism, including this principle of the unintended consequences of human action. The value judgment is that there is something good *per se* about servicing or satisfying human desires. The market is efficient only if this is assumed. But since free men and women also make bad judgments – fire or hire the wrong people, buy the wrong things, work less hard than they should, etc. – one can see that the market is efficient only for purposes of best fulfilling human desires. It is not necessarily efficient at making sure that these desires themselves are worthy of fulfillment.

To make out the case that the market is also efficient in that respect we would need to have it shown that people ought to be free to make their own judgments as to how to allocate their labor, income, wealth, time and so on. We would need to be shown that this is so despite the fact that they often make bad judgments. We would need to have it shown that the element of sheer market agent sovereignty found in the free market, the element of respect for individual human rights and the virtue of prudence that motivates much of commerce, is of the utmost human worth, even if it can result in some undesirable consequences.

Democracy versus individualism

I now turn to the social choice paradox but as I do so I wish to recall the point made at the outset of this chapter. This paradox is addressed not to advocates of central planning but to those who favor a mixed system, one that involves considerable democratic decision making about public policies that are supposed to serve the public in a rational, consistent fashion. It seems to me that here too the criticism lacks punch unless it is also demonstrated that there is moral importance in setting general public policies while at the same time satisfying the purposes of individuals who comprise the public.

The social choice paradox implies that a wholly democratic society with a very large public sector – for example, a mixed democratic welfare state or a democratic socialist society – will not be conducive to consistent public administration. Since such administration relies on the votes of all the people who are part of that society to reach a ranking of priorities, it will end up with results that mutually exclude one another as policy guidelines. With, say, three alternatives A, B and C, when all of the votes from the commune or democratic socialist society are in, the results will be such that the first choice is A but, depending on where B falls, C could also be first; or if the first choice is B, again, depending on where A falls, C too may get to be first. Based on second guessing and other scheming, you cannot have a consistent public policy. Roughly, this is the social choice paradox. It makes the forging of consistent public policy hopeless.

And is this not a very good picture of the kind of bloated democracies we have all over the West now? Every group is politicking to influence the setting of priorities. Lobbyists, special interest groups, cohesive groups of constituents, farmers, car workers, unmarried mothers, artists, scientists, broadcasters and hundreds of other such associations claim that their projects and concerns are the most important. Every distress of every such group puts the society into a state of crisis. And the democratic process affords no resolution at all. The public administrators are certainly not omniscient and omnipotent and able to resolve the paradoxes, so the welfare state threatens to degenerate into a Hobbesian state of nature, a war of every special interest group against every other, each fighting to reach the public treasury first![3]

One of the problems with this criticism of welfare state democracies is that it can be answered with the institution of a dictatorship. With only one person to set "public" policy, the social choice paradox is avoided because that individual person's ranking of priorities will avoid producing the conflicting priorities in "public" choice. One reason that Marx felt the feudal societies were kinder to people than market systems is that there was a kind of stability to them. This stability came from having just one royal family, in the main, set the priorities for the society. And many of these families were tradition bound enough not to cause constant upheavals. The ideal monarchy, at least, offered a vision of harmony. The market is admittedly changing constantly although, contrary to Marx, this need not destabilize public administration in a free system.

Of course dictatorship or monarchy does not actually produce stable *public* administration. It exhibits the private choices of the head of state. These are the preferences that will be honored in such a system, provided it is physically possible to bring about the desired results. There is nothing in the social choice criticism of democratic socialism, however, that excludes a dictatorship as a legitimate alternative. It is ruled out simply as a matter of fiat. There is no justification for the exclusion of this alternative apart from a traditional desire to remain democratic about public matters. However, if everyone has a right to life, liberty and private property, if everyone's life ought to be led by that person and not by others, this rules out the legitimacy of tyranny.

And then the next question is, what follows from the Arrow type of criticism? Democracy must be limited in its scope. Ranking of private, social, regional, professional and other non-governmental, non-public preferences or choices is no problem if the right to private property is protected. That would preclude making it possible to vote for resource allocation in the first place, other than what is related to the administration of justice and may be secured without confiscatory taxation.

As to the bloated idea of public policy that is addressed by the voters in welfare states and democratic socialist systems, there will be no such sphere to be concerned about. Instead, agreement based on voluntary association can be reached among property owners about what needs to be done. Public administration, in turn, will be confined to those areas that are in fact necessarily of universal concern in a society: justice, police and defense. In these areas priorities can be set without internal conflict because the ruling principle is to protect and preserve the rights of individuals in society. Whatever is required for this aim is to be public policy, and whatever is not is left for the rest of society – all people, individually and in diverse voluntary cooperation – to achieve. Indeed, the very point of having public policy at all is to make these achievements possible on the part of individuals. But once again this presupposes that individual projects are vital, morally significant, not to be overridden by some allegedly superior collective project.

No need for tragedy

Our next topic is very familiar to us in this period of widespread environmental upheaval and privatization, namely the tragedy of the commons. It consists of overuse of common resources because there are no guidelines of what is yours and mine, what I have the authority to use and what you have the authority to use. Since we do not have these guidelines, we tend to use things indiscriminately. We tend to overestimate what is our share, and to underestimate what is other peoples' share, not necessarily because we are greedy or evil, but rather because there are no sensible standards to guide us.

Tragedy in the context of Greek drama involves a morally flawed yet inescapable situation in which it is not clear what should be done, or who may be blamed. Everybody recognizes that something has gone wrong, in a moral sense, that things ought to have been done somehow differently, but no one knows specifically how that could have been done. This is what a tragedy is. A catastrophe, which is often mislabeled a tragedy, for example a hurricane or an earthquake, is something that has hurt people, but to which no moral blame can be applied. With a tragedy there is a moral wrong, yet one too ambiguous to be clearly identifiable. In the tragedy of the commons something has gone culpably, morally wrong that might have gone right, but nobody quite knows how. Privatization advocates, of course, suggest that one way that it could have gone right is by never allowing the prevalence of the public realm.

What is inadequate about employing the tragedy of the commons argument against a large centrally or collectively governed economy, for example? Of course, such a commons system will deplete resources. Rationing will have to be instituted, which quickly leads to bureaucratic regimentation, abuse of power and arbitrary rule. In most Western-style democracies this is well summarized in the budgets of the governments. An unbearable national debt would testify to the tragedy of the commons. Everyone is using the public wealth for some project deemed vital, but the overall resources do not exist to permit this. In this way the day of reckoning is postponed and our children, our grandchildren and their children are made hostages. This certainly does not square with the democratic principle of "no taxation without representation". After all, those children and grandchildren have no chance to vote on the projects financed now from their wealth! They will have been wronged.

If we point out that there is a tragedy here but do not identify and defend an alternative, the conclusion is drawn - as it was by the scholar who recently called the tragedy to our attention, biologist Garrett Hardin at the University of California, Santa Barbara - that lamentably life is tragic. In other words, instead of saying that there is a way to avoid the tragedy of the commons, the conclusion drawn is that there is a tragic aspect to life, it is unavoidable, we must live with it, we have to put up with it. There is a contention that life is somehow inherently morally absurd. It is not that people have mismanaged life, that they are often crazy in how they act and treat things, but that life is unavoidably permeated with moral absurdities. This view holds that we all have moral responsibilities but that we cannot fulfill them. We have moral conflicts, but we cannot resolve them. As a case in point, the tragedy of the commons argument leaves us merely perplexed and gloomy. It does this only, unless there is the further specification of why a privatized property system, one that gets established after government is placed in its proper role as bona fide public administrator of bona fide public issues, is morally justified.

If there is a moral justification of the institutionalization of the system of private property, and if this system is extended as best as possible to all realms where individual conduct has an impact, then at least eventually the "tragedy" can be avoided. Can it be argued that lakes, by some means or other, could be privatized? Or private property rights identified even in the air mass? This may be difficult to think through now, but certainly no one has proved it impossible and, since in other recently discovered areas (say the electromagnetic spectrum) it is possible, one of the ways to approach the tragedy of the commons is to do what one can to reduce the pervasiveness of the commons.[4]

HUMAN INDIVIDUALS: THE LOCUS OF VALUE

At the heart of the justification of the market economy is the importance of the life of a human individual as an individual, not just as a member of a species. What the market economy does, in commonsense terms, is make it possible for a social system to pay economic attention as best as possible to the importance of individuals.

Free market systems do not always do this perfectly. There are, as I have repeatedly noted, indeed some market failures, misallocations of resources, trivial pursuits, even some serious morally odious trade. But without such a free economy, the institution of the right to private property which implies a commercial system of free trade, the morally all-important task of individuals living their lives successfully, albeit in extremely diverse fashion, would not be possible. Rather, what we would have is what we actually see throughout the world: the obliteration of individual differences, the regimentation of individuals to conform by law or by regulation to certain narrow ways of life very often drawn from select individuals and arbitrarily imposed upon other individuals, and in the name of humanity!

The market economy makes it possible for us to rid ourselves of these constraints, to refuse to be regulated, to refuse to succumb to the pressure to conform by law, by force, to models of life which do not suit us as individuals and which, most importantly, we should not tolerate, however well suited they may be for others. Unless we have a philosophical, moral justification that living this individual life is good and right, no powerful case for the market economy is going to be possible.

WAYS OF UNDERSTANDING SOCIOECONOMIC SYSTEMS

We can approach gaining an understanding of socioeconomic systems from several perspectives. Economists tend, in the main, to seek an understanding of how the free market or socialism or some other economic arrangement operates. When this understanding is attained, those who carry on economic life within such societies will have a clearer idea of what they can expect from certain policies, institutions, laws and so on.

There is another way to seek understanding of such systems. One can ask whether one or another socioeconomic system is just or morally right for human community life. This kind of understanding is not solely concerned with how the system works, although there is much that must be known about that for it to be attainable. Rather the task here is to see whether one or another socioeconomic system is appropriate, right, just for a human community.

LIBERTY AND CRITICS OF THE MARKET ECONOMY

One of the greatest benefits many Western political systems bestow upon their citizens is a substantially free market economic system. In this system individuals are not legally prevented from seeking their economic advantage in the company of others who may be counted on to do the same thing. While there is no purely free economic system anywhere, surely the main difference between other political systems and Western liberal democracy is the presence of the economic opportunity afforded by a relatively free market.

There are those who dispute this, but they usually do not so much deny the presence of greater economic opportunity in the West as frown on the value of this opportunity. Critics from left and right have alleged the corrupting influence of a political system that makes commercial prosperity more likely than other systems do. These critics tend to see the free market as catering to base human inclinations, such as self-interest, greed and lust. When one is not even much hindered, let alone prevented, from pursuing wealth, one will, the critics say, focus all of one's attentions on this pursuit. Thus, we are told, free market systems give us the commercialization of everything from religion to art. Doctors worry not so much about medicine as about prospering economically. Lawyers, evangelists, educators, scientists, artists, politicians – members of all vocations and professions with talent and skill – concentrate predominantly on the bottom line.

Now there is something to this charge, if we look only at the evidence before us in most Western societies. But it is unfair to judge the matter from a narrow empirical framework. For example, it needs to be stressed that economic liberty is a recent phenomenon, following centuries of repression and oppression during which prosperity was out of the question for the bulk of people in the world. It is therefore not surprising that for a few centuries people would focus their attention on attaining reasonable material prosperity, besides a number of other goals that are important to them. Arguably, even the more than appropriate concern with material prosperity during the last few centuries could be looked upon as quite benign, at least if those examining the phenomenon consider that securing a prosperous life on earth is a worthy goal for human beings.

CHALLENGING THE HOMO ECONOMICUS APPROACH

Not only Marxists have challenged the kind of system that seems to be favored by the economic approach to understanding human social life. Theirs is, of course, the most sustained and fully developed challenge. But there are those who issue challenges based on less totalist outlooks. They find certain elements of the case for the market unbelievable and they offer in opposition considerations that seem to accord with common decency. I wish to spend some time on one such challenge because it calls to mind what many people say about capitalism outside of formal disputations.

Paul Samuelson has made the following serious charge against the free market system: "The Invisible Hand will only maximize total social utility *provided the state intervenes so as to make the initial distribution of dollar votes ethically proper.*"[5] In other words, the justice of such a system is predicated on the presence of a strong government that first distributes wealth equitably. If we start out with some people having much more than others, with no moral justification, then the results of market processes will be contaminated with this initial defect of unjust distribution. From this indictment follow almost all the other indictments levelled at the free market: the rich get richer while the poor get poorer, the important professions lack support while trivial pursuits are well rewarded and so forth. Hardly anyone can claim not to be concerned about these criticisms, coming from both left and right with only the minor difference that the left's criterion (of what is more deserving than that recognized via the market) is need, while the right's is spiritual superiority.

Defenders of the market offer different replies but one of them is very prominent, coming from the best placed group of such defenders, namely economists. Murray N. Rothbard summarized this defense most aptly when he wrote:

> There is no distributional process apart from the production and exchange processes of the market; hence the very concept of "distribution" becomes meaningless on the free market. Since "distribution" is simply the result of the free exchange process, and since this process benefits all participants on the market and increases social utility, it follows directly that the "distributional" results of the free market also increase social utility.[6]

The crux of this defense is that, apart from what people actually choose to do in a free market, there is no other measure of what is good for them. Putting it more generally, this is the well-known subjective value theory defense, one we encountered earlier from David Conway: how could we dispute the free judgments of market agents as to what are the best decisions for them to make apart from the ones they actually do make as they carry out their commercial transactions? And if there is no way to criticize those decisions, how could anyone propose that the overall results of market transactions are defective and require state intervention? There is, in short, no justification for state intervention because there is no other standard of value than what persons in fact individually and freely invoke – and thus the result of such judgments that characterizes collective or "social utility" – in free market systems.

IS A SUBJECTIVIST IDEA OF THE PUBLIC GOOD ENOUGH?

As we have already seen, there is much that is wrong with this defense. For the present, however, what concerns me is its serious implausibility.

People may often be subjectivists in their general outlook, but in particular matters they are not. They may say that everything is relative as far as value judgments are concerned; that, like beauty, goodness is merely in the eye of the beholder. But when they see someone indulging in reckless purchases such as accumulating eight Rolls-Royce, as did the late Liberace, or obtaining cocaine or pornographic books, they are perfectly willing to say that, contrary to the economists' theory, these people do not really benefit themselves in trade but are guilty of faddism, fetishism, excesses and immoderation.

They will conclude, if they are without a contrary theory that accepts the legitimacy of ethical criticism of market behavior, that any society that makes it possible for people to be indulgent – in ways people evidently are in systems with substantially free markets – must be ethically flawed. People often enough and quite reasonably dispute that "[the exchange] process benefits all participants on the market and increases social utility", at least as they observe the market in their particular situations. They then go on to share the view of social critic John Kenneth Galbraith that the market produces many failures of distribution; people often fail to benefit themselves and their society when they produce and sell in the free market. Would it not be better if the money spent on pornography or heroin or even video arcade games went to medical research, the arts or economic education? Perhaps they will not know how to give a thorough philosophical defense of this conviction, but they will nevertheless hold it. Moral sensibilities cannot be extinguished by social science.

And they are right. Free men and women can indeed make very bad, even evil judgments; there is no guarantee that, when people enjoy freedom from the dictation of others, they will always, even in markets, choose to do the right thing. Anyone who proposes this view, as some economists do, will fly in the face of unshakable convictions and common sense. The very idea of freedom implies that one can do both good and evil, including while carrying on as a market agent. The details could only be known from close up, but they are no mystery; self-indulgent people are a dime a dozen. Misallocation of resources, therefore, is easy to conceive in free markets.

But does this not concede the case to those who would wish to intervene in the market? Not by a long shot.

SOME NORMATIVE "PUBLIC CHOICE" INSIGHTS

Just as market agents can make bad judgments, so can those who would intervene in the behavior of market agents. And there are fewer pressures on these latter than on the former, since they enjoy "sovereign immunity"; for example, government regulators cannot be sued when a mishap occurs in an industry they regulate, as is clear from the recent industrial accidents in airline transportation and chemical manufacturing. But even more importantly, it is meaningless even to talk of morally good human conduct without freedom. Persons who are fully or even only partially enslaved, dictated and forced to behave by others, simply cannot be given credit for morally good or evil conduct. They are in effect reduced to the status of robots.

Thus an unfree system is to the extent of its lack of freedom a dehumanized system. The utopian dream of making persons perfect through the limiting or regulation of voluntary, self-regarding conduct is a dangerous dream, not some beautiful ideal as many suppose. So the free market society must be seen as the best that we can do. Whatever failures it is exposed to can be resisted only by education, exhortation and example, not by coercion. It will not do either to deny that it is open to failure, as economists sometimes do, or to try to eliminate the failure by way of state intervention. And this should not be surprising; the quintessential human characteristic is, after all, our capacity for good or evil. Why should we expect otherwise from such a perfectly human and proper endeavor as the pursuit of economic welfare?

REFLECTIONS ON THE DISMAL "SCIENCE"

Must the dismal science remain such? It looks like there is no reason to think that to remain scientific economics has to avoid the problems most of its early practitioners tried to solve.

Classical economists, including Adam Smith, Thomas Malthus, David Ricardo, Karl Marx and John Stuart Mill, concerned themselves in part with the problem of value. A version of this problem was that, although the market value of something like water or food is usually quite low, the same is not true in the case of, say, diamonds, even though one should ordinarily regard water or food as far more important than diamonds, in the sense that people need the former more than the latter or they are of greater value to them. Similarly, contemporary lamentations about the real versus market value of education, environmental quality, science or art, versus entertainment, sport or narcotics bear on this issue. In general, some things fetch a great deal more in the market than others, even though by different measures the former are taken to be worth far less than the latter. High price does not always translate into great worth.

Smith, as well as others, tried to resolve this version of the problem by ascribing value to commodities on the basis of the labor that is required for their production; at first, labor *per se*, then later command over labor. Marx, especially, went a very long way to spell out a definition of the value of commodities by reference to the socially useful and necessary labor required to produce them, the last idea being explained by reference to a very complex system of dialectical human development.

Eventually most economists proposed to solve this problem of value by abandoning the search for a standard or measure independent of the market itself. They adopted the subjective utility analysis of value which held, in effect, that anything has value by virtue of someone's valuing it.

As Professor Don Bellante put it, "with the values and motives of individuals being entirely subjective it is impossible for an analyst to pass judgment on the optimality of the individual's chosen actions." And someone's individual and unique ranking of items or services, among other alternatives available to him or her, is the only "measure" of value something has. No objective, intrinsic or real value or worth, apart from the subject's valuation in his or her unique way, can be spoken of reasonably, according to the eventual resolution of the problem of value in mainstream economics. Market value, in turn, is determined by reference to the marginal subjective value placed on something within the membership of the potential consumers of the marketplace, in relationship to their other valuations. Given various constraints, so many people will want to have something at a given price but not above; many would readily want the thing even if it cost more, but there are not enough of those to make production economically feasible.

For our purposes what is crucial is that from the dominant version of the neo-classical economic point of view – embraced especially by those who have made breakthroughs in extending the economic approach to studying human behavior to several areas not traditionally believed to yield to economic analysis – values are the marginal aggregates of individual subjective valuations. In other words, from the economic point of view, values are equal to price.

None of this would be objectionable, except for the claim of some economists that there is no other discipline outside economics which makes good sense of human behavior in general. That is to say, it is not only market behavior that economists study, but human behavior as such. And as it turns out, according to many prominent economists – including, by way of punctuating their prominence, several Nobel prize winners – human behavior is always market behavior. As stated by Professor Roger Meiners, "the linchpin of economic analysis is . . . utility maximization with 'constant tastes'. This framework of analysis may thus be extended to any sort of situation explainable in terms of a comparison of altered constraints on action." [7]

The peculiarity of this imperialistic economic perspective is not that it is false but that it is nearly true. Much of the time people try to improve on their own lives, to prosper and to make deals with others who are aiming for the same. Indeed, why should they not?

Yet claiming that this is what they do all the time is, as I argued before, either quite false or meaningless. It is false if it means that people in fact always first try to improve their own circumstances. They simply do not, whether rightly or wrongly. They often aim to improve the circumstances of others, or worry about things other than themselves, at times even at their own expense. Everyone knows this well enough. It is simply incredible to deny it and any theory that does so will remain unconvincing to most of us. But if to this it is replied that utility maximization does not mean "improving one's own circumstances", or "benefiting oneself" in any objective sense – that is, in any sense whereby it is possible to determine on independent grounds that the agent has in fact benefited from some action – but only that people aim to do what to them seems to be the best alternative in their situation, then the claim is vacuous. Milton Friedman's statement, quoted earlier, attests very poignantly to this.[8] If we accept Friedman's conception of what people always do, namely serve their private interest, we have to explain how this amounts to anything determinate enough to be informative, to say something definite about some class of human actions. If the serving of one's private interest includes such obviously self-destructive conduct as excessive smoking or reckless driving, as well as the constructive tasks of trading on the stock market, producing corn, running a bank and writing a novel, what is "serving one's private interest" to be compared to? What kind of behavior does this distinguish in the human world? What would its opposite be? And what kind of explanation is it that gives the same factor for explaining the bank robber's and the bank executive's actions?

If we interpret the observation differently, focusing on the point that the private interest is what drives everyone, what is the point of calling it a "private" interest? Does this serve to distinguish it from some other possible motive? Evidently not, since everyone is always being driven by just this motive. So it does not really offer an informative explanation to make the point.

In short, the imperialistic economic hypothesis about human motivation either is false or makes it impossible to make clear, useful sense of the notion of utility maximization or selfishness, of working towards the enhancement of oneself, of profiting or prospering by making all chosen ends prospectively profitable, prosperous and beneficial for anyone. Just as the concept of "truth" requires such other concepts as "false" and "probable" in order for it to make sense, so the concept of "selfishness" (or "maximization" and "private interest") requires "selflessness" and "indifference" for it to make sense. If there could be no selfless human conduct, there plainly could be no selfish conduct either. And so while the imperialist economists are partly right that people pursue their self-interest, understood in some determinate way, they are just wrong to think that they do so always.

We need also to note, briefly, that the modification of the idea of self-interest accomplished by adding the qualifier "as perceived by the actor" will not help unless we can make sense of "self-interest" itself. If I say that something seems to me to be a chair, this makes snese because there is the possibility or at least the conceivability of something actually being a chair. But is there in standard imperialistic economic metatheory any objective sense to "private interest" or "utility" or "self-interest"? In each case the subjective approach is supposed to carry the whole weight of the analysis, so that any non-subjective sense of "private interest", "utility" or "self-interest" is excluded from the start. Yet if that is so, these terms have no clear meaning.

That this is actually admitted by some imperialist economic theorists should be evident by reference to the idea of revealed preference. If A prefers something, as understood ordinarily, it would be possible for A either to do what he or she prefers or to do something else. But in the imperialistic economist's analysis a preference is exactly what is done by a person. How do we tell what someone prefers? By looking at what the person is doing. But this leaves the designation of the behavior as "preferred" a mere pointless exercise. Preferring to do X and doing it needs to be distinct from not preferring to do X and doing it nevertheless. Then preferred versus not-preferred behavior might be a useful, meaningful distinction. But if all of what one does is preferred, the designation is uninformative. We should leave it at A having done X, never mind preference (or private interest or self-interest or utility). It is entirely open whether the agent preferred to do what he or she did or actually preferred to do something else.

Of course, there is a danger if the imperialist economist admits to the possibility of distinguishing selfish and unselfish conduct, (objective) utility-maximizing and not-utility-maximizing, private-interested or not-private-interested conduct. The scientific, value-neutral posture that so many economists claim for economic science is threatened. Once we admit that actions could be selfish or unselfish and so on, we can quite meaningfully pose the question as to which they *should* be and how we could know which they are. We can ask, furthermore, whether a system of economic relations that enhances selfish conduct or thwarts it is more desirable, better or more just. If the soundness of the system depends on the answer to this sort of inquiry, surely the value-free "scientific" stance cannot be upheld by those who wish to endorse it. Imperialist economists know this.

Since common sense tells us readily enough that not all actions are selfish, and since imperialist economists insist that they are, such economists are either not believed or, more often, denounced for inadvertently, even disingenuously, advocating narrow selfishness. Although all that most economists claim is that people in fact behave selfishly (pursue their private interests), when we understand this in terms of common sense it becomes a form of endorsement of selfishness, a kind of advocacy of, or as

Marxists like to characterize it an "apology" for, free market capitalism.[9] This is especially true when economists hold that letting such selfish conduct prevail in society will most likely lead to the general welfare. And this addition is often made by economists, even though it means that the scientific posture of these scholars is thereby weakened.

My own suggestion for avoiding the problems perpetrated by imperialist economic theorists, namely that they are just plainly wrong or embrace a vacuous model, is that the basic assumption of this kind of economics needs to be rethought quite drastically. Since economics is not the field which validates these assumptions, the suggestion does not pit me against economists. They too should prefer working with correct assumptions, so they should not object to the effort to unearth them.

Of course, there are those, following the lead of Milton Friedman's famous essay on economic methodology,[10] who would protest that the assumptions of economic analysis need not be true, but only productive of testable and useful predictions. If the assumption that all people are eternal utility maximizers, whatever this is taken to be, yields this result, surely nothing can be objectionable about the idea.

This is a tempting move but there are troubles with it. Firstly, the broader theory of the free market will still be wedded to this assumption, especially by its critics, regardless of whether economists insist on its truth. Lacking any independent source of justification of this political economic system, since the prevailing ones (e.g. Lockean) tend to start from different assumptions, those who scrutinize it will freely associate the system with the postulate of eternally economic – that is, utility-maximizing or greedy – man. Secondly, there is a very plausible charge that has to be taken seriously in connection with the Friedmanite approach to treating the assumptions of economic analysis. This is that since no reference to truth is available, since no independent criterion of what counts as truth versus falsehood is attached to the theory, the method of testing the prediction advanced from the assumptions becomes suspect. The theory may very well bias its own testing, so that it is not possible to tell, in terms of this approach, what will count as a successful versus an unsuccessful prediction because what counts as a test is determined within the theory itself. We often note this, somewhat hesitantly because of all the jargon and mathematics now included in the discussion of economic issues, when we come up with what seems like a counter example to an economic prediction.

Imperialist economists postulate that people do whatever maximizes their utilities. From this they predict that, if an option arises, a person will choose what benefits him or her most rather than what does not or does so less. But if someone chooses what in ordinary terms seems like a disadvantageous option – cigarette smoking, an unhealthy diet, an unfulfilling job – this is explained away either by noting that it must have "seemed" advantageous to the agent or, even more vacuously, by asking who else is to say what is of advantage to the agent. So the prediction is itself vacuous since the ambiguous or vacuous meaning assigned to "advantageous" (or "utility maximizing") makes it impossible to determine whether people choose the advantageous, or utility-maximizing, course.

Let me return, however, to the deeper worry about the scientific character of economics. If the assumption of imperialist economists concerning the selfish or utility-maximizing nature of human behavior is open to question, perhaps even unsound, will this not destroy the scientific nature of economics? That worry is also unfounded, yet it is widely entertained since many economists have a conception of science that is itself seriously flawed.

Here, too, it is not the economist's business to make sure of the nature of science. Most economists take their understanding of science from others, mainly their professors in undergraduate and graduate schools. Consider, as a possible instance, that Friedman's positivism in economics followed by several decades the positivist movement in the philosophy of science, and by several centuries the empiricist turn in British–American philosophy. His instrumentalism also followed by several decades the instrumentalism of Karl Popper.

To date the most prominent mainstream economists understand that science requires that we assume human behavior to be fully determined, explainable by reference to various observable causal factors which behave according to identifiable laws. This view of science, probably a rough expression of positivism, has played a significant role in imperialist economic thinking. But it is certainly debatable and probably quite wrong.

SCIENCE RECONSIDERED

The crux of science, its essence, is the organized, systematic study of some integrated sphere of reality. It involves the gradual development of appropriate methods of study. What science does not require, however, is the acceptance of various philosophical assumptions for such study, apart from some very general notions about knowledge, reality and so forth. In short, science must not be prejudicial. And it must avoid prejudice especially about its subject matter.

Accordingly, if economics is a science, it must discover the facts that are important about what it studies, not impose certain assumptions and then derive theorems and predictions from such unproven assumptions. Not that at times proceeding in such a fashion could not yield valuable results.

There are enough similarities between men and mice, for instance, that sometimes what is true of men will be true of mice, and vice versa. In connection with imperialist economics it is probably true that what people do in the marketplace is done by them elsewhere as well. There are economic facets to be found in noneconomic circumstances; a scientist, concerned with truth, needs also to watch the budget, just as a nun, aside from mainly wishing to serve her order, must also consider the cost of the habit. So taking what is true of market behavior and assuming that it is true of all other sorts of human behavior can at times lead to fruitful insight.

Actually, another of the appealing features of this imperialism involves the fact that people do often behave as pure economic agents even when they should not. Thus no doubt many people sell their loyalty and integrity; some sell their sexual affections; some sell their very souls, to speak in old-fashioned term. And though they should not, it is tempting to say that, well, everyone really does, when all is said on the matter. This cynical viewpoint is given extensive intellectual ammunition from within that phase of the history of Western thought that derives from Thomas Hobbes, claiming we are just being driven by set passions to seek power, to self-aggrandize.

Economists will object that there cannot be any basis for the "should not" in what was said above, let alone for such notions as loyalty and integrity. Yet economists as such are not experts on whether there is or is not a basis for such talk. Arguably, their very respect for science should impel them to stay away from prejudging the prospect for objective normative judgments. As economists they need to leave that open for possible discovery and demonstration by people versed in other fields. Just as there is a lot of economic ignorance among philosophers, so there is a lot of philosophical ignorance among economists. Just as philosophers often spin theories that flatly contradict economic reality, such as a vision of a prosperous socialist economy, economists spin theories that flatly contradict moral and political reality, such as that all persons work only for the bottom line when it comes to "public" service. True, one might sell one's best friend (i.e. one's loyalty) for a pound of flesh, but it could very well be morally wrong to do so. And it may further be true that this is not a subjective value judgment but an objective moral claim. By this I mean that, when one says that one is morally wrong to betray a genuine friend, this may well be true, though the truth might have to be shown differently from the way truth is shown in, say, physics, biology or even economics. To object that this is impossible is certainly to depart from economics and to enter into metaethics, something in which the imperialist economist rarely engages or has training.

Yet among imperialist economists, especially, this kind of talk is heresy.

Only some Marxist economists have proposed that we can talk intelligently about values even in the midst of discussing economics. Most Marxists and theists have defended normative economics recently. And in this the Marxists and the theists have managed to steal the thunder and gain the attention of millions of human beings throughout the world, while mainstream economists have essentially been left to talk amongst themselves. This is no wonder. The concern with values, the ordinary conviction that some values or norms are objectively valid, sound, even universal: this view is too well embraced to be given up for some grand tautology which constitutes the imperial science of economics.

The main point to be made here is this: from the perspective of science, there is a question about the nature of human behavior that economists have not actually answered with any discoveries or demonstrations but have simply assumed away. They have not actually observed everyone behaving selfishly – that is, engaging in utility maximization – inasmuch as the meaning of "selfish" is, as indicated earlier, entirely ambiguous or vacuous. Indeed, the nature of self-interested behavior is not even discussed by economists. Behavior is what it is, but economists simply decided to call it selfish. It may well be true that when people go to market they wish to make a deal. Some will fulfill this wish better than others, but it is very likely that 90 percent of them will try, more or less successfully, to make a deal in the marketplace. Of course, there will be those who are there merely to wander about. Some, as in actual markets, are simply getting out of the rain; others are too hurried to engage in bargaining or dealing, and simply do what is necessary within their constraints to get what they require; still others are sloppy economic agents. But the bulk will, no doubt, try to do more or less well by economic standards. What is crucial, however, is that there are realms of human life other than the marketplace. In such places what they do may have very little connection with making a deal.

MISCONCEIVING HUMAN ACTION

Contrary to George Stigler and his followers, when scientists try conscientiously to describe what they observe, they aim at truth, not at some empty goal to be designated as maximum utility. When composers try to create a new tune, they aim at beauty, not a deal. When educators try to do their job conscientiously, they aim at ridding their pupils of ignorance, not at maximizing their own utilities. And one would hope that, when economists are trying to identify the relationship between monetary policy and the rate of employment, they want to get this right, not simply to make a good deal. And in all these cases one would suppose that those who put making a deal ahead of the considerations that should motivate them are acting immorally, unless they have very good moral reasons for doing so. Faking the evidence for money is morally wrong, even though it might clinch a deal. Indoctrinating or pleasing students might yield more money at times, but it would be degrading, morally. But since "maximizing utilities" is left so empty of specificity – what does it mean other than that someone is doing what he or she can and is doing? – it may be unfair even to contrast the pursuit of these various proper objectives with what the economists seem to be saying people are doing. Suffice it to say they are not making it clear, as they would seem to be suggesting they are doing in their imperialistic aspirations, why people do what they do. Their explanations of human actions are empty gestures, not informative claims or theories.

These are our ordinary reflections, at least those of some people and the question is whether there is anything scientifically wrong with them. I wish to suggest that only if we misconceive the demands of science must we conclude that viewing economics along the lines sketched above is unscientific.

NOTES

1. Mishan, "Fact, faith, and myth: changing concepts of the free market", p. 66.
2. Hayek, "The uses of knowledge in society".
3. This, as I understand it, is the thesis of Mancur Olson, noted for his *Logic of Collective Action* and *The Rise and Decline of Nations*.
4. See Machan, "Pollution and political theory".
5. Samuelson, *Collected Scientific Papers*, p. 1410 (emphasis in original).
6. Rothbard, "Toward a reconstruction of utility and welfare economics", p. 251.
7. Meiners, "Economic considerations in history", p. 98.
8. Friedman, "The line we dare not cross", p. 11.
9. Wood, *Karl Marx*, p. 233.
10. Milton Friedman, "The methodology of positive economics". For a thorough critique of the philosophy of science that underlies Friedman's approach, see Rappaport, "What's really wrong with Milton Friedman's methodology of economics".

Chapter 8

Business and Society: Why Anti-corporatism?

CORPORATIONS: WITHOUT FRIENDS

One of the puzzles I have tried to address in this work is why economists are so eager to distance themselves from objective human values. Granted, they derive this inclination from philosophers who espouse the fact-value or is-ought gap, Humeans and positivists. But there are other philosophers they might have followed but did not. And it is notable that the economists most inclined to eschew values are actually quite sympathetic to certain very general values or moral principles, such as the doctrine of individual liberty and private property rights. Why would they still engage in what psychologists might actually characterize as a kind of perverse denial?

I believe now it has to do with the fact that the field they study, namely human commerce, has had a very bad reputation – indeed, has been roundly denounced – throughout the better part of recorded human history. Wealth has never been hailed as a noble objective; Plato and Aristotle denied that it is, and most Western and Eastern religions have had little good to say about it. If one were to allow value judgments in economics, they would generally have to be negative ones, based on the traditions prevalent in our culture. It is best, then, to be rid of such adversity and proceed in a value-free fashion. But this is all very sad and wrong and in the following passages I wish to explore why.

There is no denying that a good many Westerners, among them some who are very vocal and influential, abhor commerce, especially its corporate, "big" variety. On the face of it, this might appear to be fully justified. Catastrophes such as occurred at the Union Carbide plant in Bhopal, India, would appear to lend support to the views of those who regard corporate commerce as a menace.

Apart from those with a special hatred for corporations, such as Ralph Nader in the United States and the bulk of the leaders of the Labour Party in Britain, the entire Hollywood writing community is hostile to commerce. A reading of Ben Stein's penetrating book *The View from*

Sunset Boulevard, or a viewing of the PBS documentary, *Hollywood's Heavies*, aired on 25 March 1987, will immediately confirm this. With, ironically, the corporate support of the television industry and the support of both the popular and the university intellectuals, the anti-corporation mentality is dominant.

The first disturbing thing about this is that, in an atmosphere of virtual war, the genuine problems of corporate commerce cannot be focused upon. When charges against businesses are as unjust as they are these days, those who manage them stop listening. They become cynical and begin to dismiss all criticism as a case of prejudice, even when that criticism has some merit. When the Ralph Nader brigade of corporation hecklers organizes a Big Business Day, thereby indicting all corporations, indeed the whole of large business, how can those in the business community begin to take him and his ilk seriously? They cannot and will not. And this is too bad because the nature of corporate business is such that there could be considerable merit to discussing the way such an institution ought, morally, to be managed in modern society.

Add to this the fact that almost all so-called business ethics texts used in the academic community, including business schools, discuss the nature and role of corporations with hostility toward commerce. They leave students preparing for careers in business morally numb. They are not going to decide against a business career, yet they cannot cope with the barrage of sophistic "moral" harangue. Their situation would be quite pathetic if it were not so tragic.

Millions of people are sent into a business world with their moral sensitivities blocked by exaggerated condemnations of the institution of which they will be part. Clearly, they are not convinced by the lectures they hear and the books they read. And their common sense is sound: they should not be. Commerce and commercial corporations are not akin to enslavement or gulags. Firms are not bureaus of some twentieth-century dictatorial governments; they do not have the power of force, only at times that of relentless persuasion. They are means by which human beings in modern society try to secure their economic well-being. Their conduct can be open to criticism, but their existence is morally justified. Theories to the contrary notwithstanding, the corporation is a bona fide human institution, and business an honorable human activity.

HISTORY OF ANTI-CORPORATISM

What is the background to the hatred of commerce and of commercial corporations? Some suggest the explanation lies in the fact that there was a time when big corporations were really creatures of the state. It was during the mercantilist, feudal era that governments established some of the great joint stock companies with an eye to improving their nations' economic posture in the world community. In those days the legal and moral foundations of free enterprise had not yet been developed. Constitutional individualism was just coming onto the intellectual scene. Corporate commerce began before such individualism, the doctrine of individual rights, had taken root in Western culture.

What was the purpose of government-created corporate commerce? The strengthening of the wealth of nations. It was Adam Smith who in 1776 published his *The Wealth of Nations*, mainly to refute the belief that nations could be made wealthy by means of state run commercial endeavors. Paradoxically, he argued, it is by not doing much about commerce that nations become wealthy. *Laissez-faire*, or what came reasonably close to it at one time, made the best sense for purposes of enhancing the wealth of a community.

Despite the great theoretical and practical influence of Smith's masterpiece, the legal status of corporations has never been absolutely clear. Even as the USA was born, corporations were seen to be between the citizenry and the state, somewhere in limbo. The American government has always acted somewhat schizophrenically when it comes to corporate commerce. On the one hand the government began with the view that individual rights should be protected and beyond that people ought to be left to their own resources. Largely, though with major exceptions, this is the viewpoint that governed American culture for about a hundred years. Yet oddly, even by 1867, the free trade association of America had complained about excessive government intervention.

And this complaint was fully justified. Around the middle of the nineteenth century in the United States, for example, the various states and the Federal government began to be very active in subsidizing business, especially large commercial concerns. Most notably, the government gave all sorts of benefits to those corporations which took on some of the tasks that accorded with the politicians' own image of a bustling commercial society. For example, the transcontinental railroad was built with extensive government support and hardly any genuine free enterprise. Land grants were made to the railroads, in violation of the property rights of thousands of farmers. The eminent domain law was used extensively to benefit private commercial interests. In general, the constitution of the United States simply did not sufficiently restrain the government from going to the aid of corporate America.

In a more technical vein, corporations were also granted limited legal liability by government, something they might have but did not attain through contractual negotiations. Corporations are not fully liable for damages they cause. Strict or even less than absolutely strict liability does not apply. This is one of the reasons why many people are very upset by nuclear-power-generating firms, since the harm these might cause would exceed by a considerable amount the limitations on their liability. In general, corporations received extensive government protection, to which small interests were not privy. This in itself is a justly infuriating aspect of corporate commerce. But it does not seem to explain the deep-seated hostility since corporations also promise much that is very helpful to us.

CORPORATIONS AND THE PUBLIC INTEREST

Corporations are immensely useful. They are an unsurpassed means by which large enterprises can be conducted. Dams, factories, massive shopping centers, huge aircraft, saving and loan services, franchising establishments, hotels and motels, credit cards, newspapers, hospitals, resorts, television and thousands of other products and services would not be capable of being financed in a free society without the institution of corporations.

Individuals must combine in order to fund the risky massive ventures which corporations undertake. Only by getting the government involved in economic life, in a way intolerable in a free society, might these endeavors be manageable without corporations, yet that approach, as Eastern Europe has shown, is hopeless. The cost of a plant such as that which Union Carbide built in Bhopal could not be borne by individuals. And the responsibility for mishaps could not be borne by individuals either, judging by what is now the well-publicized figure of the first lawsuit filed against Union Carbide, namely $15 million. Governments, which enjoy immunity from such suits, would not be a very accommodating culpable entrepreneur, given the objectives and responsibilities of corporate commerce. And when governments do take on such tasks, they usually must turn their societies into slave labor camps since, if the prospect of prosperity does not motivate people to combine to achieve the usual corporate feats, then fear will have to be tried to that end.

Interestingly, the proliferation of corporations is also due, in part, to the increasing surge toward economic equality. Without massive individual wealth to carry out the gigantic economic projects needed to achieve what an abundant society requires for its well-being and enjoyment, wealth needs to be pooled. And corporations are the most efficient way for pooling wealth without letting the state, the agent of legally organized force within a society, have this power as well.

Indeed, it is partly because of their usefulness that politicians were, and often still are, so eager to support corporations with extra legal privileges. You and I might like to be bailed out of our financial troubles, but Chrysler Corporation could go to Washington and obtain such money, even from an administration rhetorically committed to free enterprise. The reason is that a lot depends on corporations for many people, and politicians are always sensitive to that fact. So how could they refuse, without an explicit legal, constitutional prohibition? And in the United States constitution there is no such prohibition. Government cannot aid the Church, but it may help commerce. It may, then, also regulate commerce, while it may not regulate the Church.

There are more basic reasons than those mentioned thus far why many people despise corporations. Of course, some just do not like big things. Some do not like the idea of seeking profit, and the bigger the effort to seek it, the less they like it. Then there is envy, which eats away at the hearts of many, including intellectuals (who find it revolting that corporations are so powerful while they can only talk, talk and talk some more, with very little immediate result). When we consider that intellectuals, most of whom work outside the sphere of corporate commerce, are our teachers, writers, novelists, composers, pundits, editors, commentators and so forth, it becomes evident that they influence our moral climate. And they are not known for their love of commerce and commercial firms.

But here again the question remains, why would they want to affect negatively the image of commerce? What seems to be the very powerful impetus behind the hostility towards business and its biggest representative, the commercial corporation?

CORPORATIONS SERVE IGNOBLE ENDS

The chief reason that corporations are despised is that they represent a concern for something for which very few people are comfortable admitting they have a concern. This is earthly pleasure and satisfaction.

The attorney who filed the first major lawsuit against the American firm Union Carbide, in connection with the Bhopal disaster, expressed the point poignantly. Melvin Belli, who often sues big corporations on behalf of private individuals, said in an interview, "The American businessman is . . . concerned with the profit and that's all. . . . I think we should be more concerned with safety than the dollar." This is a revealing comment.

Corporations are massive efforts to please people. They get rich when they read the market correctly. And the market is where people express their desires most forcefully, through the way they spend their money. Corporations cash in on what the bulk of people in relatively free societies actually desire, never mind what they preach! People may sing the praises of altruism, the joys of spirituality, the nobility of self-sacrifice, but they also want to live well. They want to go shopping; they want to have a decent, prosperous, enjoyable life. And corporate business is there to do this for them in a very big and efficient way indeed.

But it is one thing for people actually to seek pleasure and satisfaction, and another thing for them to be happy about their doing so. In short, we ourselves tend to be a bit schizophrenic. We want to live well, we seek joys and delights, but we also claim to honor and respect those who care very little for such trivial things and feel and express disdain for people and institutions which explicitly, unabashedly pursue the satisfaction of desires, or make a living from such pursuits.

Corporations are, of course, the main institutional means by which these earthly goals are pursued. They do not question whether what we want is good or bad, they just try to capitalize on our wanting it. Corporations, oddly enough, treat us as adults. We want Michael Jackson gloves, we get them. We want pornographic books, we get them. We want Disneyland and Disneyworld, and pet rocks and cabbage patch dolls, and Nehru jackets and Pac-Man software, and we get them all, usually at a reasonable price. We are the boss, the corporation says, and we must decide what we will have. They try to entice us, but if we change our minds they will change their product and service lines, and in a jiffy.

THE PHILOSOPHICAL SOURCE OF ANTI-CORPORATISM

But why would all this be resented, even while encouraged at another level? Mainly because from the time of ancient Greece, encouraged by many subsequent features of Western civilization, human beings have been struggling to reconcile what they have believed to be opposite elements of their nature: the spiritual and the material.

This fight is really but a version of what we so often experience when we talk about how our better judgment is defeated by our urges and drives and instincts. When we think we ought to do such and such but end up, for lack of fortitude, doing the opposite, we tend to explain it as a battle between mind and body, spirit and matter, the intellectual and emotional or appetitive side of us. Indeed, we have, to a large extent, managed to come to characterize this conflict as the conflict between good and evil; the mind is noble, the body base or evil.

Now this may seem a specious hypothesis, but I suggest that the anti-commercial, anti-corporate mentality is an outgrowth of the view that what satisfies our bodies, our earthly, base nature, is in conspiracy with the Devil, while what guides us towards otherworldliness is indeed the godly. Corporations mainly concentrate on serving our earthly needs. The few which do serve our spiritual ones are rarely under attack; the major orchestras and opera houses, the large private universities, the think tanks, the newspapers, magazines and television and radio stations tend to be exempt. But when there is a combination, as with the major movie companies which produce "art" and may be construed as serving sheer, crass pleasure, the fact that the organization makes money by suiting our immediate, earthly needs serves to condemn it for certain. All this may strike some people as odd, and for good reason. The most fervent ideological opposition to corporate commerce comes, after all, from a fundamentally materialist source: Marxism.

CORPORATIONS AND THEIR FOES

Marxism regards capitalism as the adolescent phase of humanity's development. As with adolescence in general, so with capitalism, what is lamentable is its recklessness, anarchy and irrationality. Marxists would point to the incredible productive energy consumed for such trivial purposes as I have already mentioned: game shows, gas-guzzling cars, horror films, most of television. But for Marxists this reckless production is explicable, just as the wildness of adolescence is. It all has a vital function, namely to build muscle which the next, more rational phase of the growth process will put to good use.

I do not wish to return to a long discussion of Marxism here. But I do wish to mention that Marxism, like capitalism and corporate commerce, makes room for materialism. While capitalism finds materialism an inherent part of human life, however, Marxism and other anti-corporate viewpoints regard it as either just a phase or a disease. For the Marxist, the future here on earth should usher in the more spiritual life for us all, while for others that spiritual life awaits us elsewhere. In either case, the life which satisfies our natural, earthly or actual human demands is inferior.

To put the matter rather differently, what is brazen and offensive about corporate commerce to many who reflect on these matters in public is that it unabashedly regards the satisfaction of our mundane desires as perfectly worthwhile. And what is more, corporations, as they now exist, tend to make it possible for everyone just to jump right in there and pursue prosperity without apology.

Whereas, in its inception, corporate commerce was under the jurisdiction of the state, in a near-capitalist society it is not. In a near-capitalist or capitalist society, corporations are creatures of individuals who wish to prosper. Shareholders invest and hire experts to make their investments pay. Of course the managers also invest but, in principle, corporations are companies of human beings aiming to flourish economically, to prosper, to profit.

This makes of the profit motive – or, as some might rather refer to it, greed or ambition – a respectable trait. It gives it a legitimate role in human community life. It is for many, even among those who participate in the institution, a kind of legitimation of sin. As with the modern role of sex as an unabashed source of joy, so with business, we seek self-satisfaction from it.

One escape from this implication is offered by scientific economics, which tells us that we always pursue profit no matter what we think we are doing. But, as we have already seen, this doctrine of "everyone is selfish" just will not wash. We know too many counterexamples of people who have forsaken their own interest for some other goal, good or bad. And the doctrine is even more fundamentally unpersuasive: it denies that we have any choice in the matter of what goals we pursue. To defend capitalism and corporate commerce this way is ultimately to help dig their graves.

OUR DILEMMA: CORPORATIONS, MORAL OR AMORAL?

So the point can be summarized thus: commercial corporations were born of the state and received privileges from it (as, of course, did all other institutions for much of human history). That is one count against them, but it is not the most fundamental. Another and more important indictment of them, at least in the view of some, is that they flourish by satisfying people's wants, regardless of the quality of these wants. They serve people's economic aspirations, their desire to prosper in life. That is the most lamentable fact of corporations. It rubs many of us, steeped in a culture that looks either to the supernatural world or at least to the world of pure intellect for salvation, the wrong way.

Business, especially big business, would not be despised if people did not have the belief that there is something lowly about attaining worldly satisfaction. If people held their earthly life in high esteem, if they could in good conscience accept their own desires for pleasure, fun and happiness as these are available here on earth, then perhaps commerce and commercial firms would begin to gain a standing and Ralph Nader, their arch enemy, would not be the saint he is today. In that case there could emerge a somewhat more admiring as well as palatable view of commerce.

Whenever some institution or practice is regarded with total disdain, yet is also felt to be indispensable, it remains outside the scope of morality. This is well illustrated by the underground economy, for example in drugs. When a business is driven outside the law, it begins to be conducted in a criminal fashion. During prohibition, the business of making wine, beer and other alcoholic beverages became thoroughly demoralized. Those associated with it were placed outside the law and thus no distinction could be made between those who participated in the business and acted decently and those who were crooks. In any underground economy we find this to be the case. Institutional support for doing business decently is lacking and then the entire industry tends to get corrupted.

A somewhat milder version of this phenomenon occurs in connection with corporate business and, indeed, business itself. In the eyes of many who discuss moral issues in our society, business is regarded as wholly base or, at best, tolerable because necessary. Even those in the business world often reinforce this picture when they talk about the need for realism and the lack of room for naive idealism in business. In short, people in business, managers, executives and employees of corporations tend often to accept the view that they see depicted on television, in the novel and by the verbalists in our community. They see their profession as amoral, virtually immoral.

When this happens, is it surprising that business does not behave itself very decently? Is it any wonder that everyone is suspicious of corporations? Since they are in fact indispensable yet are held in contempt by those who forge the moral opinions in the land, the very idea that there could be decent corporate conduct, that we could in fact discover the standards of how corporations should behave, vanishes.

Not long ago I had a conversation with the anti-trust attorney of one of our major corporations. I was shown an internal booklet in which the firm discusses its policy as far as foreign business conduct is concerned. One item in this booklet struck me as tragic yet understandable. It was the declaration that the firm regarded any conduct vis-à-vis foreign countries as permissible unless legally forbidden. Legality alone, not morality or ethics, is of primary concern. Of course, the law is itself impure and often the source of moral failure.

Those who wonder why many firms simply do what is legally permissible when it comes to trading with the Soviet Union, Cuba, South Africa or other foreign countries or firms in those countries should know this. When a society tends to hold an institution as inherently amoral and even immoral, that institution begins to accept that picture and refuses to bother itself about questions which are relevant only for people and institutions which could be decent, which could act ethically, morally.

It is not my purpose here to develop the case for the proper moral standards of corporate commerce, although I believe that there is such a case.[1] I am simply interested in presenting a picture, one that I think is disturbing and worth thinking about. It is tragic that an institution in our society that seems to be vitally necessary is also widely held in contempt. And since the only friends of commerce, economists, eschew moral discourse as "mere music", the only source of help to boost the morale of those associated with this vital and honorable institution tends to be impotent in a crucial respect.

There is a particularly notable area where this tragedy appears, namely in the role business plays in environmental pollution. Business is supposed to produce for us efficiently, so that what we want we can get at the lowest price. But in doing this business will make use of the public realm. Making use of the public realm requires political permission. How much soot may go into the skies over New York and Los Angeles, or how much effluent into lakes or oceans, is something politicians and their bureaucrats decide. Business just does not do this on its own. The government determines or helps determine the limits.

Of course, business tries to get a good deal from the government. Everyone will benefit from that, since if you can dispose of your wastes with lower cost, your employees can get more pay, products can be sold at a lower price, shareholders will receive higher dividends and the manager can get promoted. But, in the meantime, the air gets dirtier, the lakes die and fewer beaches can be used for recreation. Firms try to do the right thing and get caught in the middle. Naturally, people do not blame the regulators or sue the government, which, as we have already noted, enjoys sovereign immunity and cannot be sued even if it contributes to pollution; instead they turn on the irresponsible, immoral corporations.

Again, it is not that corporations do everything right, but that it is almost impossible, some argue entirely impossible, to determine what is the right thing for them to do. If we want to appreciate the problem, we can begin with these two matters: corporations are held in contempt, yet everyone helps to make them rich; and they are blamed for ruining the environment, yet everyone wants them to charge lower prices.

When Charles Baudelaire, the famous nineteenth-century French novelist, wrote that "Commerce is satanic, because it is the basest and vilest form of egoism", he was expressing a sentiment shared by many people both left and right on the political spectrum. Marx too railed against capitalism in his early writings, when he still believed in morality, saying that "The right of man to property [the fundamental principle underlying capitalism and corporate commerce] is the right to enjoy his possessions and dispose of the same arbitrarily, without regard for other men, independently from society, the right of selfishness." (As I have already observed, no capitalist could survive if he or she disposed of property "arbitrarily, without regard for other men, independently from society".) It is true that in a capitalist system one has the right to do this. And, more importantly, in many relationships in such a society one is concerned not with other persons, not primarily with whether others will in fact benefit, even if one has to be concerned with whether others believe that they are being benefited.

So the charge that capitalism and its most visible institution, corporate commerce, is selfish rings quite true. One of this century's most ardent defenders of capitalism, novelist-philosopher Ayn Rand, proudly defended this system by observing that it accommodates the ethics of rational self-interest. But by this she did not mean reckless disregard for others, only a sensible, prudent concern with one's life as a human being, including one's economic welfare.

And, yes, corporate commerce does rest, ultimately, on the view that human beings are doing the right thing when they concern themselves with their own well-being, with the welfare of those whom they love (more than with the welfare of strangers or even neighbors), and with their own community before the communities of others. If this be morally offensive, capitalism and corporate commerce must plead guilty. In a moral climate dominated by pleas for self-sacrifice, though not necessarily acts of benevolence, it is no wonder that corporations receive a bad press. Frankly, I do not envy those speaking for corporations. I would not wish to be one myself.

NOTES

1. See Machan (ed.), *Commerce and Morality*.

Chapter 9

Living with Capitalism

THE MORAL-POLITICAL STRUCTURE OF A FREE SOCIETY

The main purpose of this work has been to argue that, as an alternative to the problematic *homo economicus* argument for capitalism, there is a more powerful case to be advanced, one that acknowledges the moral nature of human life and views the free market system as the sociological framework most accommodating and supportive of this moral nature. Indeed, that framework is a logical extension of this moral nature, as Abraham Lincoln observed:

> All this is not the result of accident. It has a philosophical cause. Without the *Constitution* and the *Union*, we could not have attained the result; but even these, are not the primary cause of our great prosperity. There is something back of these, entwined itself more closely about the human heart. That something, is the principle of "Liberty for all" – the principle that clears the *path* to all – gives *hope* to all – and, by consequence, *enterprise*, and *industry* to all.[1]

What Lincoln saw clearly is that capitalism, the free enterprise system, is not what is fundamental in a free system. Capitalism is, rather, a consequence of the deeper, more general principles that all human individuals have the right to life, liberty and property – "Liberty for all".

The ground of that universal principle of human individual liberty is, of course, in much dispute. Many different traditions have tried to claim it as their prerogative to provide these foundations. I have argued that the prominent *homo economicus* – or Hobbesian – individualist or egoist foundation is flawed. I have proposed that a different kind of individualism or egoism, which I have dubbed "classical", is more true to the facts of human nature and also serves better to keep the moral nature of human life in clear focus.

The central premise of my argument is that human beings are moral agents who ought to live to achieve happiness in their lives here on earth, with this happiness understood to involve their success as rational yet also unique natural beings. Each person has as his or her proper goal to seek this happiness. A society that aims to serve the common good through its legal system will, then, have to incorporate in its basic constitution the principles that uphold this objective as proper for each person. The tradition of Lockean natural individual rights comes closest to doing this by preserving the social conditions for everyone to seek his or her happiness as a human individual through the institution of the rights to life, liberty and private property.

A crucial aspect of the thesis that human beings are moral agents is that human beings are able to make fundamental choices in life; that they possess free will and are the ultimate cause of their most important actions. (This does not mean that these choices are easy to make, since free choices can be very difficult to exercise.) This is what requires for them, as a matter of the logic of their moral nature, certain conditions of community life. These would be upheld by everyone's respect for the moral nature of human life and by the institutions giving expression to that respect. The standards that identify that moral nature for the purpose of community life are individual natural rights. They require being treated not as mere means to others' goals, being accorded our autonomy and independence; that is, that neither masters nor slaves shall we be!

The economic consequence of this kind of system is that human beings are respected in their right to make choices about the disposition of what belongs to them: their labor or skills, their products, their wealth, their creative energies; that is, their lives. Capitalism is, then, the by-product of a system of liberty for all, not the main social objective of the system. The social objective that is central in a system wherein capitalism can flourish is to preserve the individual's decisive role in his or her life, to avoid the individual's subjugation (against his or her will) to the projects of other individuals.

Of course, individuals can make commitments, obligate themselves of their own free will, and thus form extensive communities – and, indeed, from the moral point of view that underlies the capitalist system, that is exactly what they very often should do. Family, fraternity, collegiality, professional community, science, art, recreation, religion and all the rest of a rich cultural life can grow from such freely chosen associations and obligations. Yet at the foundation of all this lies the fact that a person is his or her own "master" – or should we say moral or ethical first cause? – and ought to be involved even with the wisest and most noble human community objectives as a matter of his or her own decision. Such is the nature of a just human community, one that honors the nature of the beings comprising it, one that services their morally proper purposes in life.

It is in coming as close as possible to this kind of social setting, where individuals can be moral (and, incidentally, also legal) first causes, that a system securing for them their "space" is ultimately naturally justified. The right to private property is no mere instrument for efficient wealth production, although that is one of its likely consequences, as so many experiments with collectivized economies have strongly suggested. That right is the means of securing for each person a realm of exclusive jurisdiction, one that may not be trespassed upon lest the individual's capacity to be the major moral force in his or her life become obscured. Since we live in nature, this right secures for us a literal as well as a figurative sphere of jurisdiction: there will be things and events over the disposition of which one will be the final authority.

Yet there is a total lack of utopianism about this idea of a human community, mainly because the mere securement of such a jurisdiction for everyone – be it meager or extensive – will not ensure the wisest, best, most honorable approach to what will be disposed of. In other words, the free society is a necessary but not a sufficient condition for a good or virtuous human community. That element must be supplied by the flesh and blood unique men and women who live fully within that society.

As this work has argued, the individuals who comprise a human community are unique and genuine human beings. They have the common characteristic of being able to order their lives by rational understanding, as well as being morally responsible for doing so. They have a lot in common as a result, around which human community life can and ought to be forged: first of all, their ultimate moral precepts and their basic legal institutions. Their nature as human beings serves to make them, as Aristotle so clearly knew, social and political animals. Yet they are also essentially individuals who draw on their unique situation, talents, opportunities, attributes, fortunes and misfortunes so as to create their version of a human life, good, mediocre or evil. This individuality is central to each person, even where the person or even his or her larger community might not yet acknowledge it, and it emerges in the incredible variety of approaches people have been taking to living a human life since its dawn on earth. It accounts for enormous achievements and immense difficulties. It produces clarity of insight as well as baffling confusion about the nature of human existence. It gives, I submit, the best meaning to the phrase "the mystery of human life", since it defies fixedness or long-range prediction about the course of human existence on both individual and community dimensions. Yet it does not prevent understanding and practical (political) preparedness for community life.

Precisely because individuality is an essential feature of humanity, it is individual rights that remain at the core of the proper or optimal social organization of human living. Collectivization – not, however, community – belies the actuality of good human living because it rests on the distorted idea that "the human essence" is, as we have seen Marx declare, "the true collectivity of man", that is, the absence of the ongoing factor of differentiation, of the recreation and rebuilding that we witness from generation to generation even in the most primitive communities. Indeed, this is one reason why it is futile to try to preserve original or early forms of human society, as some try to do when they encounter groups that exhibit early human customs and traits. (Oddly, Marx's entire life as a unique revolutionary spearheader serves as a counterexample to his own conception of human life as fundamentally collective.)

Individual rights are the principles by reference to which a human community can be true both to every person's essential community with every other person and to every person's essential individuality as the source of his or her moral character. Rights, as Marx realized, place borders around persons – or, rather, they are the acknowledgment in our moral vision that such borders need to be granted. But the administration of our lives need not, therefore, proceed regardless of other persons, by disposing of our lives and properties "arbitrarily".[2] Rather, we each have the task to judge clearly what disposition is most appropriate under our circumstances. And we have the general tenets of morality, drawing on virtually any moral system that has been advanced or on common sense, to provide us with some initial clues as to how that disposition should be made.

The rights we have to begin with are, of course, the most basic ones, but they will not, by themselves, suffice to order our communities in line with good judgment. The ordering of human society and the elaboration of these basic individual rights – which we have by nature (i.e. the respect of which is a basic moral duty of all persons in society) – will result in complex legal documents as well as elaborate legal traditions, changing with the combination of the basic principles and new developments in human living. Just how does the right to property apply to frozen embryos whose creators are in the process of divorce? Such a question cannot be answered simply by consulting natural rights, but neither can it be answered by ignoring them. Is abortion homicide or the killing only of a potential human being? Should adulthood begin around the age of eighteen? Should it be proper to enter into a contract involving *in vitro* fertilization? Can the electromagnetic spectrum be privatized? How should we deal with the kinds of productive activity that leave side effects that cannot yet be contained and will thus amount to dumping upon some other's person or property?

The central issue to be considered aside from natural rights is, however, not unrelated to natural rights theory. Indeed, this is what natural rights theory is itself dependent upon, namely an ethical perspective on human life. Only if this ethical perspective is kept close enough at hand – so we know, as it were, from where we derive natural rights – can some hard cases be decided in a sufficiently consistent, coherent and complete fashion to satisfy our needs in consulting basic theories of justice.

We have seen throughout this work that a big problem with the economic imperialist position has been its narrow conception of human nature, along Hobbesian lines. Hobbes claimed that

> whatsoever is the object of any man's appetite or desire, that is it which he for his part calleth good: and the object of his hate and aversion, evil. . . . for these words of good and evil . . . are ever used with relation to the person that useth them: there being nothing simply and absolutely so; nor any common rule of good and evil.³

The economic imperialist position holds virtually the identical view about human morality. The basic rights that can be defended from that position are ultimately derivative of a subjectivist ethics, one in terms of which each person is sole judge – no, author – of what for him or her is right or wrong. With John Locke some effort was made to produce an ethical foundation that is more robust and escapes subjectivism and its self-defeating implications. But Locke merely asserted that there is a Law of Nature, which is Reason. He did not defend this view and in his own more extensive ethical writings he advances a view almost identical to the one embraced by Hobbes.

However, there is something instructive about both the Hobbesian and the Lockean efforts that will help us understand what is the best ethical grounding of natural rights. Both thinkers stressed the motivating power of self-interest or self-aggrandizement. Hobbes saw it as a necessary drive or motive and thus robbed it of any possible moral significance; that is, of being something one ought to or should do. Ought implies can, so that if one ought say, to, serve one's own interest, one must be free to do so or not to do so. If a person inescapably or automatically serves his or her interest, it can be neither morally right that he or she does so, nor morally wrong that he or she does not.

But if we reject the Hobbesian framework and discover that there is an alternative without its metaphysical and epistemological liabilities, we may find that what to Hobbes seemed automatic may indeed be morally right and open to choice. Thus, pursuing one's self-interest, especially when viewed in the light of a broader, more robust conception of the human self than Hobbes embraced, may turn out to be a moral priority for each person. Understood in terms of the naturalist rather than nominalist view of human nature, this would mean that each person ought to be rational with respect to his or her life on earth. And from this it is also evident that a social setting requires that each person be sovereign within a given jurisdiction.

Now problems in mapping those jurisdictions often arise with borderline cases, or yet uncharted topics of concern to human beings in society. Suppose there is a question of where to lean with decisions concerning environmental matters, ecological questions, health and safety control, containment of diseases, freedom of expression, property rights and so on.

When that occurs, we need to recall that what animates the apparently successful and theoretically superior natural rights political perspective is the ultimate need for people to run their own lives in their own best (or rational) interest, so that they have as good a chance for happiness in life as possible given the stage of progress or development reached thus far by human beings on various fronts.

A case in point involving the right to life might be the handling of extraordinary situations, such as involved the well-known case of *Queen* v. *Dudley and Stephens* (1884). Two English seamen were charged and convicted of cannibalism when they killed and devoured a young and very sick man so as to save their own lives. The defendants received the death sentence, but it was afterwards commuted by the Crown to six months of imprisonment! It is undoubtedly the extraordinary nature of the "crime" that led to the commutation of the death sentence. The case had this resolution – and there are records of many similar ones – because "to preserve one's life is generally a duty" (14 QB 273).

Another case in point, this time involving the right to liberty, is long-range risk from environmental defilement. We are nowadays frequently urged to restrict the right to freedom of human beings because it might turn out that its exercise will violate the rights of future generations. (The emphasis here is on "might", on there being a discernible chance or possibility of that happening. If there is solid evidence of this, of course, then the situation changes. It becomes a clear and present danger of rights violation.) I would suggest, however, that the security of knowing that the right of everyone to private property is fully protected would provide greater resistance against environmental harm – including such cases as the erosion of the ozone layer or the destruction of the Amazonian rain forest – than the kind of political special-interest juggling carried out in the context of the welfare state. These matters can be considered only comparatively, not with an eye to a final solution, and the private property system would appear to have more promise in offering long-range solutions than alternatives being proposed.[4]

In any case, the point here is that, if we keep in mind the ethical underpinnings of natural rights, this will guide us always to consider first the interest of those now alive; that is, actual human beings. If no proof of actual wrongdoing exists to show them to have violated anyone's rights, there is no justification for such restriction. If the lives and thus the liberty of actual human beings are of primary value in the legal system, there is no justification for some people to impose burdens on innocent others for example the government on its citizens). Indeed, the whole point of even worrying about members of future generations is that their lives too will be of primary importance within the legal system. To forget this point in regard to members of current generations is to lay a precedent for neglecting those of future ones when the time comes that they need legal protection.

The right to property may be dealt with similarly. When someone engages in the sale of goods or services, it is often thought that restricting his or her right to do this might be of help to others. In arguments about censorship, it is often claimed that pornography or blasphemy, or some other form of objectionable speech or publication, might harm someone other than the user. Yet to restrict it is to violate the actual rights of the user. If we keep in focus that rights are in the service of individuals who ought voluntarily to strive for their happiness – even when they do it mistakenly or even immorally – the conclusion we will reach in complex cases (e.g. restricting the use of DDT) is that the onus of proof must weigh heavily on those who would restrict the exercise of property rights; no individual is a resource of the rest of us, however panicky we might be. The courts would not yield, even when mass opinion is tempted.

At this point we should consider the efforts of some thinkers to graft rights theory onto a non-individualist ethics. Such persons stress not natural negative but natural positive rights, meaning that each person has the right to be provided with services by the society; that is, by his or her fellow human beings who will be commanded to offer the provisions even if they refuse, just as under the negative rights framework one may be ordered to abstain from intruding on others even when one wants to. But since such positive rights effectively render some persons the possibly unwilling providers of their own services to others – or, at least, unwilling yielders of what are initially their creations and products – they violate natural individual negative rights. They treat persons as resources available to all who need them, whether or not the agent of the service chooses to be such a resource. So it seems clear that, if the basic rights we have are negative, then positive rights cannot be basic.[5]

However, positive rights can be a valid feature of a legal system where they rest on prior commitment or contract. Services from parents to children are clearly due, but this is the function of the parents' choices, which can, of course, be implicit, tacit and thus sometimes even unacknowledged by the parents.[6] More direct ways of "creating" positive rights are legally enforceable contracts and obligations: a partnership, a club with dues or fees, employment agreements, military service, etc. But this is where the idea noted earlier, that ultimately a person, an adult, must be the source of his or her own community relationships, appears very starkly. In each such case of creating positive rights, one's negative rights must have been respected and protected. Without that no freedom of choice would obtain for becoming obligated to fulfill such an initially granted right.

So the basic rights within the Lockean natural rights tradition precede all legally enforceable duties or obligations to others, indeed even to oneself (if one may even speak of obligations to oneself; responsibilities would be more natural). Yet, as we saw above, that is not to claim, as some do, that rights are morally (as distinct from politically) prior. Everyone has moral responsibilities, sometimes to others, which may not be the subject of legal enforcement. To be generous to one's fellows, to act with charity towards those who are in desperate need and to remain loyal to friends are all moral but not legal obligations. The areas where many thinkers forget this, such as business ethics, might be contrasted with areas where almost everyone remembers it: artistic integrity cannot be morally enforced upon authors or composers, yet it is widely understood that it is morally demanded. And the most basic moral responsibility to strive to live a happy life precedes the moral category of basic natural individual rights. It is, as we saw, on that moral responsibility that the very idea of natural rights rests; to have the opportunity to choose to live happily, one has rights in society to use and govern one's life, to act freely and to control one's belongings.

WHAT IS THE FREE AND MORAL LIFE?

Even after claiming that there is a moral case for the free system and arguing that case, I still perhaps have a question to answer: how does one carry out the task of living a moral life within the kind of free community of individuals we have been considering here? There is a way to answer this question but it needs to be prefaced by some cautionary remarks.

The idea that human beings ought to strive for their happiness in life allows for – indeed, as a form of individualism it would require – enormous diversity of conceptions. Consider that anyone may live a good human life who is in his or her profession an artist, a dancer, a business executive, a political leader, a philosopher and so on, and in his or her personal life single, married, with or without children, gregarious or tending towards the solitary, with many hobbies or with few, in rough or in mild climates, with troubled children or with untroubled ones. Surely this can suggest, already, that what a good human life amounts to can vary tremendously. A free society is hospitable to this great variety of ways of doing well at living one's life. So as far as the detailed objectives of a good human life are concerned, there is no ultimate generalization that can be made beyond this: to succeed as a rational individual.

But there are, of course, valid generalizations about what virtues we should all support, embrace and cultivate in our lives and in the lives of those whom we care about (provided they accept such loving "meddling" from us). These are really the familiar virtues of honesty, generosity, courage, prudence, moderation, temperance, frugality and so forth. Each of us in his or her circumstances may take these as suitable rules of thumb, as the guiding ethical principles whatever are the detailed objectives of the life he or she is leading.

Let me state the point bluntly at first. I am embracing here moral objectivism: the virtues of human life are not authored but discovered by us by means of an understanding of our human nature and the nature of the world we live in. Moral matters, such as what we ought to do, our obligations and our rights, are all matters of fact. They are, of course, matters of very complex fact, not simply such as that there are printed pages before us, but they are still factual concerns and they can be dealt with dispassionately when one is engaged in analysis.

Most of those who criticize the free society for its various "market failures" tend, often only implicitly, to presuppose the objective (or at least intuitive) reality of values and virtues, although their characterization varies. Some talk of the public interest, some of moral imperatives, some of values, some of virtues – but in most cases the free market is deemed to be an arrangement that fails to deliver sufficiently on what is morally important in human life. Thus regulation or even revolution is recommended; the market must be steered or even abolished to set matters on the objectively right course. Affirmative action, safety and health regulation, sanctions against doing business in South Africa, prohibitions of trade in drugs, pornography or sex, and related government edicts amount to the former alternative, whereas proposals for economic democracy or democratic socialism or sometimes even theocracy express the latter.

Those who tend to favor the former alternative from the political left include such philosophers as John Rawls, Ronald Dworkin, Alan Gewirth and all those talking about positive rights and duties that need to be protected and enforced by the state. It seems that there is a desperate attempt to shore up the case for an aggressive state that will guarantee the performance of the virtues, values and moral obligations, even while there is a protection of a reasonably substantial measure of negative liberty.

Some of this may be due to promises made from the classical liberal corners which have not come true. At one time *laissez-faire* was supposed to bring panacea, utopia, and it has not brought it. The pursuit of self-interest, even understood in the vein in which I champion it, did not occur, and even with the radical new stress on individual liberty in the last two hundred years, we cannot be said to have permanently solved the problem of social evil, of lack of charity or generosity, or of injustice in personal and economic relationships. Since many still desire just that – to stop all the waste, all the superficiality, all the neglect, all the irresponsiblity, all the abuse – they hold that, if *laissez-faire* cannot do it, we must have a different system and maybe that will do the trick. In short, the objective moral values that we apprehend need to be produced somehow, even if not freely.

If what I have been arguing is right, that is a futile expectation. It was unwise to promise it with *laissez-faire* and it is unwise to promise it with government regulation or with wholesale planning. Human beings have not evolved to be guaranteed to be perfect. They are the sort of creatures who can do right and wrong, and they will continue to be that until they become extinct. This desperate effort to construct a political system and a public policy agenda which accommodates that futile hope is very sad, and sometimes evil.

It is a mistake to think that immorality can be forcibly remedied, that you can somehow make out of callous, rich people charitable or magnanimous individuals by having laws that tax them without your paying an enormous cost somewhere else, such as in civil liberties or due process of law. Just as the lynch mob seeks swift penalty at the expense of justice, so the regimented polity seeks its various benevolent objectives at the expense of the very basis of morality, namely human choice. (Oddly enough, civil libertarians with leftist economic views often admit this when they discuss governmental attempts to handle drug abuse or even more serious crimes. The same holds with all vice.)

This is all futile. One need not be an economic determinist of the public choice variety to know that it is hopeless to try to make people charitable, make them generous, make them moderate in their behavior. That is a matter of their own choices, of their interaction with others, of what kind of education they get, of what kinds of culture support they have around them, but not a matter of some social engineering system of a government regulated or regimented society and economy.

But this is not to throw up our hands and despair of any function or prospect of virtue in a free society. The privatization movement that is booming all over the world right now is a testimony to the revolt against the disutilitarian consequences of collectivist policies, and to the destruction of many of our values stemming from neglect of individual rights. Aside from utility, the market alternative to government regulation or planning also has serious moral implications. For one, it restores to individuals their moral dignity; that is, their authority as moral agents who have the responsibility and right to run their own lives, to form cooperative business or other ventures, to be free to make moral choices. Then also, when the government relinquishes its powers and the people of a country assume the responsibility for their behavior, this tends to encourage, but not guarantee, better behavior. A kind of moral tragedy of the commons is avoided, one whereby the responsibility for individual behavior is not ascribable to anyone, or whereby the consequences of that behavior are not linked clearly enough to individual moral agents. When this is made more and more likely in a society, it would seem reasonable to expect that members of that society will come to understand better the quality of their judgments, choices and actions, come to heed that quality more than otherwise.

Of course, what is mostly emphasized now about planned or authoritarian societies are the shortages, the constant embarrassing economic downturns of what used to be the Soviet bloc and the dissident movements such as the growing revolt against apartheid. Some of these – those stressed mostly in the media, especially when it comes to the Soviet Union and Eastern Europe – are economic woes. But when we focus on the political, intellectual and artistic disenfranchisement of millions of citizens, the moral dimensions of the foibles of the planned alternative also become clear. In socialism, indeed, there are serious moral and psychological problems: consider Vladimir Bukovsky's *To Build A Castle* as a demonstration, especially the chapter "The Soul of Man in Socialism".

It is fair, then, to conclude that almost everywhere that there are genuine political upheavals, at the base there is either a total confusion about, or a total abrogation of, individual rights. For example, in the Palestinian–Israeli conflict, confusion abounds, compounded by all sorts of historical contingencies. Yet there is the outstanding complaint that some people's homeland has been violated, which can be translated into concern about property rights. Solving that problem will need a thorough recapture of the concern for individual or private property rights and the kind of legal system that ought to preserve them.

The tragedy of the commons arising from environmental pollution can be translated as the failure to extend the concept of rights into new domains. We have been preoccupied with other political and legal agendas instead of trying to make as many areas as possible accessible to individual rather than collective responsibility. (Perhaps this is because many people are attracted to the promise of final solutions to problems and will not settle for something that can only be considered the best available alternative by which to reach a current solution.) Those are the consequences of not taking individual rights really seriously.[7]

Within the confines of a legal system based on individual rights, the improvement of human life either at the individual or the community level is especially promising. This is due to what I have alluded to earlier, namely the consistent possibility of protecting against dumping. "Dumping" is a concept often associated with environmental misbehavior, but we can extend the use of the concept to cover a kind of moral dumping, letting unwilling others shoulder the impact of our moral wrongdoings. Collectivization produces the climate, making it more likely that those who choose to live by ignoring or defying moral principles will, nevertheless, experience no discernible adverse effect, not even clear-cut personal rebuke. When it is systematically unclear who is responsible for what, since all our spheres are united and no borders are maintained between us, it is risky to say who is guilty and who is innocent. That way a kind of tragedy of the commons exists everywhere that the individual rights of persons are ignored or trampled upon.

Within the framework of classical egoist ethics, wrongdoing ultimately boomerangs, by way of either losses or lost opportunities. In the last analysis discernible immorality brings self-destructive results. In this framework, the locus of morality is the individual – you, him, her, me. From this locus of morality flow natural rights. If I have a right to life, what that means is that you may not murder me or enslave me. But in order to make this concrete, the "me" has to be identified. This is where property rights come in, in spelling out what is "me" in the extended sense that I have jurisdiction over it. My life, my works, my labor, my skill – this all begins to sound like property rights. If I have the right to liberty, you may not intrude upon my actions, my conduct. Actions are usually carried out somewhere, so you may not intrude on somewhere that is mine – property rights again. Take liberty of the press: you may not take my typewriter or my computer from me, you may not take away the electricity I pay for, you may not shut down the machines. Take the copyrights to musical arrangements: you may not use my arrangement without compensation and without an agreement from me for some entertainment project that you have. Property right is not just the right in estates, but also property right is right in mental products, computer programs, novels, etc. It is implicit in almost all of the complaints that persons have against one another, complaints that are not based on some sort of misconception of tribal unity, but where there is a genuine respect for individuality.

So we have a number of reasons why even if we cannot make predictions about the way people would act in a free society – how morally good they might be – we might think that they would be more inclined towards virtue. Firstly, when their right to liberty is protected, people are recognized as moral sovereigns, as agents responsible to make choices that are morally praiseworthy. Secondly, their choices have traceable impact on them, so that both their virtues and their vices are consequential. Thirdly, the possibility of not shouldering the errors of one's ways is limited – an implication of the first two reasons. Fourthly, the legal system will have a basic rudder in case the normal tools of the law are insufficient for purposes of settling disputes or solving problems.

More generally, it is less likely that the consequences of vice could be avoided. Thus virtue would be a more pressing preference. In a free society it would also be an encouragement to human moral virtue that the entire system of law underlying such a society would rest, firstly, on the recognition of the vital significance of human virtue (by making the right of choice of conduct a paramount legal principle) and, secondly, on the importance of the pursuit of happiness or prudence – the virtue that renders, among other matters, commerce a morally upright institution (it is when we act prudently in our lives that we get embroiled in commerce).

Prudence, the first of the cardinal virtues, has been denigrated as not even a moral virtue in the nineteenth and twentieth centuries. Immanuel Kant considered prudent activity to be something that people do automatically. So businessmen are out to succeed because they are driven. But in fact they are not all driven; they have to think, they have to focus, they have to concentrate and they have to apply their initiative and their intelligence. And what do they get from this? Mostly condemnation, contempt from politicians, preachers, ecumenical councils, popes and, most of all, the popular media where the smoking guns are found mostly in the hands of those who strive to make a profit.[8] Prudence and one of its consequences, namely the pursuit of prosperity, have to be recognized as righteous activities by the very people who follow them. Furthermore, a culture of capitalism would do: for example, assert that generosity is noble since you cannot wait for government redistribution, and that courage is glorious because you cannot depend on the state to stand up for your values.

So the virtue of prudence, as well as other moral principles, would be re-asserted within the culture of a morally grounded free, capitalist society. Of course, defending prudence as a virtue might be very difficult because one must go on the offensive against the egalitarians and the Marxists and those who want either to sap the energies of commerce or to conscript it into the service of some higher good. To say of commerce only, "Occasionally it makes us rich so why don't you leave it be?" is just not enough.

The general theme of these last passages is, then, that the "privatization of virtue", to quote Quentin Skinner – including prudence or the pursuit of happiness in life – would be a good thing all round. It would recapture the idea that the basis of morally good conduct is the individual agent, not collective authority. And it would encourage more responsible conduct, since misconduct would in the end have self-destructive consequences. This would not guarantee overall good human conduct, but it would, it seems, be a necessary condition for it, one that is under severe neglect in our times.

In the last analysis, the morally good human life can be lived only in freedom, just as can the morally bad one. While this may appear a rash claim – after all, are there not morally good persons in tyrannies or concentration camps? – the central point of it is evident enough. In absence of the respect for and protection of our natural rights, the moral and immoral can be distinguished only when some *de facto* personal sphere of jurisdiction can be identified: a courageous act involving one's own life, a generous act involving possessions one may choose to part with, a prudent act involving the postponement of present enjoyment for later. That we find moral, indeed heroic, conduct in circumstances of attempted totalitarianism shows the ultimate futility of such a political arrangement: people will often be able to carve out some sphere of personal authority even in the face of the greatest obstacles placed before them.

At the heart of this work is the notion that in any case we would be better off in freedom since then, at least, we would know who we were and could learn from it and there would be the chance to choose virtue over vice and amorality. Without that freedom, we face the present kind of demoralization that is natural when the individual and his or her impact on life are obliterated. There is a field in current academic philosophy that well illustrates my point. The term "applied ethics" would suggest a concern with how individuals ought to act. Thus when courses in medical or business ethics proliferate as they have, one would suspect that their focus would be on the morality of individual actions. But within the current political climate this is just what they mostly avoid. Instead they pursue studies of public policy: what should the government do about ethical problems in medicine, law, business, education, etc.? The very idea of improving individual conduct drops out of focus when politically we have turned away from a system of individual rights. That is what I mean by "demoralization", the robbing from our culture of the element of individual moral responsibility. (Of course, this is something to which many academic and social scientific disciplines have contributed during the last two centuries.9)

So when we try to answer the question of how we should act in a system of politics that makes capitalism possible, our answer has to be this: we should lead a life of moral virtue so as to make the best possible progress in our individual lives towards our own human happiness, the fullest development of ourselves as rational beings in the context of the world in which we live. And it seems quite plausible that such a life would be more widely encouraged in a free society, based on individual rights, than in all varieties of enforced collectivism.

NOTES

1. Quoted in Jaffa, *How to Think About the American Revolution*, p. 2.
2. Marx, *Selected Writings*, p. 53.

3. Thomas Hobbes, *Leviathan*, p. 48. This very same idea has been overhauled many times, by Locke, Hume and of course contemporary economic scientists. A particularly imaginative effort at developing an enriched version of the Hobbesian idea is made in Frank, *Passions Within Reason*. Frank argues that the apparently purely altruistic acts and practices of many people that seem at first to defy the *homo economicus* account of human behavior do, ultimately, conform to the idea of self-interested rationality. Yet Frank still insists that this is best understood in terms of the Hobbesian model of reason, whereas I have argued that to appreciate the rationale for such behavior one requires the Aristotelian conception of reason that shapes our passions, as well as the classical egoist notion of right conduct, in terms of which our goal is to live rational lives as human individuals, a goal which is intimately connected with our social values and objectives.
4. The issue of how to adjudicate conflicts arising from environmental problems within a private property rights framework is discussed in Machan, *Private Rights, Public Illusions*.
5. For more on this, see Machan, *Individuals and Their Rights*.
6. *Ibid.*
7. See further Machan, "The virtue of freedom in capitalism".
8. While there are some who appreciate the impact such a cultural disdain can have on a profession, others find it merely trivial to "moan" about the matter. Yet they would probably not find it trivial to moan about a culture in which scientists, educators, authors or composers were widely held in contempt. They would probably recognize that such contempt is demoralizing. The reason for the lack of concern with such attitudes toward business is itself the incomplete appreciation of the virtue of prudence; it is in our time treated by most philosophers and ethicists as morally irrelevant. For a good example, see Nagel, *The Possibility of Altruism*. This important book follows the Kantian trend in maintaining that looking out for oneself must be morally irrelevant since it must stem from a natural or automatic desire and not from principled choice.
9. For a discussion of this theme, see Chain, *The Science of Behavior and the Image of Man*.

Bibliography

Arblaster, A. (1984) *The Rise and Decline of Western Liberalism*, Oxford: Basil Blackwell.
Aristotle (1966) *Metaphysics*, trans. H. G. Apostle, Bloomington, IN: Indiana University Press.
Arrow, K. J. (1981) "Two cheers for government regulation", *Harper's*, March, pp. 18–22.
Austin, J. L. (1970) "Other minds", in *Philosophical Papers*, 2nd edn, London: Oxford University Press.
Baker, C. E. (1975) "The ideology of the economic analysis of law", *Philosophy and Public Affairs*, vol. 5 (fall), pp. 3–48.
Bambrough, R. (1979) *Moral Skepticism and Moral Knowledge*, Atlantic Highlands, NJ: Humanities Press.
Becker, G. S. (1968) "Crime and punishment: an economic approach", *Journal of Political Economy*, vol. 76 (March/April), pp. 169–217.
Becker, G. S. (1976) *The Economic Approach to Human Behavior*, Chicago, Ill.: University of Chicago Press.
Bell, D. and Kristol, I. (eds.) (1971) *Capitalism Today*, New York: New American Library.
Bellah, R., Madien, R., Sullivan, W. M., Swidler, A. and Tipton, S. M. (1984) *Habits of the Heart: Individualism and commitment in American life*, New York: Harper & Row.
Berlin, I. (1958) *Two Concepts of Liberty*, London: Oxford University Press.
Beversluis, E. H. (1975) "The not so brief history of ethical egoism", *The Personalist*, vol. 56 (spring), pp. 199–206.
Bissell, R. (1974) "Dual-aspect theory of agency", *Reason Papers*, no. 1, pp. 18–39.
Buchanan, E. (1962) *Aristotle's Theory of Being*, Cambridge, Mass.: Greek, Roman, and Byzantine Monographs.
Buchanan, J. M. (1975) "Boundaries of social contract", *Reason Papers*, no. 2, pp. 15–28.
Buchanan, J. M. (1986) "Why governments 'got out of hand' ", *New York Times*, 26 October.
Buchanan, J. M. and Tullock, G. (1962) *The Calculus of Consent*, Ann Arbor, Mich.: University of Michigan Press.
Buchanan, J. M., Tollison, R. D. and Tullock, G. (eds.) (1980) *Toward a Theory of the Rent-Seeking Society*, College Station, Tex.: Texas A & M University Press.
Chain, I. (1972) *The Science of Behavior and the Image of Man*, New York: Basic Books.
Christian, S. (1983) "Real policy vs. applause lines", *The Atlantic*, August, vol. 252, no. 2, pp. 10–24.

Conway, D. (1987) *A Farewell to Marx*, New York: Penguin.
Dawkin, R. (1976) *The Selfish Gene*, New York: Oxford University Press.
Ehrenfeld, D.W. (1978) *The Arrogance of Humanism*, New York: Oxford University Press.
Ekelund, R. B., Jr. and Tollison, R. D. (1981) *Mercantilism as a Rent-Seeking Society*, College Station, Tex.: Texas A & M University Press.
Fisk, M. (1973) *Nature and Necessity*, Bloomington, Ind.: Indiana University Press.
Frank, R. H. (1985) *Choosing the Right Pond*, New York: Oxford University Press.
Frank, R. H. (1989) *Passions Within Reason: The strategic role of the emotions*, New York: W. W. Norton & Co.
Friedman, M. (1953a) *Essays in Positive Economics*, Chicago, Ill.: University of Chicago Press.
Friedman, M. (1953b) "The methodology of positive economics", in Friedman (1953a).
Friedman, M. (1962) *Capitalism and Freedom*, Chicago, Ill.: University of Chicago Press.
Friedman, M. (1974) "An interview with Milton Friedman", *Reason*, vol. 6 (December), pp. 4–7.
Friedman, M. (1976) "The line we dare not cross", *Encounter*, November, pp. 8–14.
Galbraith, J. K. (1973) *The Affluent Society*, 3rd edn, Boston, Mass.: Houghton Mifflin.
Gauthier, D. (1986) *Morals by Agreement*, Oxford: Clarendon Press.
Gewirth, A. (1979) *Reason and Morality*, Chicago, Ill.: University of Chicago Press.
Gordon, B. (1975) *Economic Analysis Before Adam Smith*, New York: Barnes & Noble.
Gracia, J. J. E. (1988) *Individuality: An essay on the foundations of metaphysics*, Albany, NY: State University of New York Press.
Gray, J. (1987) "The economic approach to human behavior: its prospects and limitations", in G. Radnitzky and P. Bernholz (eds.), *Economic Imperialism*, New York: Paragon House.
Guzziardi, W., Jr. (1979) "Judges discover the world of economics", *Fortune*, vol. 99, pp. 58–66.
Hardie, W. F. R. (1965) "The final good in Aristotle's *Ethics*", *Philosophy*, vol. 40, no. 154, Oct, pp. 277–95.
Haworth, A. (1989) "Capitalism, freedom and rhetoric: a reply to Tibor R. Machan", *Journal of Applied Philosophy*, vol. 6, no. 1, pp. 97–107.
Hayek, F. A. (1948) "The uses of knowledge in society", in *Individualism and Economic Order*, Chicago, Ill.: University of Chicago Press.
Hayek, F. A. (1960) *The Constitution of Liberty*, Chicago, Ill.: University of Chicago Press.
Hayek, F. A. (1975) "Economics, politics and freedom: an interview with F. A. Hayek", *Reason*, February, pp. 4–12.
Hayek, F. A. (1984a) "Equality, value and merit", in C. Nishiyama and K. R. Leube (eds.), *The Essence of Hayek*, Stanford, Calif.: Hoover Institution Press.
Hayek, F. A. (1984b) " 'Social' or distributive justice", in C. Nishiyama and K. R. Leube (eds.), *The Essence of Hayek*, Stanford, Calif.: Hoover Institution Press.
Hemmermesh, D. and Soss, N. M. (1974) "An economic theory of suicide", *Journal of Political Economy*, vol. 82 (January/February), pp. 83–98.

Hessen, R. (1979) *In Defense of the Corporation*, Stanford, Calif.: Hoover Institution Press.
Higgins, R. (1984) "British philosopher says self-interest corrupts Western liberty", *Boston Sunday Globe*, 28 October.
Hobbes, T. (1962) *Leviathan*, New York: Collier Books.
Howard, J. A. (ed.) (1984) *On Freedom*, Greenwich, Conn.: David-Adair.
Hunt, L. H. (1982) "Some advantages of social control: an individualist defense", in T. R. Machan (ed.), *The Libertarian Reader*, Totowa, NJ: Rowan & Littlefield.
Jaffa, H. V. (1978) *How to Think About the American Revolution*, Durham, NC: Carolina Academic Press.
Jaffa, H. V. (1981) "A conversation with Harry V. Jaffa at Rosary College", *Claremont Review of Books*, vol. 1, pp. 1-5.
Joseph, H. W. B. (1916) *An Introduction to Logic*, 2nd edn, Oxford: The Clarendon Press.
Kalt, J. and Zupan, M. (1982) *The Politics and Economics of Sentate Voting on Coal Strip Mining Policy*, Cambridge, Mass.: Energy and Environmental Policy Center, John F. Kennedy School of Government, Harvard University.
Kelman, S. (1983) "Regulation and paternalism", in M. Bruce Johnson and T. R. Machan (eds.), *Rights and Regulation*, Cambridge, Mass.: Ballinger.
Lee, D. R. (1985) "Public choice: the rest of the story", *The Freeman*, January, pp.29-30.
Letwin, S. R. (1976) "The achievements of Friedrich A. Hayek", in F. Machlup (ed.), *Essays on Hayek*, New York: New York University Press.
Letwin, S. R. (1977) "Romantic love and Christianity", *Philosophy*, vol. 52 (April), p. 135.
Letwin, S. R. (1982) *The Gentleman in Trollope: Individuality and moral conduct*, Cambridge, Mass.: Harvard University Press.
Leube, K. and Moore, T. G. (1986) *The Essence of Stigler*, Stanford, Calif.: Hoover Institution Press.
Lyons, J. O. (1978) *The Invention of the Self*, Carbondale, Ill.: Southern Illinois University Press.
McCloskey, D. N. (1985) *The Rhetoric of Economics*, Madison, Wis.: University of Wisconsin Press.
Machan, T. R. (1974) *The Pseudo-Science of B. F. Skinner*, New Rochelle, NY: Arlington House.
Machan, T. R. (1975) *Human Rights and Human Liberties*, Chicago: Nelson Hall.
Machan, T. R. (1976) "Prima facie versus natural (human) rights", *Journal of Value Inquiry*, vol. 10, no. 2, pp. 119-31.
Machan, T. R. (1977) "Human dignity and the law", *DePaul Law Review*, vol. 26, pp. 807-832.
Machan, T. R. (1980) "C. S. Peirce and absolute truth", *Transactions of the Charles S. Peirce Society*, vol. 16 (spring), pp. 151-61.
Machan, T. R. (1981) "Wronging rights", *Policy Review*, no. 17, pp. 37-58.
Machan, T. R. (1982) "Epistemology and moral knowledge", *Review of Metaphysics*, vol. 36 (September), pp. 23-49.
Machan, T. R. (1983a) "Individualism and the problem of political authority", *The Monist*, vol. 66, no. 4, pp. 500-16.
Machan, T. R. (1983b) "Should business be regulated?", in T. Regan (ed.), *Just Business*, New York: Random House.
Machan, T. R. (1983c) "Social contract as the basis of norms: a critique", *Journal*

of *Libertarian Studies*, vol. 7, no. 1, pp. 141-5.
Machan, T. R. (1984) "Pollution and political theory" in T. Regan (ed.), *Earthbound*, New York: Random House.
Machan, T. R. (1986) "The virtue of freedom in capitalism", *Journal of Applied Philosophy*, vol. 3, no. 1, pp. 49-58.
Machan, T. R. (ed.) (1987) *The Main Debate: Communism versus capitalism*, New York: Random House.
Machan, T. R. (1988a) "A new individualist basis of the free market", *International Journal of Social Economics*, vol. 14, no. 1, pp. 27-39.
Machan, T. R. (ed.) (1988b) *Commerce and Morality*, Totowa, NJ: Rowman & Littlefield.
Machan, T. R. (1988c) "Ethics vs. coercion: morality or just values?", in W. Block and L. Rockwell (eds.), *Man, Economy and Liberty: Essays in honour of Murray N. Rothbard*, Auburn, Ala.: L. von Mises Institute.
Machan, T. R. (1988d) *Marxism: A bourgeois critique*, Bradford, England: MCB University Press.
Machan, T. R. (1988e) *The Moral Case for the Free Market Economy*, Lewiston, NY: Edwin Mellen Press.
Machan, T. R. (1989a) *Individuals and Their Rights*, LaSalle, Ill.: Open Court.
Machan, T. R. (1989b) *Liberty and Culture*, Buffalo, NY: Prometheus Books.
Machan, T. R. (1990) *Private Rights, Public Illusions*, New York, Holmes and Meier.
MacIntyre, A. (1984) *After Virtue*, Notre Dame, Ind.: University of Notre Dame Press.
Mack, E. (1973) "Egoism and rights", *The Personalist*, vol. 54, no. 1, pp. 5-33.
McKenzie, R. (1983) *The Limits of Economics Science*, Boston, Mass.: Kluwer-Nijhoff.
Marx, K. (1967) *Writings of the Young Marx on Philosophy and Society*, ed. by L. Easton and K. Cuddat, Garden City, NY: Anchor.
Marx, K. (1971) *Grundrisse*, ed. by D. McLellan, New York: Harper Torchbooks.
Marx, K. (1973) *Grundrisse*, trans. by M. Nicholas, New York: Vintage Books.
Marx, K. (1977) *Selected Writings*, ed. by D. McLellan, London: Oxford University Press.
Meiners, R. E. (1987) "Economic considerations in history: theory and a little practice", in G. Radnitzky and P. Bernholz (eds.), *Economics Imperialism*, New York: Paragon House.
Melden, A. I. (1977) *Rights and Persons*, Berkeley, Calif.: University of California Press.
Mill, J. S. (1871) *Principles of Political Economy with Some of its Applications to Social Philosophy*, 7th edn, New York: D. Appleton.
Miller, F. D., Jr. (1974) "The state and community in Aristotle's *Politics*", *Reason Papers*, no. 1, pp. 61-9.
Mises, L. von (1949) *Human Action*, New Haven, Conn.: Yale University Press.
Mishan, E. J. (1986) "Fact, faith, and myth: changing concepts of the free market", *Encounter*, November, pp. 65-7.
Morgan, L. C. (1923) *Emergent Evolution*, New York: Holt.
Morris, C. (1972) *The Discovery of the Individual 1050-1200*, New York: Harper & Row.
Mueller, D. (1979) *Public Choice*, Cambridge: Cambridge University Press.
Nader, R., Green, M. J. and Seligman, J. (1976) *Constitutionalizing the Corporation: The case for federal charting the giant corporations*, Washington, DC:

Corporate Accountability Research Group.
Nagel, T. (1970) *The Possibility of Altruism*, Oxford: Clarendon Press.
Norton, D. L. (1976) *Personal Destinites: A philosophy of ethical individualism*, Princeton, NJ: Princeton University Press.
Norton, D. L. (1977) "Individualism and productive justice", *Ethics*, vol. 87 (January), pp. 113-25.
Oakeshott, M. (1975) *On Human Conduct*, London: Oxford University Press.
Pasour, E. C., Jr. (1980) "Liberty, and possibly wealth", *Reason Papers*, no. 6, pp. 53-62.
Preston, L. M. (1984) "Freedom, markets, and voluntary exchange", *American Political Science Review*, vol. 78 (December), pp. 959-70.
Rachels, J. (1974) "Two arguments against ethical egoism", *Philosophia*, vol. 4 (April/July), pp. 297-314.
Radnitzsky, G. and Bernholz, P. (1987) *Economic Imperialism*, New York: Paragon House.
Rand, A. (1967) *Capitalism: The unknown ideal*, New York: Signet.
Rand, A. (1971) *Introduction to Objectivist Epistemology*, New York: New American Library.
Rappaport, S. (1986) "What's really wrong with Milton Friedman's methodology of economics?", *Reason Papers*, no. 11, pp. 33-62.
Rasmussen, D. B. (1973) "Aristotle and the defense of the law of contradiction", *The Personalist*, vol. 55 (spring), pp. 149-62.
Rawls, J. (1971) *A Theory of Justice*, Cambridge, Mass.: Harvard University Press.
Ripley, C. (1980) "Sperry's concept of consciousness", *Inquiry*, vol. 23, pp. 399-423.
Roberts, P. C. and Stephenson, M. A. (1973) *Marx's Theory of Exchange, Alienation and Crisis*, Stanford, Calif.: Hoover Institution Press.
Rothbard, M. N. (1956) "Toward a reconstruction of utility and welfare economics", in M. Sennholz (ed.), *On Freedom and Free Enterprise*, Princeton, NJ: D. Van Nostrand.
Samuelson, P. (1966) *Collected Scientific Papers*, Cambridge, Mass.: MIT Press.
Schwartz, B. (1986) *The Battle for Human Nature*, New York: W. W. Norton & Co.
Shue, H. (1980) *Basic Rights*, Princeton, NJ: Princeton University Press.
Skinner, B. F. (1953) *Science and Human Behavior*, New York: Macmillan.
Skinner, B. F. (1971) *Beyond Freedom and Dignity*, New York: Bantam.
Skinner, Q. (1978) *The Foundations of Modern Political Thought*, New York: Cambridge University Press.
Sowell, T. (1985) *Marxism*, New York: William Morrow & Co.
Sperry, R. W. (1965) "Mind, brain, and humanist values", in J. R. Platt (ed.), *New Views of the Nature of Man*, Chicago, Ill.: University of Chicago Press.
Sperry, R. W. (1974) "Mental phenomena as causal determinants in brain function", in C. C. Globus, G. Maxwell and I. Savodnik (eds.), *Consciousness and the Brain: A scientific and philosophical inquiry*, New York: Plenum Press.
Sperry, R. W. (1976) "Changing concepts of consciousness and free will", *Perspectives in Biology and Medicine*, vol. 19, pp. 9-19.
Sperry, R. W. (1983) *Science and Moral Priority*, New York: Columbia University Press.
Stigler, G. (1978) "Wealth and possibly liberty", *Journal of Legal Studies*, vol. 7 (June), pp. 213-17.
Stigler, G. (1980) "Economics or ethics?", Lecture II, Tanner Lectures, Harvard

University, April; published in Leube and Moore (1986).
Stigler, G. (1982) *The Economist as Preacher, and Other Essays*, Chicago, Ill.: University of Chicago Press.
Stigler, G. (1984) *The Intellectual and the Marketplace*, Cambridge, Mass.: Harvard University Press.
Stigler, G. (1988) "The Adam Smith Lecture: the effect of government on economic efficiency", *Business Economics*, vol. 23 (January), pp. 7–13.
Tanner Lectures on Human Values, The (1980) Salt Lake City, Utah: University of Utah Press.
Tawney, R. H. (1926) *Religion and the Rise of Capitalism: A historical study*, New York: Harcourt, Brace & Co.
Thomas, L. (1974) *The Lives of a Cell*, New York: Viking.
Topitch, E. (1987) "How enlightened is 'dialectical reason'?", in Machan (1987).
Walker, M. (ed.) (1988) *Freedom, Democracy, and Economic Welfare*, Vancouver: Fraser Institute.
Wood, A. W. (1981) *Karl Marx*, London: Routledge & Kegan Paul.

Index

After Virtue (MacIntyre), 6
aggregate demand, 119
aggression, 78, 113, 115, 116, 162
alienation, 66, 104, 119
altruism, 35, 103
amoralism, 17-20, 150-3, 167
anti-collectivism
  critique of planned systems, 118-29
  'dismal science', 134-9
  homo economicus approach (challenged), 131-2
  human action (misconceived), 141-2
  human individuals (locus of value), 129-30
  market economy, 130-1
  normative public choice, 133-4
  public good (subjectivism), 132-3
  science reconsidered, 139-41
  socioeconomic systems, 130
anti-corporatism
  amoralism and, 150-3
  capitalism and, 149-50
  corporations (goals), 147-8
  corporations (reputation), 143-4
  history of, 144-6
  philosophical source, 148-9
  public interest, 146-7
anti-humanism, 72
anti-individualism, 7, 65-70, 120
Aristotle, 7, 62, 66-71 *passim*, 119, 143, 156
Arrow, Kenneth J., 90
  social choice paradox, 118, 119, 126-7
atomistic materialism, 2
Austin, J. L., 57
Austrian school, 5, 18-19, 99
authoritarianism, ix-x, 49-51, 81
authority, sovereign, 73, 76, 77, 80
autonomy, 71, 108-9, 155

Balanced Budget Amendment, 29, 31
bankruptcy, 31
basic needs, 121
Baudelaire, Charles, 152
Becker, Gary, 19, 21, 26

behaviorism, 4
Bell, Daniel, x
Bellah, Robert, 7
Bellante, Don, 135
Belli, Melvin, 147
Berger, Peter, 7
Bernholz, Peter, 7
Berns, Walter, 7
Bhopal disaster, 146, 147
Bohm-Bawerk, E. von, 99
Bork, Robert, 78
bourgeois society, 6, 9, 106
Buchanan, Emerson, 67, 69
Buchanan, James, 17, 18, 19, 43, 91
  public choice theory, 20-2, 24, 28, 31
Bukovsky, Vladimir, 164
business
  government regulation, 88-96
  society and (anti-corporatism), 143-53

calculation problem, 118, 119-22
Calculus of Consent, The, 20-1
capital accumulation, 87
capitalism, 6-11, 13
  anti-corporatism and, 149-50
  background of study, ix-xiii
  classical individualism and, 76-7
  corporate commerce in, 149-50, 152-3
  criticisms, 84-96
  diversity, 81-3
  living with, 154-67
  market system (justice in), 83-4
  morals, coercion and natural rights, 77-8
  paradox of, ix-xiii
  property rights and morality, 79-81
  vindication of, 96-7
capitalism (living with)
  moral-political structure, 154-61
  morally good life, 161-7
capitalism (moral superiority)
  freedom (free economic system), 107-16
  limitations (paradox of), 99
  main debate, 98-9
  Marxism, 100-7

175

Carey, Henry, 9
causal principles, 63, 106
causality, 68
Center for the Study of Public Choice, 20, 91
central planning (criticisms), 118-29
chaos theory, 60
Chicago school, 5, 18
choice
　free, 37, 39, 42, 64, 67, 108-9, 115-16
　moral, 6, 52, 64, 163
　public see public choice
　social (paradox), 118, 119, 126-7
Christian salvationism, 119
Christianity, 63
civil rights, 64, 84
civil society, 48, 71, 77, 82, 105
class, 3
　consciousness, 67
　working class, 86-7
classical individualism, 76, 77, 154
　anti-individualism, 65-70
　epistemological themes, 56-9
　metaphysics of, 59-65
　political individualism, 70-4
classical liberalism, 2
coercion, 12, 42, 49-51, 52, 70, 73, 77-8, 109, 114, 134
Cohen, G. A., 113, 114
collectivism, 52-3, 156, 163, 164-5
　Marxism and, 102-7
　political individualism and, 71, 73
　see also anti-collectivism
college student scholarships, 23, 24, 30
Collingwood, R. G., 5
command economy, 34
commons, tragedy of, 29, 82, 118, 119, 127-9, 163
commonsense thesis, 22, 31, 34, 35, 45
communications network, 122-3
communism, xi, 66, 81, 83, 120
　Marxist, 98-107
community, 7, 11, 78, 106
　loss of, 8
　moral-political structure, 155-7
　political, 64, 69, 71-3
competition, 89
conditionality, 34-40
consciousness, 67, 103, 113
　rational, 66, 68, 105
consequences, unintended (doctrine), 118, 122-6
consumer goods, 120
contracts, 122
　social, 18, 19
contradictions, 62
Conway, David, 10, 12, 132

coordination problem, 118, 119-22
corporate commerce, 95-6
　see also anti-corporatism
corporations
　amoralism, 150-3
　critics of, 149-50
　goals, 147-8
　public interest and, 146-7
　reputation, 143-4
corruption, 9, 38, 71, 96, 151
cost, 27
cost-benefit analysis (social), 82, 90, 94, 95
culture, 45, 105
　of capitalism, 166, 167

death (value concerns), 46
deliberation process, 110, 111-12
demand, 12, 119
democratic solution, 8, 127
democracy, individualism and, 118, 119, 126-7
Democritus of Abdera, 36
'demoralization', 167
deregulation, 90
Descartes, René, 56
desire (satisfaction of), x-xi, 1-2, 9, 21-2, 41, 45-6, 48, 125, 150
determinism, 36, 39, 48, 85
dialectic approach, 10, 66, 100-101, 102, 112, 134
dialectical materialism, 63, 119
dictatorship, 126-7
dissidents, 110, 164
diversity, xiii, 81-3
divestiture program, 95
division of labor, 69
doctrine of unintended consequences, 118, 122-6
drug addiction, 115-16
'dumping', 82, 83, 86, 90, 94-5, 164-5
Dworkin, Ronald, 98, 162

Economic Approach to Human Behavior, The (Becker), 19
economic exchange, 8, 51, 70, 108, 115
economic imperialism, 7, 10, 20, 25, 36, 38, 112, 136-41, 158
economic individualism, 6-9
economic life (scientific/moral nature), 40-46
economic man, see homo economicus model
economic science
　amoralism, 17-20
　'dismal science', 134-9
　public choice teaching, 31-2
　public choice theory, 20-2
　reforms (consequences), 29-30

science reconsidered, 139-41
vested and public interest, 24-8
welfare state (services), 22-3
economic science (metaphysical recasting)
economic value theory, 53-4
market failures, 51-3
scientific/moral nature of economic life, 40-6
scope (normative perspective), 33-40
scope of economics, 46-7
values and liberty, 47-51
economic value theory, 53-4
economic welfare, 12
economics (scope of), 46-7
economists (rejection of morality), 17-20
efficiency, 120
  in business, 88-9, 90, 91-2, 93
  in resource allocation, 119
egoism, 6, 8, 48, 71, 77, 152, 154, 165
  see also classical individualism
Elster, J., 113
empiricism, 11, 13, 58
epistemological themes, 56-9
epistemology, 4, 13, 67-8
ethical relativism, xiii
ethics, 10, 35, 69, 151, 153, 158, 167
  metaethics, ix, xiii, 56
evil, 5, 6, 37, 51, 61, 67, 84, 133-4, 148-9, 158
exchange, economic, 8, 51, 70, 108, 115
exchange economy, 10, 12, 104, 119
existentialism, 98
expansionism, 104
exploitation, 10, 87
externalities, 82, 83, 90, 93-4

fact, 57, 72
'fair wage', 93
family, 8, 58, 66, 69, 72, 102-3, 105-6, 155
Ferguson, Adam, 122
feudalism, 95, 127, 145
Feyerabend, Paul, 58
foundationalism, 56-9
fractionalism, 86
free choice, 37, 39, 42, 64, 67, 108-9, 115-16
free economic system, 107-16
free exchange, 121
free market, 5
  critics of, 6-9
  defense of, 9-14
  process, 64-5
free and moral life, 161-7
free rider problem, 93
free society, 7-8, 52-3, 77
  moral-political structure, 154-61
free trade, 86, 93

free will, 39-40, 61, 63, 68, 72, 112
freedom
  of capitalism, 107-16
  right to, 49, 165
  see also liberty
Friedman, Milton, 5, 17-18, 21, 26, 43, 44, 53, 71-2, 136, 138, 139
friendship, 8, 11, 42, 70, 161

Galbraith, John Kenneth, 44, 89, 133
Gauthier, David, 11
geopolitics, 98
Gewirth, Allan, 89, 98, 162
gift-giving, 70
glasnost, 104
Goldwater, Barry, 7
good, x, 5, 36-8, 67, 134, 148-9, 158
  moral goodness, 6, 51, 61-2, 64, 70, 115, 161-7
goodwill, 72
government
  corporate commerce and, 145-7, 151-2
  intervention, 86, 92
  political individualism, 4, 65, 70-4
  regulation of business, 88-96
graduate scholarships, 23, 24, 30
Green, T. H., 113
Grundrisse (Marx), 102, 107

Hardie, W. F. R., 69
Hardin, Garrett, 118, 119, 128
Hayek, F. A., 5, 17-18, 53, 83, 84, 99, 109
  calculation problem, 118, 119-22
  doctrine of unintended consequences, 118, 122-6
Hegel, G. W. F., 113
Hessen, Robert, 95
Hobbes, Thomas, 2, 3, 5, 48, 140, 158
Hobbesian individualism, 36
  critical analysis, 1-2
  critics of economic individualism, 6-9
  Hobbesian answer to critics, 9-14
  quantitative individualism, 2-6
Hollywood's Heavies (PBS documentary), 144
Holmes, Oliver Wendell, 94
homo economicus model, 9, 44, 49, 83, 93
  amoralism, 17, 18-19
  challenged, 131-2
  imperialistic, 36, 112
  public choice theory, 18-19, 25, 28, 132
human action (misconceived), 141-2
Human Action (von Mises), 19
human beings
  conditionality, 34-40
  definitions, x-xi, 18
  economic individualism, 7-8

human beings (continued)
  quantitative individualism, 2–4
  species-beings, 6, 66, 67, 69, 103, 104, 121
human essence, 52, 66, 73, 83, 102, 156
human individuals (locus of value), 129–30
human life (free and moral), 161–7
human nature, 10, 18–19
  conditionality, 34–40
human rights, 8, 92–3
humanity, 102–5
Hume, David, 35, 123
humility, 44–5

ideas (consequences), 29–30
ideology, 25, 26, 27, 28, 30
imperialism, economic, 7, 10, 20, 25, 36, 38, 112, 136–41, 158
individual rights, xii, 157, 163–5
individualism, 86
  anti-, 7, 65–70, 120
  background of study, ix–xiii
  calculation problem, 119–22
  democracy and, 118, 126–7
  economic, 6–9
  Hobbesian (problems with), 1–14
  numerical, 2–6
  political, 4, 65, 70–4
  qualitative, 56–74
  quantitative, 2–6
individuality, xiii, 52–3, 103, 104, 105–7, 156–7
individuals
  locus of value, 129–30
  moral nature, 77–8
information, 18, 112, 114, 125
instrumentalism, 62, 139
integrity, 42, 62, 92, 96, 140
intention, 111, 112
interest groups, 23, 28, 30, 126
international free trade, 86
interventionism, 72
intrinsic values, 45, 50
Invention of the Self, The (Lyons), 6
'invisible hand', 123, 131
Islamic fundamentalism, xi, 8

Jacob J. Javits National Graduate Fellowship Program, 23, 24, 30
Jaffa, Harry V., 7, 66, 69
Javits Program, 23, 24, 30
job security, 87
jobbing, 88
justice, 11, 27, 28, 82, 157
  individualism and, 7, 8
  of market system, 83–4
  natural, 5

political, 94
qualitative individualism, 63–5, 71

Kalt, Joseph, 25
Kant, Immanuel, 3, 11, 35, 99, 106, 166
Kelman, Steven, 89
Kirk, Russell, 98
knowledge, 18, 34, 56, 58, 67–8, 72, 112
  moral, 49, 50, 57, 89
Koop, C. Everette, 121
Kristol, Irving, x, 7, 53, 98

labor
  employee protection, 89–93 *passim*
  at risk, 85–7
labor market, 87–8
laissez-faire economics, xii, 31, 145, 162–3
Lavoie, Don, 119
law, 124, 151, 164–6
  natural, 5, 123, 158
Lee, Dwight, 26
legal system, 164–6
legality (of corporate commerce), 151
liberalism, x–xi, xiii, 2
liberty
  capitalism and, xii–xiii, 101, 113–15
  critics of market economy, 130–1
  negative, 1
  political, 52–3
  right to, 49, 165
  values and, 41, 42, 47–51
Lincoln, Abraham, 154
living standards, x, 87, 114–15
lobbyists, 24, 30, 126
Lochner v. New York, 94
Locke, John, ix, 18, 63, 64, 82, 99, 116, 158
Lockean tradition, 7, 9, 70, 77–8, 89, 155, 160
love, 7, 8, 42, 70
loyalty, 9, 42, 140, 161
Lyons, John O., 6

MacIntyre, Alasdair, 6, 105
McLaughlin, Andrew, 114
Macpherson, C. B., x
Malthus, Thomas, 134
Marcuse, Herbert, 53
market economy (critics of), 130–1
market exchange, 8, 51, 70, 108, 115
market failures, 44, 51–3, 120, 125, 162
  business regulation and, 89–90, 91–2
market mechanism, 125
market socialism, 121
market system (justice in), 83–4
markets (definition), 41–2
Marshall, A., 113

Marx, K., 3, 96, 134, 157
  on capitalism, x, 6, 84–7, 98–9, 101–5, 107, 113–15, 152
  Hobbesian answer, 9–10, 12
  human essence, 52, 73, 83, 102, 156
  species-being, 6, 66–7, 69, 103, 104, 121
Marxism, 6–8, 10, 52–3, 149
  capitalism and (moral superiority), 98–9, 100–107, 111, 112–16
Marxist-Leninism, 108, 120
materialism, 2, 11, 149
  dialectical, 63, 119
  mechanistic, 3, 4–5, 106
  metaphysical, 40, 58
  reductive, 3, 5, 13, 40, 63
matter-in-motion, 2, 3, 4–5
mechanistic individualism, 3
mechanistic materialism, 3, 4–5, 106
Meiners, Roger, 135
Melden, A. I., 89
mercantilism, 95, 127, 145
mataeconomic notion, 45, 46
metaethics, ix, xiii, 56
metaphysical materialism, 40, 58
metaphysics, 11, 13, 39–40
  of qualitative individualism, 56, 59–65, 67–8, 72
  of quantitative individualism, 2, 4, 5
Mill, John Stuart, ix, 18, 89, 134
minimal state, 65, 70, 72
minimalism, x, 18
Mises, L. von, 19, 99
  calculation problem, 118, 119–22
Mishan, E. J., 120
monarchy, 127
monism, 59–60, 62, 63, 67, 69, 72
monopolistic industries, 90, 91–2
moral
  choice, 6, 52, 64, 163
  equivalence thesis, 111
  evaluation, 33–4
  foundation of free society, 7–8
  good, 6, 51, 61–2, 64, 70, 115, 161–7
  knowledge, 49, 50, 57, 89
  life, 161–7
  objectivism, 162–3
  philosophy, 99
  -political structure, 154–61
  responsibility, 161, 163–4, 167
  skepticism, 50, 53
  sovereignty, 52, 73, 165
  space, 64, 78, 80
  standards (of commerce), 151–2
  structure (free society), 154–61
  system, 10–11
  virtues, 70, 72
moral nature
  of economic life, 40–6
  natural rights and, 77–8
morality, 5
  conditionality, 34–40
  property rights and, 79–81
  rejection of *see* amoralism
Morals by Agreement (Gauthier), 11
Morris, Colin, 105
motion, laws of, 2, 3, 4–5
motivation, 21–2, 136
  subjective, 1, 9–10
  see also private interest; public interest; self-interest; vested interest
Mueller, Dennis, 18

Nader, Ralph, 95, 143, 144, 150
natural law, 5, 123, 158
natural rights, 3, 48, 93, 165
  Lockean theory, 7, 9, 77–8, 155, 160
  in moral-political structure, 157–61
  private property, 79–81
  qualitative individualism, 61, 63–4
needs, 48, 121
negative liberty, 1
negative rights, 8, 160
neo-classical economics, 6, 7–8
  alternative view, 9–14
neo-Hobbesian individualism, 1–2
  answer to critics, 9–14
Nielsen, K., 113
nominalism, 2, 4, 36, 63, 73, 158
non-governmental rights, 93
non-reductionist approach, 59
Norton, David, 2, 3, 68, 70–1
Nozick, Robert, 70, 71, 99
numerical individualism, *see* quantitative individualism

objective values, xi, 28, 47, 141
  classical individualism, 61–2
  conditionality, 37–8, 39
  economic life, 43, 45–6
  Hobbesian individualism, 1, 5–6, 12
  market failure and, 52–3
Olson, Mancur, 29
ontology, 2, 3, 11, 46, 56, 59, 60, 62, 105
'organic body', 102

paternalism, 70, 72, 89
perestroika, 104
personal integrity, 42
personal sovereignty, xii, 64, 73, 115
philosophical positivism, 13
philosophical source (anti-corporatism), 148–9
philosophically objective value, 45
planned systems (criticisms), 118–29

Plato, 7, 63, 66, 103, 113, 114, 119, 143
pleasure, 147-8
   see also satisfaction (of desires)
pluralism, 58, 59, 60, 61, 63, 69, 72
polis, 69-70
political anti-individualism, 68, 69-70
political behavior, 28
political community, 64, 69, 71-3
political economy, 12
   background of study, ix-xiii
   of capitalism, 99-100
   Marxist, 101
political failure, 51, 90, 91
political individualism, 4, 65, 70-4
political justice, 94
political liberty, 52-3
political sovereignty, 73, 106
political structure (free society), 154-61
Pollock, Jackson, 47
pollution, 82-3, 86, 90, 93-5, 152, 164-5
Popper, Karl, 139
positive rights, 160, 162
positivism, 4, 11, 13, 18, 139
potentialities, 61
poverty, 105, 115
power, 73
Preston, Larry, 108-16 *passim*
price system, 123, 124-5
private interest, 12-13, 21-8, 48, 136-7
   see also self-interest
private property see property rights
private service, 22-3
privatization, ix, x, 12, 128, 129, 163
productivity, 48
professional responsibility, 22
professions, 8
profit-seeking, xi, 48, 147-8, 150
prohibition approach, 93-4, 95, 122
property rights, 41-2, 127
   abuse of, 84-5
   capitalism and, ix-x, 9, 94, 114, 155-7, 159-60, 164-5
   morality and, 79-81
   privatization, 128, 129
prosperity, 18, 34, 35, 41-2, 48, 131, 166
   see also wealth
prudence, 41, 166, 167
psychophysics, 39, 67
Public Choice (journal), 20
public choice
   normative, 133-4
   teaching, 30-2
   theory, 18, 19, 20-32
public good, 82, 91
   subjectivist idea, 132-3
public interest, 24-8
   corporations and, 146-7

public service, 20-8, 140

qualitative individualism, 76, 77, 154
   anti-individualism, 65-70
   epistemological themes, 56-9
   metaphysics, of, 59-65
   political individualism, 70-74
quantitative individualism, 2-6, 14, 71, 106
quarantine approach, 93-4, 95
Queen v. Dudley and Stephens, 159
Quine, Willard Van Orman, 3

Rachels, James, 8
Radnitzky, Gerard, 7
Rand, Ayn, 45, 57, 153
rational consciousness, 66, 68, 105
rationality, 64, 66-7, 68
rationing, 128
Rawls, John, 8, 89, 98, 162
reality, 39, 58, 59, 60, 61, 69, 72
realpolitik, xii
redistribution, 70-1, 91
reductionism, 36, 39, 58, 60, 62, 68
reductive materialism, 3, 5, 13, 40, 63
reductivism, 101
reforms (consequences), 28-30
regulation (of businesses), 88-96
resources
   allocation, 119, 127
   common (tragedy of), 29, 82, 118, 119, 127-9
responsibility, 11, 94
   anti-collectivism, 124, 125, 129
   capitalism and, 76-7, 78
   conditionality and, 38, 40
   moral, 161, 163-4, 167
   professional, 22
   self-, 106
revealed preferences, 10, 137
Ricardo, David, 134
rights
   to freedom, 49, 165
   individual, xii, 157, 163-5
   natural, see natural rights
   negative, 8, 160
   positive, 160, 162
   property, see property rights
   protection, 41-2, 89, 90-3
risk, 85-8, 92
Roemer, J., 113
Rothbard, Murray, N., 132
Rousseau, J. J., 113

Samuelson, Paul, 131
Sartre, Jean Paul, 98
satisfaction (of desires), x-xi, 1-2, 9, 21-2, 41, 45-6, 48, 125, 150

Index 181

scarcity, 48
science of economics, 139–41
scientific nature (of economic life), 40–6
scientism (demise), 99
self-destruction, 76, 165
self-determination, 39–40, 69, 78, 106, 108–9, 112, 114
self-development, 69, 113
self-indulgence, 132–3
self-interest, xi, 8, 10, 12–13, 26, 30, 136–7, 141, 153, 158, 162
self-regulation, 71, 72
selfishness, 136–7, 139, 141, 152
sell outs, 42
Shakespeare, William, 7
Shue, Henry, 89
skepticism, moral, 50, 53
Skinner, B. F., 38
Skinner, Quentin, x, 18, 51, 166
slavery, 79, 80, 95
Smith, Adam, ix, xii, 18, 35, 116, 122, 134, 145
social choice paradox, 118, 119, 126–7
social contract, 18, 19
social control, 70
social cost-benefit analysis, 82, 90, 94, 95
Social Statics (Spencer), 94
social utility, 131, 132, 133
socialism, xi, 86, 116
  Marxist, *see* Marxism
socialization, 116
socially objective value, 45
society, business and (anti-corporatism), 143–53
socioeconomic systems, 130–4
sovereign authority, 73, 76, 77, 80
sovereign immunity, 133, 152
sovereignty, 81, 82, 93
  market agent, 125
  moral, 52, 73, 165
  personal, xii, 64, 73, 115
  political, 73, 106
Sowell, Thomas, 10
'species-being', 6, 66, 67, 69, 103, 104, 121
Spencer, Herbert, 94
Sperry, Roger, 39, 67, 69
state, minimal, 65, 70, 72
state of nature, 18, 48, 77, 126
Statecraft as Soulcraft (Will), 66
statism, 18, 32, 53, 71
Stein, Ben, 143–4
Stigler, George, 6, 10, 19, 24, 38, 43, 141
Strauss, Leo, x, 7
subcontracting, 88
subjective motives, 1, 9–10
subjective values, xi, 19, 47, 54, 134–5, 158
  classical individualism, 61–2, 71, 73

conditionality, 34, 36, 37
economic life and, 43, 44, 45–6
Hobbesian individualism, 9–10
liberalism and, xiii
liberty and, 48, 50
public good, 132–3
substitutability, 37
Surface Mining Control and Reclamation Act (1977), 25

'talents', 61
tautological approach, 12, 27, 34, 141
Tawney, R. G., 3
taxation policy, 92, 127, 128
Taylor, Charles, 114
terms of trade, 81
theocracy, xi, 141
Thomas, Lewis, 66
To Build a Castle (Bukovsky), 164
Tocqueville, Alexis de, 7
totalitarianism, 100-1, 106–7, 167
trade, 19, 81, 86
trade unions, 51, 86, 87, 88
tragedy of the commons, 29, 82, 118, 119, 127–9, 163–5
truth, 5, 36, 37, 39, 57, 59, 67
Tullock, Gordon, 20
tyranny, 50, 53, 97, 127

unemployment, 85, 88, 92, 122, 123, 124
unintended consequences, doctrine of, 118, 122–6
Union Carbide, 146, 147
unity (of sciences), 59–60
universal values, 52
universality, 68, 103
utilitarianism, 90, 94
utility, social, 131, 132, 133
utility maximization, xi, 1, 6, 9–13, 18–19, 24–5, 27, 135–9, 141–2

value
  judgements, 27–8, 43, 47, 49–50, 52, 125, 143
  problem of, 134–5
value theory, economic, 53–4
values, 5
  defense of, xi–xii
  economic science, 40–7
  intrinsic, 45, 50
  liberty and, 47–51
  locus of, 129–30
  objective *see* objective values
  subjective *see* subjective values
  utilitarian, 90, 94
vested interest, xi, 21–8
vice, 13, 165, 167

vice (*continued*)
    see also evil
victimization, 94–5
View From Sunset Boulevard, The (Stein), 143–4
virtue, 13, 64, 70, 72, 165–6
    see also good

wages, 87, 88, 93, 122, 123, 124
wealth, 2, 41, 42, 48, 86, 128, 143, 145
    distribution, 115, 131
    maximization, x, 11, 21, 113
    see also prosperity
Wealth of Nations, The (Smith), xii, 145
welfare, 48, 86, 106, 153
welfare state, 17, 22–3, 28–31, 91, 98, 126, 159
Will, George, x, 7, 66
women's liberation, 50, 113
Wood, A. W., 113
working class, 86–7

Zupan, Mark, 25